P9-CRN-615

Praise for *Go Green, Live Rich*

"Great news: there is no green premium! By demonstrating how going green can fit any budget, David Bach shows that good environmental and financial decisions go hand-in-hand. *Go Green, Live Rich* gives great tips, useful to everyone, about how to save money and the planet at once." —Robert F. Kennedy Jr.

"*Go Green, Live Rich* is as much about saving money as it is about preserving our world of natural wonders for future generations. This is the rich-green-book of a promising tomorrow." —Matthew Modine, Founder: Bicycle for a Day

Praise for *The Automatic Millionaire Homeowner*

"[Bach's] cheery, can-do message . . . cuts through the intimidating challenge of buying a house for the first-timer . . . for a newcomer, it's fundamental reading."

—*USA Today*

"If you read only one real estate book this year, it should be *The Automatic Millionaire Homeowner* . . . This is one of the few real estate books that cannot be recommended too highly for both beginners and experienced homeowners."

—Robert J. Bruss, *Miami Herald*

Praise for *Start Late, Finish Rich*

"Financial wizard David Bach's new book, *Start Late, Finish Rich*, offers solid advice for getting our finances in order, no matter how old we are." —AARP

"With feel-good sensibilities, David Bach delivers levelheaded strategies for reaching financial goals. . . . Bach's clever approach will make readers feel as if they're having a one-on-one conversation with a friendly personal financial counselor. . . . Powerful, poignant and pleasing, *Start Late, Finish Rich* can't be read fast enough." —*Bookpage*

Praise for *The Automatic Millionaire*

"*The Automatic Millionaire* is an automatic winner. David Bach really cares about you: on every page you can hear him cheering you on to financial fitness. No matter who you are or what your income is, you can benefit from this easy-to-apply program. Do it now. You and your loved ones deserve big bucks!"

—Ken Blanchard, co-author of *The One Minute Manager®*

"*The Automatic Millionaire* gives you, step by step, everything you need to secure your financial future. When you do it David Bach's way, failure is not an option."

—Jean Chatzky, Financial Editor, NBC's *Today*

"*The Automatic Millionaire* proves that you don't have to make a lot of money or have a complicated financial plan to get started—you can literally start toward your financial dreams today, in a matter of hours, with just one life-changing secret: Pay yourself first and make it automatic! Equally important, this book shows you how to simplify and automate your entire financial life."

—Harry S. Dent, Jr., investment strategist and author of *The Roaring 2000s*

Praise for *Smart Couples Finish Rich*

"*Smart Couples Finish Rich* teaches women and men to work together as a team when it comes to money. Bach's nine steps are powerful, yet easy to understand and fun to implement. The entire family can benefit from this great book."

—Robert T. Kiyosaki, author of *Rich Dad, Poor Dad*

"I know how hard it is to make a personal-finance book user-friendly. Bach has done it. *Smart Couples Finish Rich* picks up where *Smart Women Finish Rich* left off. . . . This is an easy, lively read filled with tips that made me smile and at least once made me laugh." —*USA Weekend*

"David Bach offers a prescription both to avoid money conflicts and to plan a harmonious future together. . . . The bottom line is action, and Bach's chatty writing style helps motivate you to that end." —*BusinessWeek*

Praise for *Smart Women Finish Rich*

"Inspires women to start planning today for a secure financial future. Every woman can benefit from this book. . . . Bach is an excellent money coach."

—John Gray, bestselling author of *Men Are from Mars, Women Are from Venus*

"David Bach is the one expert to listen to when you're intimidated by your finances. His easy-to-understand program will show you how to afford your dreams."

—Anthony Robbins, author of *Awaken the Giant Within* and *Unlimited Power*

"[David] Bach gets across some complicated stuff: how to organize a portfolio, keep the taxman at bay, invest in yourself, and earn more, all of which makes this book one of the best overall." —*Working Woman*

FIGHT FOR YOUR MONEY

Also by David Bach

Smart Women Finish Rich

Smart Couples Finish Rich

The Finish Rich Workbook

The Finish Rich Dictionary

The Automatic Millionaire

The Automatic Millionaire Workbook

Start Late, Finish Rich

The Automatic Millionaire Homeowner

Go Green, Live Rich

FIGHT FOR YOUR MONEY

HOW TO STOP GETTING RIPPED OFF AND SAVE A FORTUNE

DAVID BACH

DOUBLEDAY CANADA

Copyright © 2009 by David Bach

All rights reserved. The use of any part of this publication, reproduced, transmitted in any form or by any means electronic, mechanical, photocopying, recording or otherwise, or stored in a retrieval system without the prior written consent of the publisher—or in the case of photocopying or other reprographic copying, license from the Canadian Copyright Licensing agency—is an infringement of the copyright law.

The Automatic Millionaire Homeowner, The Automatic Millionaire, The Latte Factor, Smart Women Finish Rich, Smart Couples Finish Rich are registered trademarks of FinishRich, Inc.

Doubleday Canada and colophon are trademarks.

This book is designed to provide accurate and authoritative information on the subject of personal finances. While all of the stories and anecdotes described in the book are based on true experiences, most of the names are pseudonyms, and some situations have been changed slightly for educational purposes and to protect each individual's privacy. It is sold with the understanding that neither the Author nor the Publisher is engaged in rendering legal, accounting, or other professional services by publishing this book. As each individual situation is unique, questions relevant to personal finances and specific to the individual should be addressed to an appropriate professional to ensure that the situation has been evaluated carefully and appropriately. The Author and Publisher specifically disclaim any liability, loss, or risk which is incurred as a consequence, directly or indirectly, of the use and application of any of the contents of this work.

Book design by Ralph Fowler / rlf design

Library and Archives Canada Cataloguing in Publication

Bach, David.
Fight for your money / David Bach.—Canada ed.

ISBN 978-0-385-66623-7

1. Finance, Personal. I. Title.

HG179.B3124 2009 332.024 C 2008-906905-6

PRINTED AND BOUND IN THE UNITED STATES OF AMERICA

10 9 8 7 6 5 4 3 2 1

To my son, Jack Bach—

you are the best thing that ever happened in my life.

I love you more than the "whole world"!

CONTENTS

FIGHT FOR YOUR MONEY A–Z

Do you feel like you're being ripped off . . .

. . . or scammed every time you open your wallet, pay a bill, read your email, or take a trip? You're not alone!

What if I told you that there are simple things you can do RIGHT NOW to get a better deal on almost everything you pay for—and if you devoted just a few hours to a handful of them, you might be able to cut your overall expenses by 10 to 20% this year?

What if I told you that by using this book and spending just a few hours of your time learning how the major corporations take advantage of you (legally), you could put hundreds, if not thousands of dollars back in your pocket?

What if I told you that you don't have to be the victim of a bad deal, rip-off or scam ever again?

Would I have your attention?

Spend a few hours with me and use the tools inside this book as your guide. Let me share with you the secrets that big businesses don't want you to know. Then see for yourself how quickly you can start keeping more of your hard earned paycheque for yourself once you learn to FIGHT FOR YOUR MONEY.

Are you ready? Then turn the page. Let's get started.

—David Bach

Introduction

Why Fight for Your Money?

You hold in your hands a book that could change the way you think about and deal with money from this day forward for the rest of your life.

That's a pretty major statement, because virtually everything you do every day of your life has something to do with money. Think about it. What are the odds that you will go the next 24 hours without spending any money? What are the odds that you will go another five minutes?

And don't think that just because you're not taking out your wallet and forking over a few dollars for something that you're not spending. Are the lights on as you read this? Is there a cell phone in your pocket? Do you own or rent a place to live? Are you covered by insurance of any kind?

I thought so. Just sitting there, you're spending money. And the unpleasant truth is that though you may not realize it, you are spending too much.

Everything You Do Every Day That Involves Money Is a Battle

The great truth about money is that, in order to keep it and grow it, you have to fight for it. For years, I have said that it doesn't matter what you earn, it is what you keep that determines whether you will be financially free. Yet each year our money has become harder and harder to keep. That's because, at every turn, the companies we deal with every day in every aspect of our lives are working as hard as they can to take as much money from us as they can.

Whether you realize it or not, we are all engaged in a never-ending battle with giant corporations and economic institutions whose only goal is to separate us from our hard-earned dollars.

This is a battle we consumers have been losing because they are better equipped to take our money than we are to keep it.

Lose the Battle and You Lose the War

Think about it. We live in a world now where even once-respectable institutions like banks and brokerage houses, insurance companies and hospitals no longer seem to have any scruples about how they accomplish the task of separating us from our money. Whether you let them do it will ultimately make a huge difference in the way you live.

When you pay just 10 or 20% too much for the products and services you use every day, you will have to work ten to twenty extra years before you can retire. Or, to put it another way, if you let yourself be overcharged by ten to twenty percent for the things you buy, you are in effect spending one or two months a year working without pay for the companies that rip you off. ***And trust me—until you fight for your money, you will overpay for almost everything you buy.***

My hope is that this book will change your life by giving you the tools to FIGHT FOR YOUR MONEY and WIN.

The World Has Changed Financially

I have no idea when you will actually read this book, but as I sit here writing it in October 2008, the world is going through tremendous financial turmoil. In a single week this month, the U.S. stock markets plunged 18%, the biggest drop in their history, and the Canadian stock market was reeling as well. At the same time, U.S. real estate prices were falling catastrophically. Canada's real estate markets were not so severely affected, but even here house prices and sales in many cities were down 20% or more from their peak in 2005 and 2006. As Canada's government struggles to insulate the country from the worst effects of the economic turbulence in the United States—and coordinate its efforts with other governments around the world to break the worst credit logjam since the 1930s—ordinary people can't help but worry about what new crisis tomorrow might bring.

The fact is, this turmoil has already hit you and me in our homes, in our wallets, and in our bank accounts. Most likely, you have less money today than you did a few years ago. If you're a homeowner, you probably have less equity in your home than you did a few years ago. There's also a real possibility that you not only owe more than you used to but that you also have fewer options for paying off that debt than ever before in your life.

It's also possible that your income from your job or business is less secure than it has been in years, maybe in decades.

No wonder a Conference Board of Canada survey reported in October 2008 that consumer confidence had fallen to a 26-year low.

The point of all this is not to depress you, but simply to be real about what is happening. And whether we like it or not, it is happening.

A War for Your Money Is Raging

With easy money no longer so easy, companies are struggling to remain profitable and continue to grow. The challenges they face are immense. At a time when everyone is stressed financially and has zero confidence, they can't just raise prices. Instead, they've got to be creative—they've got to figure out how to get more money out of you and me without us realizing it.

In an effort to solve this problem, companies have spent billions and billions of dollars developing ways to sneak money from us. The techniques they've come up with include hidden fees, obscure rules, misleading come-ons, and, occasionally, outright fraud. Some people call this unfair. Others call it infuriating. I call it a war.

Who Am I to Help You Fight Back?

For the better part of two decades now, I have devoted myself to helping people live better by being smarter about their money. This book is the tenth one I've published in the last ten years. The previous nine were all focused on how to live and finish rich. Chances are, you may have read one or more of them. There are currently upward of 7 million of my FinishRich books in print *worldwide*.

Most people know me for my take-action advice about money. Because I tell it like it is—and make it simple and doable—millions of people have used my books to change their lives completely. If you are one of those whom I've helped, thank you for giving me the opportunity to inspire you again. If this is our first time together, then let me say, "Welcome, and thank you for inviting me to be your financial coach."

My life is completely dedicated to the mission of helping people live a great life—a life of meaning and hope. I have spent so much time and energy teaching millions of people how to be smarter with their money for one simple reason: I believe with all my heart that acting positively to get your financial life together is the best and fastest way to achieve the great life you want and deserve. Fix your money problems, and it will be so much easier to live your life more powerfully and purposefully.

Financial Knowledge Is Power

For us as consumers, this age of global economic uncertainty is especially challenging. In order to survive in these tough times, the companies that sell us goods and services have launched a new war for our wealth. The battle to separate us from our hard-earned money has been going on for a long time, but now it's been kicked up to an entirely new level, with companies becoming trickier and more ruthless than ever, not just nickel-and-diming but nickel-and-*dollaring* us to death.

What this means is that you have to be smarter with your money and take your finances more seriously than ever before. Financial ignorance is now a luxury none of us can afford. And I'm not just talking about getting a better handle on the stock market or the housing market. I'm talking about being smarter about how you spend money every single day on every single product and service you use.

Companies Need Your Money—But You Need It More

Never before have corporations been so successful at taking us financially without our really realizing it.

Here's what I mean:

You take your credit card company up on its invitation to skip a payment without penalty—not realizing they will still hit you with a finance charge for the unpaid balance.

You sign up for basic local phone service at $13 a month—not realizing that a laundry list of fees (for things they never told you about or bothered to explain) will inflate your actual monthly bill to nearly twice what they promised.

You buy an extended warranty for a new appliance—not realizing there's virtually no chance you'll ever use it enough to justify the cost.

You agree to pay an extra $12 a day for insurance on your rental car—not realizing that you're already covered by your credit card company.

You say "Sure!" to the nice sales clerk at the department store who urges you to "save 10 % right now" on the clothing you're buying by signing up for a store credit card—not realizing that they charge 29% interest and won't even discuss lowering the rate.

You trustingly sign on the dotted line when the tax preparation firm offers to give you an immediate "convenient" advance on your refund—not realizing the interest and service fees they're charging you may equal 500% or more in annual interest.

You buy a new car and thank the dealer for getting you financing even though he said your credit rating was poor—not realizing that he lied to you about your credit score and that you could have easily gotten a bank loan for thousands of dollars less.

They Are Taking Us for Billions—And We Are Now Working for Them

In the past, when times were good, it was easier to shrug off this sort of thing. To tell ourselves that's the way the world is and there isn't anything we can do about it. We were busy and flush with cash and so we let much of this go. But times have changed. *And in truth, being ripped off is never okay.*

If we don't fight the fight and protect ourselves from the companies that rip us off with sneaky fees and absurd systems, we end up working for them. What happens when you're forced to spend more than you should on everything you pay for? Well, not only do you wind up getting less for your money—you also end up working longer and harder to simply get by.

Here are a few facts to consider while you're thinking about how hard you have to work to keep your head above water these days.

- The banking industry can take $5 from our pockets in overdraft fees for withdrawing as little as a few extra pennies beyond our account balance, which adds up to millions of dollars a year.
- By playing games with payment deadlines and bamboozling customers into inadvertently breaking the rules, the credit card industry can shake us down for millions of dollars in penalty fees.
- In 2008, major airlines including Air Canada hit up travellers for well over $1 billion in unprecedented new charges for checked baggage, in-flight meals, and a variety of other services they used to provide for free.
- Payday lenders (those places with the neon signs that say "Cash Cheques Here") claim to be helping strapped wage-earners, but they actually gouge them out of $1 billion a year in fees—charging what amount to annual interest rates of *1,000%* and more.
- Between the end of 2001 and the summer of 2008, as gasoline prices soared from just over 50¢ a litre to nearly $1.50 a litre, oil industry profits totalled upward of $23 billion in 2008 alone. Globally, Exxon Mobil earned US$40.6 billion—"the highest profits ever recorded by

any company," according to *The New York Times*—and its 2008 profits were expected to be even higher.

- Manufacturers tempt consumers into buying their products by offering as much as $100 off the price of a product, but they make the process of collecting the rebates so difficult that as many as 50% of them are never redeemed.

And It's Not Just the Corporations Taking You—It's the Swindlers!

What may be most outrageous about these sorts of rip-offs is that they are all perfectly legal. Factor in the criminal con men who bombard us with enticing come-ons over the phone, via email, or even in the form of a car parked by the side of the road with a "For Sale" sign stuck in the windshield, and your head begins to swim.

According to the RCMP, which tries to keep track of such things, 10,000 Canadians a year complain about fraudulent telemarketing alone. Credit card fraud costs customers and issuers as much as $500 million a year.

What this means is that unless you are *extremely* careful, it's a virtual certainty that you will be scammed at least once in your lifetime.

Fight for Your Money—Shop for Your Money

The fact that you are reading this book right now tells me that you are truly hopeful and that you believe you can do better financially. My mission with this book is to give you the knowledge, the tools, and the action steps you need to make you an advocate for your own financial rights. The FIGHT FOR YOUR MONEY goal is for you to be smart and in charge of your money so others can't separate you from what you have worked so hard to earn.

The first step in this process is recognizing that while there is a problem, there is also a solution—that you have the power to do something about it. The challenge of keeping yourself from being ripped off is not hopeless. It is, in fact, HOPEFUL.

You deserve to be in control of your money.

Why give up control to some powerful corporation that doesn't care about you personally? You know you are smart. All you need are the right tools.

As you read this book, you may notice there are some general rules that apply to almost every single financial or consumer issue we cover—from buying a used car on eBay to paying for your groceries with a debit card. Most are plain old common sense. The trick is not just to know them but to live them. If you can, you'll never have to worry about being ripped off again.

The "Fight for Your Money" Rules

- THERE IS NO SUCH THING AS A FREE LUNCH. If a deal sounds too good to be true, it probably is.
- FIGURE OUT THE TOTAL COST. The price they advertise isn't necessarily what something really costs. Make sure you know what the advertised price covers, what it doesn't cover—and how much you'll have to pay for the stuff you're going to need that isn't included.
- DON'T TAKE ANYBODY'S WORD FOR ANYTHING. Guarantees and promises don't mean anything unless they are in writing.
- DO YOUR HOMEWORK. Comparison-shop, educate yourself about the product, and unless you know whom you're dealing with, check them out before you send them a money order or sign a contract.
- BE CAREFUL WHAT YOU SIGN. Read *all* the paperwork, including the small print, and make sure you understand it.
- RESIST EFFORTS TO PRESSURE OR INTIMIDATE YOU. Not every salesperson who employs the hard sell is a crook. But honest ones rarely do. When they badger you to "Act now!" that's a sure sign you shouldn't. When they urge you not to tell anyone else about this "very special opportunity," you definitely should—preferably someone who carries a badge.
- IF YOU THINK YOU'VE BEEN SCAMMED, REPORT IT TO THE APPROPRIATE AUTHORITIES. As an official for a U.S. consumer organization put it in an interview with consumer reporter Bob Sullivan, "Complaining is to being a good consumer what voting is to being a good citizen. If there are no complaints, there's no impetus for legislative change and the enforcement officers don't know what's going on. If you only complain to friends but don't report something . . . then nobody who can do something about it knows what happened to you."
- THERE IS NO SUCH THING AS A SET PRICE. With most services and many consumer goods (cars, cable TV, gym membership), not everyone pays the same price. How much often depends on when you signed up, what incentives you were offered, and how well you negotiated. As a consumer, you have more power than you think.
- PACKAGE DEALS ARE OFTEN NOT GOOD DEALS. They may sound great, but they typically require you to buy something you don't really want or need.

- MONEY GIVES YOU CONTROL, SO HOLD ON TO IT AS LONG AS YOU CAN. It's easier to reverse an unfair charge than to try to get a refund once you've paid out cash. So don't agree to automatic debits—use a credit card instead. Similarly, parcel out payments to repairpeople and contractors, and avoid years-long service contracts.
- PROTECT YOUR IDENTITY. Personal information, such as credit card and bank account numbers, should be shared only with salespeople and companies you know and trust—and never by email.

Rich or Poor—The Odds Are Against You Until You Fight Back

You might think this book was timed to coincide with the current economic crisis. It actually wasn't. I had been thinking about writing it since January 2004, when I appeared on *The Oprah Winfrey Show* to launch my fifth book, *The Automatic Millionaire.* That show inspired millions, as Oprah's shows always do, and *The Automatic Millionaire* went on to become the top-selling business book of the year. The experience I had while taping *Oprah* that day changed my life. It opened my eyes even more to all the financial challenges tens of millions of Americans face on a daily basis.

Appearing along with me on the show were several couples with serious financial issues. My job was to diagnose the nature of their problems and create a plan to solve them—to do what we called a money makeover. Over the next few years, I would do a half dozen shows like this with Oprah and ultimately dozens more money makeovers on other TV shows.

Doing these money makeovers inserted me into a world that was both eye-opening and heartbreaking. When I was a financial planner and senior vice president at Morgan Stanley, which is what I did before I began writing books, I never had clients who owed $50,000 to $125,000 in credit card debt. I never worked with people who'd taken out payday loans that were costing them 900% annually. I didn't even know such rip-off products existed.

I had never known anyone who paid 35% too much for a car, then got it financed at 15%, then was talked into buying an insurance policy to pay off the debt, and then took out another loan, also at 15% to pay for the insurance policy.

I had never known anyone who had gone to what was supposed to be a non-profit credit repair agency—only to have her money stolen and her credit destroyed completely. I had never known anyone who bought a home with little money down, a second mortgage and a third mortgage carrying interest rates north of 10% that changed every month—plus a 10% early payment penalty, meaning it would cost them tens of thousands of dollars to get out of that terrible deal and into a better one.

To put it simply, until I appeared on *Oprah* that day and met a bunch of real people leading real lives of daily financial desperation, I hadn't been exposed on a daily basis to what so many of us are really up against when it comes to our money. I hadn't realized how many Canadians are being taken to the cleaners EVERY SINGLE DAY by companies, banks, and brokers all operating PERFECTLY LEGALLY.

Doing those makeovers opened my eyes to the enormous odds that the average person has to battle every day simply to survive financially. And it left me determined to try to do something to help.

You Don't Deserve to Be Taken

I believe you should have a fighting chance to avoid being ripped off, even if those "rip-offs" are legal. Whether you are rich or living paycheque to paycheque, you don't deserve to be taken financially—EVER!

But to be able to protect yourself effectively, you must have the mind-set, the attitude, and the action plan of a FIGHTER. How do you acquire all that? This book will be your guide.

How to Use This Book

The heart and soul (and most of the pages) of *Fight for Your Money* consists of a guide to protecting yourself from financial rip-offs. This guide is divided into 11 sections, each of which concerns a basic area of financial life (Automobiles, Banking, Credit, and so on). Within these sections, you will find a number of entries devoted to specific consumer issues, such as car buying or travel packages, that tell you how to find a good deal, what to watch out for, and where you can go for help if things go wrong. At the end of the book, we have included a concise toolkit filled with sample letters—the specific tools you will need to become your own consumer advocate.

We chose the topics we did because we felt that they represent the most critical areas for most people. In fact, some of them may not seem particularly relevant to you right now. Maybe you are single and the topic of divorce holds no interest for you. If this is the case, simply skip that section. (Then again, if you know someone going through a divorce, maybe you should give it a look—you could wind up saving your friend some unneeded heartache, not to mention a lot of money.)

Unlike my previous books, which were written to be read straight through, this one can be read cover to cover or it can be dipped into where and when it serves your particular needs. So scan the list of topics and go straight to what matters to you most right now. Taking action based on one idea in just one chapter could easily save you 10 to 20 times the cost of this book. For example:

- Don't rent a car at the airport (take a cab to a nearby location), and save $300 in a week.
- Use a credit card, not a debit card, and fraudulent charges will cost you $0 instead of $500 or more.
- Raise your credit score (you can do it yourself) and save as much as $50,000 in interest on a 25-year mortgage.
- Book your airline tickets one at a time and save as much as $275 per ticket.
- Cut your life insurance premiums *in half* by making one call.

And, what's more, you'll avoid huge rip-offs like:

- sneaky renewals of your cell-phone plan
- gift cards whose fees and expiration dates erode their value

In short, this book is yours to use in any way you need to use it. I hope it will become a guide that you come back to time and time again, as the need arises.

Join Our Movement of Smart, Empowered Consumers

My goal with this book is to create a movement of smart, empowered consumers who FIGHT FOR THEIR MONEY. Over the years, I have received thousands upon thousands of letters and emails from readers like you who have used my books to change their lives. These messages have inspired me—and, more important, countless readers like you—to continue to fight to live and finish rich.

I hope this book will inspire you to take action. I want to hear what has happened to you and how you have fought back. This is the first edition of a book that we plan to continue updating in the future—so if we overlooked a crucial FIGHT FOR YOUR MONEY topic that you would like to see covered, let us know. We want your suggestions and input.

Please email me at **success@finishrich.com** and visit our web site at **www.finishrich.com**. We are transforming the FinishRich site into an active community where savvy consumers like you can share what they have done to fight for their money. We will have stories from you and others that you can review to get more ideas as well as specific resources of what has worked (or hasn't).

Together, we will be a team that FIGHTS—and ultimately WINS!

Your friend and coach,
David Bach

Take Your Fight to the Next Level!

Here's a special offer for all my readers.

Visit my web site at **www.finishrich.com/ffymdownload** to access our 7-day trial for the all new Fight for Your Money Power Pack. Log on today to test drive this 13-step battle plan for living a debt-free lifestyle.

Enjoy!

AUTOMOBILES

Buying a New Car

High gas prices and an economic slowdown have decimated auto sales, but Canadians still buy roughly 1.6 million new cars, minivans, SUVs, and pick-up trucks each year. And on virtually every one of those transactions, we get taken. The Retail Council of Canada says auto dealers' 1.5% average profit margin is much lower than the profit margins of furniture, hardware, or jewellery stores. Car dealers in the United States say they actually lose $30 or so on every new car they sell. But that doesn't mean we're getting anything close to a fair bargain. That's because what the dealers lose on the cars they more than make up by sticking us with outrageous finance charges and overpriced add-ons like extended warranties, rustproofing, and paint sealants. Dealers charge as much as 60% more than third-party companies for extended warranties.

The fact is, even without the tricks and scams, buying a new car is almost always a bad investment. If you're hooked on newness and the latest technology, it makes much more sense from a financial point of view to go for a one- or two-year-old low-mileage used vehicle. That's because new cars take their biggest depreciation hit in the first year after they roll off the dealer's lot, typically losing 25% to 30% of their value. Really savvy consumers let someone else absorb that loss and buy *nearly* new cars—which are generally still under manufacturer's warranty, are equipped with most of the latest bells and whistles, and have suffered relatively little wear and tear—for less than 70 cents on the dollar.

Then again, economic common sense has never been much of a match for new-car lust. Maybe we shouldn't buy them, but we do. And if we're going to do it, we might as well do it right.

How to Fight for Your Money

There are roughly 3,800 new-car dealers in Canada. They comprise the exclusive channel through which new cars are distributed, so if you buy a new car, it will probably be through one of them.

As a group, car dealers have a pretty crummy reputation. This may not be totally fair, but it is understandable. It wasn't all that long ago that practices like rolling a stiff—urging prospective customers to take a car home overnight, only to threaten them the next morning with arrest for grand theft auto if they didn't pay for the car immediately—were practised more widely than anyone would like to admit.

These sorts of outrageous scams have pretty much been eliminated, but we still think of car salespeople as scary, and for good reason. Most of them work on commission, and many subscribe to the belief that once a customer walks into the showroom, it's their job to do whatever it takes to make sure he or she does not leave without signing a sales contract.

So if you've decided to buy a new car, understand what you're getting yourself into—the typical dealership is not a friendly oasis but rather a vicious battleground.

Here are a few key DO's and DON'Ts.

Focus on the Price

In an effort to maximize profits, car dealers try to manipulate every variable involved in the car-buying process, from the cost of the financing to the price of the floor mats. In this cutthroat environment, the best way to protect your money is to focus on one number and one number only—the purchase price of the car.

This may seem obvious, but the one thing most car dealers don't really want to talk about is the price. That's because once they commit to a price, it's much harder for them to bamboozle you into taking their money-making add-ons (like dealer financing) without the extra cost being obvious. So instead of giving you a straight answer when you ask how much a particular car costs, the dealer will ask you what kind of monthly payment you're looking for. Tell him you're not looking for a monthly payment; you're looking for a car. If he still won't name a price, take your business elsewhere.

Know the Real Price—Not the Fake "MSRP"

To get the best possible deal, you need to educate yourself in advance about what the dealer actually paid for the car you're interested in, the cost of all of the options you want, what kind of incentives and rebates the manufacturer is offering dealers, and how much of a markup local market conditions currently allow. It is these figures—and not the manufacturers' suggested retail price (the "MSRP" you'll find on the window sticker)—that should serve as the basis for your negotiations. Such information is available online from sources like **CarCostCanada.com** and the Automobile Protection Association (**www.apa.ca**). You can get similar information from **CarQuotes.ca**, if you pay $21 per report.

Keep in mind that the invoice price of a car is not the dealer's true cost, since it generally includes what's called a holdback—a fee (usually 2% to 4% of the MSRP) that most car manufacturers pay their dealers each time they sell a car. On top of this, there are often factory-to-dealer incentives—particularly near the end of a model year—that can lower the dealer's cost still further.

This is what makes it possible for dealers to make what they hope you will regard as an offer you can't refuse. If they sense you're not a pushover, they will sometimes take you aside, compliment you on your negotiating skills, and offer to let you have the car for "just one dollar over invoice." To demonstrate their sincerity, they may even show you a copy of the invoice.

All well and good, but this is definitely an offer you can and should refuse, since the invoice price is actually an artificial construct. What you want is a deal pegged to the dealer's *actual* cost—which, as a result of all those kickbacks and rebates, may be hundreds of dollars less than the invoice price.

WHAT A 2009 VW JETTA REALLY COSTS

MSRP:	$23,410
Invoice Price:	$22,350
Dealer's Actual Cost:	$22,050

Hundreds of dollars might seem like a reasonable profit for a dealer to make, but even on a $20,000 car it's actually a very narrow margin—no more than a few percentage points. This is why, as we will see, most dealers try to squeeze as much profit as they can out of service, financing, options, and extended warranties. It's because they can't make a decent profit on the sale of the car itself.

Remember, you can get all this information online. Chances are that the dealer will talk turkey once you let him know that you know how much he's getting back in manufacturer incentives.

Ask to See the Dealer's Paperwork

An easy way to gauge a dealer's trustworthiness is by assessing his financial transparency. Responsible dealers will let you see the paperwork showing the actual cost to them of the car you want, and they will tell you about any rebates, holdbacks, and manufacturer's incentives that may apply. Since you can get all this information online, checking their figures against yours is a great way to make sure you're dealing with a straight-shooter. If the sales staff gives you any doubletalk about why your numbers aren't applicable—or if they refuse to disclose their numbers—don't bother arguing with them. Just leave.

Borrow from a Bank—Not from a Car Dealer

More than a quarter of car-dealers' profits come from what they call F&I—finance and insurance. Indeed, this part of the business is so lucrative that many dealerships depend on it to make back the profits they surrender when they are forced to give customers a good deal on the purchase price.

On the finance side, what car dealers often do to boost their margins is tell customers with perfectly good credit that they don't qualify for low-interest financing and thus will have to accept more expensive loan terms. The technical term for this is "lying."

It probably happens more often in the United States than it does in Canada, but you should look out for it no matter where you live. It happened to Tom Costibile of Union Grove, Wisconsin, for example. After agreeing to a reasonable price for the car Tom wanted, the salesman went off to confer with his manager about the financing. "Eventually, he came back and told my wife and me that our credit scores were very, very low, but they could get us a loan—with a 25% interest rate."

Tom and his wife wisely fled the dealership and went home to do what they should have done before they started car shopping—check their credit rating. "I went on the Internet and ordered up my credit report," he says. "The dealership had low-balled our score by 120 points."

Here's a hard and fast rule: if you're not planning to pay cash for a new car, you should get your auto loan from a bank or credit union—not a car dealer. Take it as a given that any interest rate a car dealer quotes you is bound to be higher—often much higher—than you should be able to get from a reputable financial institution.

It's true that dealers often advertise super-low-rate auto loans (sometimes even with 0% interest) as part of a sales incentive from the manufacturer. The catch is that these loans are typically granted only to customers with the highest credit scores and then only for extremely limited terms.

Start Paying Now

A similarly misleading come-on is the "zero down/zero payments for one year" scam. Steer clear of this. All it does is defer your paying for the car for a year. This might sound appealing, but two things happen during that year. Interest accrues on your loan and the car depreciates. As a result, by the time you start repaying the loan, the amount you owe will have increased by hundreds or thousands of dollars—and your car will probably have lost somewhere between 20% and 30% of its value.

In fact, you could easily wind up owing considerably more on your car than the vehicle is actually worth. In finance circles, this is known as being upside down on a loan. This can be both uncomfortable and quite dangerous. That's because your auto insurance will cover only the actual value of the vehicle—so if your car is stolen or totalled in a crash, your insurance payout won't be big enough to pay off your loan. And you will have to continue making payments on a car you no longer have.

And Don't Buy Insurance from Them, Either

If you let them handle the financing, dealerships will also sometimes try to sell you insurance "to pay off the car loan if you die." Again, this happens more often in the United States than it does in Canada, but occasionally a car buyer in this country gets offered loan insurance. It's another deal that's great for them, terrible for you. I once did a money makeover on *The Oprah Winfrey Show* with a couple who agreed to pay $7,500 for a policy to cover their $50,000 auto loan. To make matters worse, they didn't have the $7,500, so they let the dealership finance it for them! Talk about a rip-off! Even if you're a smoker, you can get $50,000 worth of 10-year term life insurance for not much more than $100 a year.

THE CAR-LOAN INSURANCE RIP-OFF

What you might pay:	$7,500
What you *should* pay:	$0
You save:	**$7,500**

Bottom line is this, you can't be forced by a car dealer to have insurance that pays off the car if you die. And if they try to force you to buy it, then leave the car dealership and go to an ethical dealership that won't pull something like this.

Don't Trade in Your Old Car

It's certainly more convenient to let the dealer take your old car as a trade-in than to sell it separately. But that convenience comes at a huge price.

Make no mistake—the trade-in allowance is yet another variable that the dealership can and will manipulate to pad their profits and rip you off. To put it bluntly, they will lowball your trade-in to make up for the good price they gave you on your purchase. They get away with this because, with the end of the transaction in sight, most car buyers don't object.

This is why dealers often insist on taking your old car around back to be appraised. Taking away your ride home not only makes it harder for you to leave the dealership, but also puts the issue of your old car's value on the table, which takes the focus off the price of the car you are buying.

So don't trade in your old car. Sell it privately or to another dealer. Chances are, a separate sale will bring you a lot more for your car than the dealer will give you in a trade-in allowance.

What to Watch Out For

Buying into the Fantasy

The automakers spend literally billions of dollars each year on advertising designed to convince us that by changing cars, we can change who we are. This is true up to a point. Buying an expensive gas-guzzler can transform a rich person into a poor one pretty quickly. But that's about it. Driving an over-muscled SUV to soccer practice won't make you more of a hipster—or any less a Soccer Mom (or Dad)—than driving a minivan. Nor will jumping into a 4×4 for a late-night diaper run remove the spit-up from your shirt.

So don't buy into the fantasy that purchasing a particular vehicle will change who you are or even how you are perceived. Choose the kind of car you're going to buy based on what you need it for and how much it will cost you to operate—which means figuring in not only the purchase price but also fuel economy, maintenance and insurance costs, depreciation, resale value, and finance charges, if any. All the other stuff is just an excuse to spend more than you need to. Edmunds.com has a terrific "True Cost to Own" calculator (scroll down on the second page to find it) that weighs all of the key factors and tells you how much any particular model is likely to really cost you over your first five years of ownership.

OWNING A 2009 JETTA*

Monthly car payment:	$394
Total ownership cost per month:	$698

*Based on a 60-month car loan for a 2009 Volkswagen Jetta Sedan and Edmunds.com's "Total Cost to Own" calculation over five years.

Dealers Who Haggle

According to most surveys, the thing people hate the most about buying a car is haggling over the price. That's probably because most of us are not very good at haggling, while most car dealers are pros.

It used to be that you had no choice. The only way to buy a car sensibly was to walk into the dealership armed with plenty of data about invoice prices, manufacturers' holdbacks, and residual values (how much the car will be worth at the end of the lease), not to mention a strong stomach and a major attitude.

Happily, this is no longer the case. An increasing number of new-car dealers follow a no-haggle, posted-price policy. Saturn made this approach the cornerstone of its brand, so that is how all of its cars are sold. Online sites like Cars4u.com, eWheels.ca and CarCostCanada.com work in different ways, but all of them make it easier to buy a new car without impersonating a riverboat gambler playing five-card stud.

In large part, we can thank the Internet for this. In the United States, websites like Autos.com, Cars.com, CarsDirect (www.carsdirect.com), InvoiceDealers (www.invoicedealers.com), Edmunds.com, MyRide.com, and Yahoo!Autos (autos.yahoo.com) have made it possible to comparison-shop and choose the least expensive dealer without having to drive anywhere or argue with anyone. Now Canadians are catching on too with sites like auto.yahoo.ca and www.dealfinder.org.

And if you think doing online research is too much of a hassle, you can outsource the process. Drive Online (**www.driveonline.ca**) works with 60 franchised car dealers. All you have to do is specify the make, model, colour, and options you want. They do the rest, hooking you up with a dealer willing to offer "a hassle-free, time and money saving purchase/lease experience," according to the service's website.

The point is that you no longer need to haggle to get a good price on a new car. So why bother? Let the professionals duke it out for you. And avoid dealerships where they try to force you to do it yourself.

Options You Didn't Ask for and Don't Need

With their margins stretched razor thin, car dealers look for profits wherever they can find them. One big source is optional equipment. The markup on extras ranging from floor mats to theft detection systems is phenomenal. There's only one problem, as far as the dealers are concerned. It's that options are optional. There's no guarantee car buyers will order them on their own.

To eliminate this uncertainty—and maximize their bottom line—many dealers install options in virtually every car on the lot and then insist that you accept and pay for them, regardless of whether you actually want or need them. The theory is that, given a choice between a car with a bunch of unwanted options and no car at all, most customers will take the car with the options.

Dealers will also attempt to gouge you by pushing such unnecessary add-ons as paint protection and undercoating. Rustproofing is a typical scam. Even though most new cars come with six-year/160,000-kilometre rust warranties, many dealers will try to sell you on an $800 rustproofing treatment that costs them all of $40. The same is true for things like paint sealant and fabric protector. (What the dealer will do to your upholstery for $300, you can do for yourself with a $15 can of Scotchgard™.)

IS THIS OPTION NECESSARY?

Cost of dealer's "Fabric Protection Package":	$300
Cost of a can of Scotchgard™:	$15
You save:	**$285**

Fortunately, there is a simple way of dealing with this sort of thing. To quote the old antidrug slogan, "Just say no!"

Extended Warranties

One of the most unnecessary add-ons that a dealership will try to sell you is the extended warranty. Earlier I shared how "extended warranties" are huge sources of business for car dealerships (60% more expensive than comparable third-party warranties). Car salespeople like to say that such warranties provide "peace of mind." This is true only if getting ripped off makes you feel peaceful rather than angry.

The fact is that cars are built better and last longer than they used to—and, reflecting this, they come with increasingly generous factory warranties. Nonetheless, more new-car buyers than ever before—more than one-third these days, compared to only one out of five in the late 1990s—get suckered into purchasing extended service agreements. "Suckered" is the right word, since the price tag on these plans averages around $1,000, while the total repair costs they actually wind up absorbing are typically just $250 or so.

The price tags on extended service agreements average around $1,000, while the total repair costs they actually wind up absorbing are typically just $250 or so.

The typical extended warranty isn't actually a warranty. It's a private insurance policy. Essentially, you are betting that your shiny new car will suffer a catastrophically expensive failure within a specific period of time—usually, in the two or three years after the factory warranty expires. If you think your car is unreliable enough to make this a good bet, you shouldn't be buying it in the first place.

What to Do If Something Goes Wrong

If you've bought a car from an authorized dealership and are dissatisfied with some aspect of the transaction, the best course of action is to discuss the matter with the dealer's general manager. A short, clear, cordial letter outlining your concerns will generally get results. (You'll find a sample letter you can use as a model on page 325 of the FFYM Toolkit.) Avoid making threats or calling people names. This might make you feel better for the moment, but it NEVER helps your case. If anything, it will turn people off and make them less likely to want to help you.

Generally speaking, the first few weeks or months after you buy a new car are the best times to air a complaint with a dealership. Dealers do not want to be dinged on the car companies' customer satisfaction surveys, so they tend to be extremely responsive to complaints.

If your letter to the general manager doesn't provoke a satisfactory response, write a similar letter to the owner of the dealership, pointing out that you were not able to resolve things at a lower level. You can find out who and where the owner is by looking on the dealership's website or by calling the showroom and asking the receptionist. If the owner is a company, contact its CEO. Multiple-dealership owners may have dedicated customer service contacts at their headquarters, though they say that the vast majority of problems are resolved by the general manager at the dealer location in question.

If the owner isn't sympathetic and you are convinced your gripe is legitimate, you should inform the car company, through the customer service telephone number or email address you will find on its web site.

At this point, if you still haven't gotten satisfaction, then it may be time to involve the government and/or lawyers. If the problem involves fraud or deceptive practices by the dealer or the automaker, you should complain to Canada's Office of Consumer Affairs (**www.ic.gc.ca**) as well as your province's consumer protection office. (They're listed on the Industry Canada web site under Canada's Office of Consumer Affairs.) You can also file a complaint through the Consumer Information Gateway (**http://consumerinformation.ca**).

You can also contact the local chapter of the Better Business Bureau (**www.ccbbb.ca**) and possibly even a news-media outlet, such as the consumer reporter at your local television station. (His or her contact information will be on the station's website.) Car dealers hate it when a news crew rolls into their showroom wanting to know why they are cheating customers.

If your complaint is that your new car is a lemon—meaning that it has some kind of recurring, unfixable mechanical problem—you can submit your dispute to the Canadian Motor Vehicle Arbitration Plan (**www.camvap.ca**). CAMVAP's arbitration is binding on both parties.

Fight for Your Money Action Steps

- ☐ If you're not paying cash for a car, know your credit score before you apply for credit. Visit **www.canadian-creditreport.com**.
- ☐ Go online and check out the many invaluable resources for car buyers. Use them for comparison shopping, to determine dealer costs, and also to figure out how much your trade-in is really worth.
- ☐ Focus on the total cost of ownership, not just your monthly payment.
- ☐ Avoid trading in your old car. Sell it separately to another dealer.
- ☐ Just say no to extended warranties!

Buying a Used Car

There's no question that if you need a set of wheels, it makes a lot more sense to buy a well-maintained, late-model car than a new one. Why? Because if it's less than three years old, a good used car is bound to have nearly all the latest bells and whistles, not to mention the manufacturer's original warranty. And thanks to the massive depreciation that virtually all new cars suffer the minute their new owners drive them out of the showroom, you can generally get a good used one at anywhere from 20% to 50% off the new-car price.

The problem is that dealing with used-car salespeople can be a nightmare. They're not all crooks, but they are all out to take you for as much as they can. If that means selling you a car you don't really like for more than you can afford, that's just what they'll try to do.

They're pretty good at it, too. Most Canadians purchase a used car as their first vehicle, and most of them buy their car from a dealer (as opposed to private individuals). In 2007, Canadians bought 1.5 times as many used cars as they did new ones, which means they bought more than 2.3 million vehicles. Unlike new-car dealers, used-car salespeople make money on the cars they sell—the average gross margin on a used vehicle last year in Canada was $2,500 versus $1,800 for a new car. (Most new car dealers make their money on service, financing, options, and extended warranties—they actually lose a little money on the sale of the car itself.)

There's nothing wrong with a little profit, of course—as long as you make sure it doesn't come at your expense.

How to Fight for Your Money

Back in the bad old days when the big carmakers believed in planned obsolescence, automobile odometers went up to only 99,999 kilometres—and for good reason. Until well into the 1980s, most cars really weren't built to last. They began showing their age around 80,000 kilometres and were ready for the scrap heap long before they hit 160,000 kilometres.

These days, odometers go up to 999,999 kilometres. That may be a little optimistic, but the fact is that most modern cars will easily give you 200,000 kilometres or more. Indeed, according to industry analysis group R.L. Polk, in 2007 the average passenger vehicle on the road in 2007 was 9.2 years old. What this means is that a three-year-old used car with 60,000 kilometres on it has expended less than one-third of its useful life—maybe much less.

Here's what makes this statistic important to you. Even though that used car still has at least 70% of its life ahead of it, its price is bound to be a lot less than 70% of what it cost when it was new. Most likely, you can buy a car like that for just 60%—and sometimes as little as 50%—of its original price.

Older cars can be even bigger bargains. A five-year-old car with 100,000 kilometres on it probably has at least another 120,000 kilometres of good driving left in it—yet will cost you maybe one-quarter of what it did when it was new.

This is why I say used cars are generally a much better buy than new cars. Here's how to maximize your chances of getting a great deal.

Remember—They Are Called "Salespeople" for a Reason

It's no accident that used-car salespeople have such a sleazy reputation. "You know what our motto is?" one of them once asked me. *"If you ain't cheating, you ain't trying."* He later said he was just kidding, but I'm not so sure. Of course, for all the old-school salespeople like this one, there are many others who consider themselves to be transportation specialists or consultants. But whatever you call the person selling you the car, what is for sure is that he or she has been trained to sell you that car. In particular, they know all kinds of psychological tricks to keep you off balance, make you feel guilty about not trusting them, and distract you from the issues you should be focusing on.

For example, the last thing they want you to know is how much the car they're pushing you to buy really costs. So they never talk about actual price, just what the monthly payments will be. ("It's just $200 a month. You can afford that, can't you?" *Well, not if it's for 200 months.*) And they'll never admit they don't have the kind of car you're looking for. (As one salesman once told me: "If I tell the customer we have a certain vehicle even when we don't, I still have a 50% chance of making a sale. If I tell him that we don't have it, I've got zero chance.") Or if you say you need to discuss a potential deal with a spouse, parent, or friend (which is a smart thing to do any time you're making a major purchase), they'll roll their eyes, implying you must be some sort of a wuss. They may even pretend to have lost your car keys to keep you from leaving their lot.

They also like to brag that they sell more cars in a week than most people buy in their entire lives—and they use this fact to try to intimidate you into playing their game. But you know what? You don't have to fall for their bull. Do some research before you start shopping so you have at least a general idea of what you're looking for and what it's likely to cost. Talk to friends and co-workers; check out the major auto-sales websites like VMR Canada (www.vmrcanada.com), Canadiandriver.com, and Canadiancarprices.com. U.S. websites may be helpful, as well. Try Edmunds.com and Kelley Blue Book (www.kbb.com), as well as some of the reputable Canadian and U.S. consumer advocates like Phil Edmonston's Lemonaidcars.com, Consumer Reports (www.consumerreports.org), and the Canadian Automobile Association (www.caa.com) have to say. And don't take any abuse. Remember, used car dealers need you a lot more than you need them. If you don't like the way you're being treated at a particular lot, just thank them for their time and take your business elsewhere.

Check the History—Get the VIN Number and Have It Verified

How can you tell if a used-car salesman is lying?

His lips are moving.

Seriously, though, when you're shopping for a used car, there's no reason to take anything a dealer tells you on faith. Instead of wondering whether that cute Toyota that caught your eye really did have only one previous owner who never had a single accident, you can order up a vehicle history report that will tell you for sure.

One great thing about cars is that we keep records on them—billions and billions of records. Every time you bring your car in for a smog check, have an accident, register an insurance claim, or transfer the title, a record goes into a file somewhere.

For a long time, this fact did ordinary consumers like you and me no good, because those records were scattered all over the place—in insurance company offices, auto service centres, and the provincial motor-vehicle registration offices. But these days, outfits like CarProof (**www.carproof.com**) and CarFax (**www.carfax.com**) maintain vast databases containing literally billions of automobile records from thousands of government and private sources. For a fee of $25 to $45, they will take any VIN number you give them and email you a report telling you everything you need to know about that particular car's past, including all the owners it's ever had, whether it's ever been wrecked or stolen, how it did on smog tests, whether its odometer has been rolled back, and when the dealer took delivery (a piece of information that could give you some negotiating leverage if it turns out the car has been sitting on the lot for months).

Forty-five bucks may seem like a lot, but trust me—given how good used-car dealers are on taking a salvaged wreck and making it look good as new, it's more than worth it. Buying a used car without checking the history is just asking for trouble. The price of this verification is less than one tank of gas. Make the investment—you'll be glad you did.

Look for CPO Certification

While a vehicle history report can reveal a lot about a car's past, it doesn't say anything about the car's likely future. That's why you should never buy a used car without a warranty. And the very best warranties are the ones that come with cars that have been inspected and personally guaranteed by a reputable dealership. In most cases, it's the manufacturer that bestows the coveted label of "Certified Pre-Owned" on a well-maintained, low-mileage car, but some used-car chains also operate impressive certification programs. (This is one reason that it's generally not a good idea to buy a car from a private individual. You might get a good price, but you definitely won't get a warranty.)

Most Certified Pre-Owned cars tend to be upscale brands like Audi, Mercedes, Lexus, and BMW, whose long-term reliability is reflected in the fact that their original factory warranties are generally longer than the standard three years or 100,000 kilometres. But there are an increasing number of more affordable mainstream brands like Saturn, Chevy, and Ford that certify their used cars.

Certified Pre-Owned cars can cost as much as $2,500 more than less-desirable, uncertified used cars. But they're often worth the extra cost, since they tend to be the cleanest, best-maintained, most like-new used cars you can find.

Consider Mainstream Brands and Clone Cars

It may sound strange, but sometimes a car can be too reliable. If you check VMR Canada (**www.vmrcanada.com**) or **Canadiancarprices.com,** which is one of the standard references for used-car prices, you'll see that the brands with the highest resale values—BMW, Honda, Scion, Mini, and Volkswagen—are among the most reliable. That shouldn't be surprising. Reliability is one of the most important factors to consider in buying a car, so you would expect the most reliable ones to be the most in demand—and hence the most expensive.

If money were no object, you should certainly buy one of these cars. But of course money *is* an object, which means you need to think about whether the extra money you have to pay for that extra reliability is really worth it. In fact, it may not be.

Why? Because there are cars just a little less reliable that sell for a *lot* less money—which is to say, that even though they may be slightly less reliable than a BMW or a Mini, they are a much better value. Mainstream brands like Chevrolet, Ford, Nissan, and Mazda—all of which manufacture reasonably reliable vehicles—may actually be the most sensible choices for used-car buyers because their cars depreciate faster than their more reliable counterparts and therefore sell for lower prices on the used-car lot.

The same is true for some luxury North American brands like Cadillac, Buick, and Lincoln. You don't want to buy them new because their value drops like a rock the minute you drive off the dealer's lot. But for precisely the same reason, they tend to be great buys when used. Not only do they come with long factory warranties, good reliability ratings, and a nationwide network of customer-friendly dealers, but because of that awful depreciation, the price of used models tends to be quite reasonable.

And don't overlook clone cars. Clone cars are essentially identical cars built on the same assembly line but sold under different names by different manufacturers. For example, the Pontiac Vibe is a clone of the Toyota Matrix. It may be identical to the Matrix in all but name, but the name is what counts when it comes to depreciation. And since Pontiacs depreciate faster than Toyotas, a used Vibe is a better value than a used Matrix. Similarly, a used Chrysler Crossfire, which was built from the same hardware in the same factory as the old Mercedes SLK, may be a much better value used than a used SLK.

SEND IN THE CLONES

Cost of a 3-year-old Toyota Matrix:	$14,900
Cost of a 3-year-old Pontiac Vibe:	$13,875
You save:	**$1,025**

Based on Kelley Blue Book suggested retail value of 2006 Toyota Matrix Sport Wagon and Pontiac Vibe Sport Wagon, each with under 45,000 miles.

Go Online for Bargains

While the best used cars may be the Certified Pre-Owned ones you find at a big dealership, serious bargain hunters like to buy their cars directly from the previous owner. In large part, that's because you no longer have to pore over the Sunday classifieds in your hometown newspaper to find who's selling what. These days, you simply boot up your computer and surf the web.

Given the enormous popularity of online classified ads sites like Craigslist (**www.craigslist.org**) and online auction sites like giant eBay Motors (**www.ebaymotors.com**), it's no wonder that the Internet now figures in more than one-quarter of all used-car sales. Craigslist carries ads for upward of 3 million used cars each month. For its part, eBay welcomes 11 million visitors each month and sells upward of about US$18 billion worth of cars and related products each year.

There are all sorts of reasons for the popularity of these sites, but the main ones are price and selection. All things being equal, owner-sold used cars tend to be cheaper than those sold by dealerships. And the nature of the Internet means that you're not restricted to looking at ads for only the used cars that happen to be available in your town. You can see ads for cars anywhere in North America (Craigslist has separate listings for 450 cities)—which means that it's up to you to decide how far you are willing to travel to retrieve a car or how much you are willing to pay to have it shipped to you.

This is a huge advantage. A Toyota Prius might be hard to come by in Regina or Halifax, but might be more available in Winnipeg or Montreal. So the ability to consider cars from other markets can make it easier to locate the car you want.

Keep in mind that, when you buy from private individuals, you're not likely to get a warranty. That said, eBay Motors does have an online Certified Pre-Owned showroom that offers thousands of CPO vehicles.

Of course, dealerships advertise on the Internet too, and there are also plenty of good referral websites—like **Canada.motoseller.com**, Auto Trader (**www.autotrader.ca**), Used Cars Canada (**www.usedcarscanada.com**), and Auto 123 (**www.auto123.com**)—that can hook you up with a local used-car dealer who has the kind of car you're looking for. But they're not likely to get you the kind of bargains you can find on Craigslist and eBay.

You Can Also Get Good Deals from Specialists

For the most part, you should avoid independent used-car dealers—the kind of guys who have small lots filled with a jumble of old cars. The best cars tend to be snapped up by franchised dealers, who get first crack at trade-ins, leaving these guys with mainly junk. But there is one exception to this rule: independent used-car dealers who specialize in a particular kind of car, usually an upscale foreign brand.

I'm talking about the stand-alone independent dealers who sell and service nothing but BMWs, or Mercedeses or Saabs, or other similar cars. These guys generally know their cars inside and out, offer a good variety of their brand, and frequently provide a warranty. Most important, they are enthusiasts first and car dealers second—meaning they're much more fun to deal with. They also tend to buy their inventory from fanatical repeat customers who take great care of their cars, so the vehicles they sell rival those sold by franchised dealers—except that they are usually less expensive.

My friend Allan, for example, bought an old Mercedes convertible from a big Mercedes dealer for around $28,000 several years ago. Then a few months later, he saw the same year and model Mercedes at a small specialty lot for just $22,500. And the cheaper car was actually in slightly better condition!

Don't Overlook the Rental Companies

Rental car companies like to get rid of cars before the mileage gets too high—usually before the odometer hits 20,000 miles. This can happen quickly in a rental car, so rental companies regularly sell vehicles that are not much more than a year old—sometimes not even that.

Unlike the United States, rental car companies in Canada don't offer vehicles for sale on their websites. But if you ask your local car-rental agent, you can find out how to buy one from that particular company.

You might think it's a bad idea to buy a used car that's mainly been driven by people who didn't own it. In fact, rental cars are among the best-maintained vehicles on the road today. They are checked over by professionals every time they are turned in, and they are serviced religiously.

As a result, rental companies generally offer solid warranties on the used vehicles they sell. And that's on top of the original factory warranties, which, given how new these cars tend to be, are usually still several years and tens of thousands of miles away from expiring.

Rental companies sometimes charge a little more for their cars than most used-cars dealers, but given the excellent maintenance they get, their vehicles are generally worth it. In addition, most of the companies have a no-haggle sales policy, which can make the purchase process pretty painless. And some of the deals are pretty darn good.

What to Watch Out For

There are countless used-car scams, ranging from bait-and-switch advertising (where you're lured in by an ad promising the proverbial cream puff, only to be told when you arrive that it's just been sold) to selling stolen vehicles. Most of them aren't hard to spot—if you know what to look for. Here are the top red flags to avoid.

Cars with Suspiciously Low Mileage

Odometer fraud used to be one of the biggest perils facing used-car buyers.

It still is.

Carmakers thought that by making digital odometers standard equipment, dishonest dealers would no longer be able to make an old warhorse seem young and fresh by rolling back the mileage. They were wrong. Digital odometers have turned out to be just as susceptible to tampering as the old mechanical ones—and unscrupulous used-car dealers have no compunctions about taking advantage of this fact.

The statistics are astounding. According to CarFax, more than 89,000 vehicles appear with their odometers tampered with in Canada every year, at a cost to car buyers of more than $3.5 million a year in inflated prices

To make sure you're not one of the victims, be skeptical when you come across a cream puff with unusually low mileage. Keep in mind that the average car racks up around 20,000 kilometres a year. So if you're looking at three-year-old convertible and its odometer reads just 30,000 kilometres, be skeptical. Was it really owned by a little old lady from Port Credit who drove it only on Sundays? Check the tires. If the odometer shows fewer than 30,000 kilometres, the car should still have its original set. (If all four tires don't match or they're not a major brand, you'll know something is wrong.) And take a look at the gas and brake pedals. There shouldn't be much wear-and-tear if the car really is a low-mileage special.

Mismatched or Missing VIN Numbers

For several decades, every motor vehicle manufactured in or imported to North America has been required to have a 17-digit Vehicle Identification Number stamped onto a small metal plate and usually attached to the dashboard by the windshield.

The VIN number is a unique identifier as important to your car as your Social Insurance Number is to you. If a car's VIN number is missing or seems to have been altered in any way, that's a sure sign there's something fishy about the vehicle—most likely that it's either a stolen car or a salvaged wreck. Whatever the case, you want no part of it.

So before you buy a used car, make sure that all the VIN numbers are where they are supposed to be, that all match exactly, and that none of them has been filed down or otherwise tampered with.

Cars That Are Sold "As Is"

As a rule, you should never buy a used car that doesn't come with at least a 30- to 90-day warranty that will protect you against any non-obvious mechanical problems the car may have. Remember Murphy's Law: "If anything can go wrong, it will." It wasn't written with used cars in mind, but it might as well have been.

And don't be swayed by a salesperson who tells you that the dealership will take care of you if any problems arise.

No matter what the salesperson may promise, ask for the warranty in writing. Otherwise, you'll be on your own, with sole responsibility for fixing anything that may be wrong with the car—and you should not expect anyone to come to your aid if the car turns out to be a lemon.

The Car in the Walmart Lot with the "For Sale" Sign in the Window

You see them all the time: cars parked by the side of the road or in a shopping mall parking lot with those red and white For Sale signs taped to the side or rear window. The sellers usually say that it's their personal car and they just want to make a quick cash deal, guy to guy (or gal), without any middlemen or paperwork. Sometimes they are completely legitimate, but many of these sellers are what's called curbstoners—illegal, unlicensed used-car dealers who operate from the curb, rather than a legitimate lot. Most of the cars curbstoners sell are either salvage vehicles or have failed inspections. More than a few are stolen. So beware of street sales—however attractive the price may seem to be.

What to Do if Things Go Wrong

Many of the scams that dishonest used-car dealers try to pull are not simply unfair; they are also against the law. Swindles like bait-and-switch advertising, odometer tampering, and title-washing (where a badly damaged car is registered in another province and given a new title that doesn't reflect its true condition) are all crimes. So if you think you've been victimized by this sort of thing, take heart—the law is on your side.

But before you call the cops, there are a few less drastic actions you should try if you think there's something fishy about the used car you just bought.

In most cases, the first thing you should do is confront the seller and attempt to resolve the problem directly. If it's a big chain or a franchised dealer connected to one of the big carmakers, chances are they'll have a customer service department that will do its best to resolve the issue. If it's an independent dealer, you should go to the salesperson or his or her supervisor.

The important thing is to keep your cool and put your complaint—along with what you would like them to do about it—in writing.

Obviously, you shouldn't expect them to be happy to see you. In fact, most used-car salesperson will run the other way when they spot an unhappy former customer stomping onto their lot. This can be incredibly frustrating. In fact, I can't think of anything more infuriating than getting the brush-off from the same guy who pretended to be your best buddy when he was trying to sell you a vehicle just a few days or weeks earlier. But even though it might make you feel better, the way to get results isn't to call him every name in the book and threaten to have him arrested. What you want to do is send a clear, concise letter to his boss or the owner of the dealership outlining your gripe, suggesting a proposed solution, and politely expressing your hope that it won't be necessary for you to resort to legal action.

Chances are, this will produce results. If it doesn't, it's time to go to the authorities and/or hire a lawyer. In addition to contacting your province's consumer affairs department, you should also complain to your local Better Business Bureau (**www.ccbbb.ca**). And think about calling the consumer affairs reporter at your local TV station or newspaper. Consumer reporters love exposing used-car scams. (On the other hand, they are totally uninterested in "he said/she said" disputes between buyers and sellers, so if your problem isn't really a dealer who makes a practice of scamming his customers, don't bother.)

If you have issues with a used car that you bought in a private transaction (whether you found it through a newspaper ad or on Craigslist), you have fewer options. If the seller refuses to do anything about your complaint—or even respond to your letter—there's not a lot you can do short of hiring a lawyer and suing him or her. This is one benefit of doing business with a dealership.

However, there is one kind of private used-car transaction where used-car buyers do enjoy protection: vehicles sold through eBay. Under its Vehicle

Purchase Protection policy, eBay will reimburse its customers up to $50,000 if a car they bought through the site turns out to have been stolen or damaged or has otherwise failed to live up to how it was advertised.

Fight for Your Money Action Steps

- ☐ Start by using sites like VMR Canada (www.vmrcanada.com), Canadiandriver.com, and Canadiancarprices.com to research car values, prices, makes, and models. Know before you go!
- ☐ Before you buy any used car, check its history at CarProof (www.carproof.com) and CarFax (www.carfax.com).
- ☐ Always have an independent mechanic do a thorough diagnostic test before purchasing.
- ☐ Look for CPO Certification when buying from a dealership.
- ☐ Shop online for bargains at sites like www.craigslist.com and www.ebaymotors.com.
- ☐ Don't forget the car-rental company! Visit their individual sites to shop their inventory.

Car Leasing

You want to make a car dealer happy? Walk into his showroom and tell him you're interested in a lease. Car dealers just love customers who lease.

There's a good reason for this. Leasing can be so complicated and confusing that fooling customers is a breeze. Indeed, it's so easy to play games with the numbers that car dealers average twice as much profit on a lease as they do on a conventional purchase.

Leasing used to account for 40% of the new cars on the road in Canada. That figure has fallen since some car companies eliminated their subsidized lease rates. But leasing hasn't disappeared. About 20% of the new cars on the road are leased (and more than 40% of some luxury models) rather than bought. So we're talking about a lot of money—as much as $500 million a year in excess profits, according to some estimates. This doesn't mean that leasing is always a rip-off. There are situations in which it makes good sense to lease rather than buy. In fact, I have leased successfully myself. The trick is recognizing when you're in the right situation—and when you're not.

Leaser Beware!

Car dealers average twice as much profit on a lease as they do on a conventional purchase.

How to Fight for Your Money

Car leasing can sound simpler than it really is. When you lease, what you're doing is getting the use of a car for a set period of time (usually between two and five years), during which you agree to cover the cost of the car's depreciation. Let's say you lease a $25,000 Honda for three years. Since a Honda typically depreciates by 40% over three years, the car will be worth just $15,000 or so when your lease ends. So for the right to use the Honda over those three years, you have to compensate the leasing company for the $10,000 drop in its value.*

Theoretically, you could put up $10,000 in cash at the beginning of the lease and be done with it. Some people actually do this, even though it defeats one of the main purposes of most car leases, which is to minimize your upfront costs. But the vast majority of people who lease cars put little or nothing down upfront to cover the depreciation. Instead, they pay off the depreciation charge in monthly instalments—plus interest.

This is why lease payments are generally so much smaller than car loan payments. With a car loan, you're paying off the purchase price of the car—its full value. With a lease, you're paying off only part of its value—often less than half. Of course, once you've paid off an auto loan, you own the car free and clear. When you finish a lease, you own nothing. (It's true that you can usually buy a car at the end of a lease by paying the depreciated price—known in leasing jargon as the residual value. But unless the leasing company has miscalculated—which they sometimes do—it's generally a lot cheaper simply to take out a car loan and buy the vehicle new than to lease a car for several years and then buy it. That's because the interest rates on auto loans are often lower than those for leases.

So which is a better deal—paying a lot less every month but having to give up the car at the end of the lease or paying more but getting to keep the car? In fact, there is no single answer for everyone. It depends on a wide variety of factors—how you drive, where you drive, how much the car depreciates, what kind of interest you have to pay, and on and on.

Car dealers will always tell you what a great deal leasing is. They will emphasize the lower monthly payments and the lower upfront costs, the convenience of being able to walk away from the car at the end of the lease, and

*Even though you negotiate the lease with a car dealer, you actually lease the car from a leasing company. What happens is that once you and the dealer agree on the terms, the dealer sells the car to a leasing company, which then leases it to you.

most of all the ability to put yourself behind the wheel of a fancier car than you could otherwise afford.

They will talk a good game, and a lot of what they say may even be true. But keep your guard up. There's an awful lot they don't tell you—and for good reason.

When Leasing Makes Sense . . . and When It Doesn't

Leasing appeals to people because it can seem to be a lot less expensive than buying a new car. As we'll see shortly, this can be misleading. Still, there's no question that leasing can put you behind the wheel (at least for a while) of a much nicer car than you could probably afford to buy. But you shouldn't really consider it unless you fit into most if not all of the following categories.

1. YOU NEED TO HAVE A NEW CAR EVERY TWO OR THREE YEARS.
   Leasing doesn't make a lot of sense if you don't really care about having a new car. The fact is, when you're leasing, you're continually paying new-car prices without ever actually getting to own it—so if you'd just as well be driving a decent used car, why bother?

2. YOU GENERALLY DRIVE LESS THAN 15,000 MILES A YEAR.
   Since the value of a used car is directly related to how much it's been driven, most leases limit how many miles you can put on the car. You can choose the limit—generally, 10,000, 12,000, or 15,000 miles per year—and the higher the limit, the more expensive the lease. If you go over whatever limit you've chosen, you have to pay a stiff penalty, usually somewhere between 15 and 25 cents a mile. According to a study by CNW Marketing Research, more than one-third of people who lease cars exceed their annual limit—typically by around 2,500 miles a year. This may not sound like much, but over the course of a three-year lease, the overage could easily cost you nearly $2,000 in penalty fees. And if you wildly overshoot the limit, it could end up costing you so much that you would be better off simply buying the car out of the lease for the residual value and reselling it.

3. YOU'RE GOOD ABOUT KEEPING YOUR CAR WELL MAINTAINED.
   You should think twice about leasing if you like to modify or customize your car—or, conversely, if you're not good about taking care of it. You're expected to return your car in *near showroom condition* when your lease is up. Scratch a wheel rim on a curb and that will cost you hundreds of dollars—maybe thousands—depending on what kind of wheels you have. Suffer any dings, dents, windshield

cracks or nicks, worn-out floor mats—you name it and you will be charged for "excessive" wear and tear. And trust me, they charge you full value. Often the "nick fees" are simply absurd. According to CNW, wear-and-tear assessments averaged $1,700 in 2006.

> **Wear-and-tear assessments averaged $1,700 in 2006.**

With this in mind, before you give back a leased car, you should photograph it from head to toe to prove it was returned in good shape. The dealer won't do this when you bring the car in. They assess the charges later on and then send you a bill or deduct the charges from your deposit if there was one.

4. YOU'RE A BUSINESS OWNER OR SELF-EMPLOYED AND YOU USE YOUR CAR IN YOUR WORK.

   If you're a business owner or a self-employed person who leases a car for your work, the entire cost of the lease may be tax-deductible. For someone in the 35% bracket, this can reduce the real cost of the lease by more than one-third—making it hands down a better deal than buying. Regular wage-earners can sometimes deduct automobile expenses (basically, 58.5 cents for every business-related mile they drive), but they generally can't simply write off the cost of a car lease.

5. YOUR JOB IS SECURE AND YOU DON'T ANTICIPATE ANY LIFESTYLE CHANGES THAT MIGHT AFFECT THE KIND OF CAR YOU NEED.

   A car lease is a contract, and the leasing companies can be brutal about enforcing them. The fact that your circumstances may have changed—that you've lost your job, or had triplets, or been hospitalized—doesn't matter to them. Most leasing companies will not let you turn in a car early without paying huge penalties—often the equivalent of all the remaining lease payments. Indeed, once you've signed a car lease, it's virtually impossible to get out of it, short of declaring bankruptcy. So don't even think of leasing a car unless you are very sure that it will continue to be the right vehicle for you for the entire term of the lease and that you will be able to make all your payments.

How to Get a Good Deal—Focus on the Total Cost

So you've considered all these factors and you think leasing might make sense for you. Now the real work starts. There's no question that compared to financing a purchase with a car loan, leasing generally offers lower monthly payments and lower upfront costs. And, as I said, the car dealer will keep making that point over and over again. The thing is, it's not the whole story. And to make sure you get a good deal, you need to know the whole story.

It's definitely nice to have low monthly payments and low upfront costs. But what really matters is the total cost of the lease—how many of those low monthly payments will there be, what other fees are you likely to incur, and what will it all add up to.

There are several basic variables that affect the total cost of a lease. They can sound complicated, but if you don't let the jargon throw you, they are actually fairly easy to understand.

First of all, there's the actual price of the car, which is called the capitalized cost. Then there's the term of the lease (how many years it will run), the mileage limit, and the residual value, which is how much the lease company says the car will be worth when the lease ends. The difference between the capitalized cost and the residual value is the depreciation—which is the basic cost you as the lessee will have to pay. There are also upfront costs, which generally include the first month's payment, a refundable security deposit, taxes, registration fees, and other charges. Finally, there is something called the money factor, which determines how much interest you must pay on top of the depreciation.

Obviously, the smaller the depreciation, the less expensive your lease is going to be. What makes things complicated is that there is any number of different ways you can reduce the depreciation figure. One way is to lower the capitalized cost, which you can do either by haggling with the dealer or agreeing to make a down payment (known in leasing circles as a capitalized cost reduction). Typically, when you're negotiating a lease, a salesman will urge you to put a few thousand dollars down—dangling the prospect of a lower monthly payment. Don't fall for this. Sure, your monthly payment will be lower, but you'll be out a big chunk of money—and if you happen to total the car in the first few months of your lease, you won't get it back.

A better way to reduce your depreciation is to increase the residual value, which you can do by negotiating with the dealer, agreeing to a lower mileage limit, or picking a car known for retaining its value (a Lexus or Honda, say, as opposed to a Cadillac or Kia). You could also reduce the term of the lease, since the shorter the lease, the younger the car will be at its end and the less it will have depreciated.

You can also reduce the cost of a lease by trying to get the lowest possible money factor. This can be difficult since dealers are not required to disclose this number. But if you tell the dealer that you will not sign a lease without knowing what the money factor is, most will tell you. If yours refuses, take your business elsewhere.

A Simple System to Beat the Old Shell Game

Because there are so many moving parts, many car dealers turn lease negotiations into a kind of shell game, in which they keep trying to distract you with talk of low monthly payments, while they hike the capitalized cost, shave a few hundred kilometres off the annual limit, and add a few extra months onto the term—and then at the very end surprise you with a bunch of non-negotiable one-time administrative fees and add-ons.

It's not impossible to beat the dealer at his own game, but it takes real discipline and focus. Fortunately, there's a much simpler way to make sure you get a good deal on a car lease. All you need to do is decide four things in advance: what model car you'd like, how much of a down payment you're willing to make (if any), how long you'd like your lease to run, and how big or small a mileage limitation you feel you can live with. You can make these calculations with online tools at **www.cars4u.com**.

With these four variables set in your mind, you no longer need to worry about all the other complicated factors that go into calculating the total lease cost. Then you simply go online or get on the phone and start calling local dealerships.

Disclosure Checklist

The Canadian Vehicle Manufacturers Association, the Canadian Automobile Dealers Association, the Association of International Automobile Manufacturers of Canada and the Canadian Finance and Leasing Association have published a checklist that you can use to compare leasing companies' information. You can use it if you shop around for a lease rather than leasing through the dealership where you find your car.

DISCLOSURE CHECKLIST

Disclosed information	Leasing Co. Name	Leasing Co. Name	Leasing Co. Name
Acquisition Fee			
Allowable Kms and Excess Km Charges			
Annual Percentage Rate			
Gap Insurance			
Leased Vehicle Amount			
Leased Vehicle Amount Reduction			
Option to Purchase at Lease End			
Residual Value of the Vehicle			
Right for Early Purchase			
Right for Early Termination (Including charges)			
Security Deposit			
Term of the Lease			
Total Amount Due at Lease Signing			
Total Lease Charges			
Total Monthly Payment			

Tell the car dealers you contact your four specifications ("I'm looking for a three-year lease on a Honda Accord LX, no more than $2,500 down, and 12,000 miles a year"). Then ask them what's the best monthly payment they can give you.

When you approach the leasing process this way, it doesn't matter what the other numbers are or how the dealer arrived at them. Since you've already specified how much cash you will be paying upfront and exactly how many monthly payments you will be making, there's only one thing you need to find out in order to be able to calculate the total cost of the lease: the size of the monthly payment.

Once you know the monthly payment, you just multiply it by the number of months in your lease and then add your down payment. Bingo—you've got your total cost!

This system also makes it easy to figure out which dealer is offering you the best deal. When you're juggling all those different factors, every deal you're offered is bound to be structured differently, and you often wind up comparing apples and oranges. With this simplified approach, it's always apples and apples, since the only variable you're comparing is the monthly price.

If all this seems too complicated or time consuming, there are services that will handle all the calculating and bargaining for you. There aren't as many as there are in the United States, and they usually work locally. But if you can find one in your area, you might save yourself a lot of time and hassle by using the broker instead of doing it yourself. Check Google under Automobile Brokers Directory to find one in your neighbourhood.

Protect Yourself with Gap Insurance

When you lease a car, you're responsible for returning it to the leasing company in good condition at the end of your lease. So what happens if the car gets totalled or stolen? Under most standard leasing agreements, you will still have to pay the leasing company all the remaining monthly payments plus the car's residual value. You may think your auto insurance will take care of this, but most policies will pay only the car's current value—and that may be a lot less than what you owe the leasing company. (Keep in mind that the minute you drove your leased car off the lot, its value dropped as much as 20% or 30%.) On a $25,000 car stolen or totalled early in its lease, the gap between what your insurance will pay and what you might owe the leasing company could easily run as much as $7,000. And, believe me, they will expect you to pay it.

To protect yourself from this possibility, you can get what's called gap insurance, which stands for guaranteed auto protection. Gap insurance pays off the difference between what you owe and what your regular auto insurance will actually pay out. Some lease contracts automatically include it. If yours doesn't, ask your insurance company for gap coverage. The premiums shouldn't run more than $100 a year. (Warning: don't buy it from the dealer. He'll try to charge you several times that.)

What to Watch Out For

Claims That It's Always Cheaper to Lease

In the first year or two, leasing usually costs you less, but around the third year the balance begins to shift in favour of buying.

A salesperson who tells you that it's always cheaper to lease is not a salesperson you can or should trust. When it comes to leasing, there is no always. If you're likely to trade in a car before the loan is paid off, leasing is probably a better deal for you than buying. But if you generally keep driving a car long after you make the final payment (or if you paid cash for it in the first place), buying is probably cheaper. As a recent study by *Consumer Reports* showed, in the first year or two, leasing usually costs you less, but around the third year the balance begins to shift in favour of buying.

Promises That You Can Swap Your Old Lease for a New One

Salespeople eager to close a deal will sometimes tell you that if you get tired of your car before your lease is over, they will be happy to get you out of the original lease and into a new one. Don't believe them. They certainly will be happy to take care of you, but that's only because you're giving them a chance to extract even more money from you. In fact, there is no such thing as trading in an old lease for a new one. What actually happens is that the dealer will turn in your car early and roll the cost of all the early termination fees, penalties, and unpaid depreciation into your new lease. The dealer may also pocket your security deposit in the process.

Interest-Rate Confusion

Car dealers love to confuse customers by talking about the money factor as if it were an interest rate. "We're giving you a 4.6 rate on this lease," a dealer will tell you. "Try getting an auto loan for that." In fact, the 4.6 figure the salesperson is throwing around isn't a 4.6% annual interest rate. It's shorthand for the money factor, which in this case is .0046. To convert the money factor to an annual interest rate, you multiply it by 2,400. So multiplying a .0046 money factor by 2,400 gives you an interest rate of 11.04%—which is not such a great rate at all. (There's a good discussion of the money factor at

Yahoo Answers (**answers.yahoo.com**) Just type Money Factor into the question box.

Fiddling with the Figures

After spending hours going back and forth with the salesman, you've finally agreed on the terms of your lease. At this point, he disappears into a back room to write up the lease. You then spend 20 minutes twiddling your thumbs and wondering what's going on. When he finally reappears, he presents you with the lease. You glance at it and notice that the monthly payment is $30 higher than it was supposed to be. "When you and I were figuring things, we must have made a small error in our calculations," he tells you. "No biggie." Don't believe him. For one thing, on a 36-month lease, this "small error" will cost you more than $1,000. For another, it probably wasn't an error at all, but rather the result of him fiddling with the figures—for instance, trying to squeeze out some extra profit by writing down a capitalized cost $1,000 higher than what you agreed to.

Even though car lease contracts are long, complicated forms filled with tiny print and literally dozens of different numbers written in, check every figure before you sign. Make sure the administrative fees, down payment, capitalized cost, mileage limit, residual cost, monthly payment, and term are all exactly what you agreed to. Some dealers will get everything right but then write up what was supposed to be a 36-month lease as a 39-month lease—hoping you won't notice until it's too late that you've been stuck with three extra payments. Some will try to cut the mileage limit.

Assume the worst and go over your lease agreement carefully. And if you're unsure about anything, DON'T SIGN IT! Once they've got your signature, you're on the hook and there's no going back.

Unnecessary Add-Ons

Car dealers are car dealers, and whether they are selling or leasing a new vehicle, they will try to bamboozle you into paying for overpriced unnecessary add-ons like extended warranties, rust-proofing, paint sealers, and the like. Some will even suggest that the leasing companies require you to buy some or all of these protections. Don't fall for this. If a salesperson uses this line, go to another dealer.

In fact, as unnecessary as these things are for a car you buy, they are even more unnecessary for one that's leased. Remember, the car you are leasing is brand new and since you should never lease a car for a period longer than the manufacturer's warranty is in effect, you'll be protected for the entire lease period. So an extended warranty is a total waste of money. So are all the other add-ons.

I once had a salesperson look me in the eye and suggest rustproofing for a car I leased in California. I said, "You have to be kidding, right? A convertible in California—you really think I need rustproofing?" He replied, "I have to ask."

What to Do if Things Go Wrong

A variety of federal and provincial laws require dealerships and leasing companies to disclose key terms and conditions of car leases, including the capitalized cost, the residual value, the finance charge (that is, the dollar amount of interest you will be paying—NOT the money factor or interest rate used to calculate that amount), as well as things like wear-and-tear charges and early termination penalties. If you've been the victim of deceptive or unfair practices, you can fight back by contacting your province's consumer affairs office. You can find a good list of government departments and industry organizations that handle consumer complaints about cars and car leasing at the website of the Automobile Protection Association (**www.apa.ca**). And you can file a complaint through the Consumer Information Gateway (**http://consumerinformation.ca**).

A Safe, Legal Way to Get Out of a Car Lease

As I said before, once you sign a lease agreement, you're on the hook. If you try to give back the car early, they will hit you with big penalties. And if you default on the payments, they will ruin your credit. So what do you do if you lose your job or have kids or otherwise go through some change in your life that makes you desperate to get out of your car lease? The answer may be to transfer your lease to somebody else.

Taking over a lease can be a good deal, since all the upfront costs are already paid, along with a chunk of the depreciation.

For a fee that usually totals several hundred dollars, websites like **Swapalease.com**, **TakeMyPayments.ca**, and **LeaseTrader.com** put people trying to get out of a lease together with folks looking to get in.

Once a match has been made, the site verifies the buyer's credit and handles the paperwork transferring the car to the new lessee. At this point, you're off the hook. And even though you sometimes have to offer big financial concessions to entice a buyer into taking over your lease, it's still almost always a *lot* cheaper than paying those early termination penalties.

Fight for Your Money Action Steps

- ☐ Be sure leasing a car is the right decision for you. (It usually isn't.)
- ☐ Focus on the four factors that make up the total cost to get yourself the best deal financially.
- ☐ Do your homework before attempting to negotiate a new car lease. Make use of sites like **cars4u.com** that offer lots of great information and research tools.
- ☐ Take over someone else's lease for the best deal.

Car Rentals

The problem with renting a car isn't that the rates are high. In fact, they're often pretty reasonable, depending on the province and city you rent in. But car-rental companies have the same attitude toward maximizing profits as the airlines do. With intense competition making it difficult for them to raise their basic prices, they try to pick your pocket by hitting you up for all sorts of fees and special charges—many of them for things you probably don't need. This brings them billions of dollars in additional revenue—and raises the price you wind up actually paying by anywhere from 20% to 60% over their basic advertised rates.

The trick to renting a car, then, is making sure you get only what you want and need—as opposed to what the car-rental company will try to sell you.

How to Fight for Your Money

The North American car-rental business is a big one, and Canada's just a small part of it. There are half a dozen major companies operating eight continental brands—Alamo, Avis, Budget, Dollar, Enterprise, Hertz, National, and Thrifty. Together, they take in more than US$20 billion a year.

You probably have a horror story about how you were mistreated by one or another of them. I know I've got a bunch. But according to a 2007 survey by the Consumer Reports National Research Center, they all offer pretty much the same level of service. So there's no need to drive yourself crazy trying to decide which company to rent from. Just go with the one that offers you the best rates.

Here's how to make sure you get a good deal.

Shop Around and Negotiate!

Thanks to the Internet, it's easy to get price quotes from every major company and a host of minor ones. Comparison sites like **www.kayak.com/cars**, **www.hotwire.com** and **www.sidestep.com**, along with travel sites like Expedia (**www.expedia.com**), Orbitz (**www.orbitz.com**), and Travelocity (**www.travelocity.com**), can get you competing rates for any model car, on any date, at any location. Once you've got these in hand, you can contact the rental companies themselves, either through their websites or by phone, and see if they can do better. Often, they can—and will.

Basically, when it comes to renting a car there simply is not a "fixed price." What you are quoted is not what you have to accept.

Also—and this is really important—when you call the rental company directly, I recommend you have their website open and in front of you, because it's very possible that there will be a lower price on the website than they quote you. This has happened to me a half dozen times. And with that said, here's why you also need to be ready to negotiate. Sometimes, the price online can be beaten by the person you are speaking with on the phone at the same company. And now to make it even crazier—when you physically arrive at the rental counter, simply ask, "how can I get a better price" to see if you can negotiate them down a bit further.

And don't restrict your search to the major brands. There are a number of smaller car-rental companies (such as ACE, Advantage, Fox, Triangle, and even U-Haul) that may not be nationally known but still rent the same kind of late-model, low-mileage cars as the majors. You can get rate information and make reservations through web sites like Car-rental Express (**www.carrentalexpress.com**) or CarRentals.com (**www.carrentals.com**).

Lastly, book early for the best values, because you can always cancel without penalty since you're usually not required to hold a reservation with a credit card.

Rent on the Weekend—If You Have the Flexibility

You can save plenty when you rent on a weekend. Weekends are usually pretty slow for the car-rental companies, since most of their demand comes from business people who do most of their travelling during the week. So in an effort to generate traffic, they cut prices sharply on Saturdays and Sundays. And I do mean sharply. At Enterprise recently, the same compact that will cost you $78.59 a day during the week goes for just $29.89 a day on a Saturday or Sunday. So if you have any flexibility, save your rentals for the weekend.

Read Your Contract

The time you initially pick the car up is probably the most likely time something could go wrong. You absolutely must take a few minutes to read the contract before you sign. With many rental agencies now offering gold clubs that allow you to just get in your car and drive off, it's all too easy to miss something important. The contract may have insurance checked off because that's in your profile, when in fact you don't need it. Or worse—the car you drive off in could have damages, scratches or dings that you might get charged for. So before you rush off, check out the car and make sure it's in the same shape as indicated on your contract. Any damages need to be noted on the contract. Also make sure the mileage noted matches the odometer and that the gas tank is full.

Make Sure You Know What You'll Really Be Paying

The basic daily or weekly rate you'll be charged for a rental car is only part of the price you'll wind up paying. There are all sorts of extra costs that get tacked on. Some are mandatory, like:

- airport-concession fees
- special municipal surcharges
- excise and sales taxes

Others are optional, like:

- insurance premiums
- refuelling charges
- special equipment like GPS devices and satellite radios

When you add them all up, these extra charges can easily wind up doubling the cost of your rental. So ask about them in advance—and make sure that all applicable extra charges are included in your price quote. Also, don't be afraid to ask nicely, "Can you throw in a GPS?" Often the manager at the car rental lot can do just that. I regularly get "free" extras by just asking nicely. Just last week I got an upgrade and a GPS "thrown in"—saving me $75 during my rental.

RIP-OFF OPTIONAL

If you rent a Ford Taurus at Chicago O'Hare Airport:	
Your approximate total cost per day without options:	$120.94
Your cost per day with GPS and satellite radio:	$153.68
Skip the extras and, over the course of a week, you save:	**$230**

Don't Be Shy About Asking for Discounts

Do you belong to the Canadian Automobile Association? CARP? Costco or Sam's Club? If so, you probably can get a discount of 5% to 25% off the price of your rental. Most of the major car-rental companies offer discounts to members of certain organizations, employees of certain companies, customers of certain merchants —even people who attend certain conventions and trade shows. I once belonged to a gym that gave clients a Hertz discount card. There are so many of these deals available that you should always make a point of asking if any of your professional or personal affiliations qualify you for one.

In addition to these group discounts, rental companies often offer discount coupons on travel websites, in travel magazines, and at the checkout areas of big box retailers like Costco. So keep your eyes peeled. You can also visit consumer discount sites like **www.rentalcarmomma.com** for some decent savings. Lastly, ALWAYS ask at the counter, "Are you having any specials? Is there anything I can do to get a better price or better deal today?"

Members Only

- Save 25% with your Costco card at National, Alamo, and Avis; or 20% at Hertz and Budget.
- Get a guaranteed best rate with your CAA membership card at Hertz.

Renting at the Airport Can Cost You 25% More!

According to a 2005 study by Travelocity, renting at the average major airport adds more than 25% to your total bill. There's no question that it's more convenient when you're flying, but it's almost always a lot more expensive to pick up a rental car at the airport than at a neighbourhood location. That's because most airports and the local governments that oversee them impose a variety of special taxes and fees on car rentals—the idea being that the customers getting screwed aren't usually local residents, so who cares if they don't like it? Houston's George Bush Intercontinental Airport had the most outrageous charges—its taxes increased the cost of renting by more than 66%.

So if you're renting for more than a day or two, it's probably worth your while to bypass the big airport car-rental centre and instead arrange to pick up your car at a neighbourhood office near where you're staying. In recent years, the major rental companies have opened thousands of new non-airport branches, so finding one isn't usually too difficult.

TWENTY MINUTES TO SAVINGS

Renting a Chevy Impala from Avis at Minneapolis/St. Paul Airport location:	$132.36 per day
Renting a Chevy Impala from Avis at Maplewood, MN, location (a 20-minute cab ride away):	$70.13 per day
Including cab fare, which will cost you approximately $50 each way if you're renting the car for a week, you save:	**$300!**

Review Your Insurance Coverage Before You Get a Rental Car

The biggest and most profitable part of the car-rental business is rental insurance. Roughly a third of all car-rental customers sign up for it—paying as much as $40 a day for coverage most of them don't need. This is great for the car-rental companies, since most of the charges they collect are pure profit, but it's generally an expensive rip-off for you (if you already have the coverage).

Let's go through the basics of the complicated insurance coverage policies and then see if you really need them. The basic policies offered by car rental companies include the Collision Damage Waiver (CDW), the Loss Damage Waiver (LDW), the Supplemental Liability Protection, Personal Accident

Insurance (PAI), and Personal Effects Coverage (PEC). In theory, this is all perfectly reasonable. In practice, it's largely unnecessary.

COLLISION DAMAGE WAIVER (CDW)

This is actually not even an insurance policy. Rather, it's a legal agreement that relieves you of responsibility for any collision damage the car may suffer while you're renting it. This is nice protection to have—but if you happen to own a car chances are, you already have it. That's because most auto insurance policies cover accidents you have while driving not only your own car, but also other vehicles. And that includes rented ones.

LOSS DAMAGE WAIVER (LDW)

The only protection you should consider is the loss damage waiver (LDW), which protects you from having to reimburse the rental company for the income it's losing while the car is in the shop. Your gold card may cover this insurance, so check to see if it does before you pay for it.

SUPPLEMENTAL LIABILITY PROTECTION

Supplemental liability coverage provides additional liability protection if someone makes a claim against you while you're driving a rental car; for example, if you have an accident and the other driver files a claim against you for injuries and vehicle damage that exceed your regular policy limits. Again, there's a strong possibility that you already have this coverage on your own personal auto insurance policy.

PERSONAL ACCIDENT INSURANCE (PAI)

Personal Accident Insurance will cover you or your passengers for injuries sustained while driving a rental. If you already have sufficient medical coverage under your auto policy, you probably don't need this.

PERSONAL EFFECTS COVERAGE (PEC)

Personal Effects Coverage protects items and property you own if they're damaged. If you have homeowners or tenants insurance, you may already have this coverage.

Don't Own a Car? You May Still Be Covered!

If you don't own a car—and so don't have any auto insurance—you still may be covered . . . by your credit card. Many credit card companies automatically provide car-rental insurance to customers who use their cards when renting.

Don't Duplicate Efforts

Skip unnecessary car-rental insurance and you save up to $32 per day.

BUT don't assume this. Call your credit card company first to make sure you qualify, before you decline coverage through the rental agency. Be advised that most credit card companies offer insurance for only 30 days—so if you rent long term you would need to return the car on the thirtieth day, then rent a new one in order to ensure continuous coverage. Some credit cards have certain cars they won't insure at all, so again you need to know the specifics of what your credit card really covers. Make the phone call.

There is one exception to all of this—if you're renting a car abroad. Most Canadian auto insurance policies do not necessarily cover accidents that occur outside the country.

So before you rent a car, check your existing insurance policies—and check with your credit card company—to see if there's any reason for you to buy additional coverage from the car-rental firm. Most likely, there won't be. (And once you've said no, double-check your contract. Many rental clerks will automatically check the "Yes" box for insurance, even after you've told them you don't want it.)

Fill 'Er Up!

The most important advice I can give you is to make sure your car has the amount of gas in it that the car-rental company says it does. If they say the car is full and it's actually a quarter tank less than full, that's a quick financial hit of over $10 to $20 depending on the tank of the car. Go back to the counter and let them know right away—don't just drive away and assume you can fix this when you return. Also, as you know, most car-rental companies require you to return the car with a full tank of gas. If you don't, they'll fill it up themselves—and charge you through the nose for it. In fact, the rental car companies now promote this service as a perk! But you'll end up paying from $7 to $14 over and above what you'd pay if you pumped the gas yourself. And with prices around $1 a litre as I write this, aren't we paying enough for gas as it is? The refuelling fee is almost always posted in the reception area because it is such a profit centre for the car-rental companies and also such a sore issue with customers. So as you're driving away from the car-rental lot, make a point of noticing where the nearest gas station is—and then, on your way back, top up the tank before you turn in the car. If you've got an early-morning flight and you're afraid you won't have time for a refuelling stop, then do it the night before.

DO-IT-YOURSELF SAVINGS

What you'll pay to let Budget fill the tank of your Toyota Camry:	$82
What you'll pay to refuel yourself:	$68
You save:	**$14**

Returning the Car

Here's another likely place where something can go wrong—when you're returning the car. That's where you're usually rushing off—maybe to catch your flight—and you're quickly handed your bill. Now is the time to catch any final mistakes on your bill, so take a few moments to fully review it. Make sure they credit you properly for gas and for mileage.

Recently, I brought in my car and the woman looked at the mileage and noted that I drove 12,000 miles! I started laughing, because that just wasn't possible—I hadn't even driven 500 miles. The contract was wrong—and even she recognized instantly it couldn't be possible. Fortunately for me, I didn't have to argue the point.

What to Watch Out For

Unwanted Upgrades

It's funny how times change. It used to be that savvy rental customers would always reserve a car a little smaller than they really wanted. The idea was that since most rental agencies have a lot more intermediate and full-sized cars than compacts and subcompacts, they'd probably wind up getting a free upgrade to a larger model. But now, with gasoline prices sky-high, the situation is reversed. Most rental customers want economy cars, not big sedans and SUVs. Since there aren't enough to go around, it's become increasingly common for customers to be pushed into larger cars against their will.

That's exactly what happened to me recently in New York. Having just recently written a book on the environment called *Go Green, Live Rich,* it's important to me to drive a hybrid car—it's better for the environment and it saves me money on gas. I don't want to drive a gas-guzzling SUV. So recently I rented a Toyota Prius from Hertz. Because they are so in demand in New York, a Prius is very difficult to get, so I reserved mine nearly two weeks in advance. When I showed up to get my car, they let me know that they were going to do me a wonderful favour and upgrade me at no extra charge to a luxury SUV. Normally, the SUV rental was nearly $50 a day more—and I should be thrilled. But I wasn't thrilled—in fact, I was very upset. I had reserved the Hybrid two weeks early and I wanted that specific car, not an SUV. I insisted they find a Prius somewhere else and get it delivered to the rental location I was at. After about 15 minutes of searching, they found a car and had it sent over to the car location I was at. It would have cost me twice as much to drive the SUV just in gas costs alone.

Given how heavily their fleets are weighted toward big cars and SUVs, it will probably take the car-rental companies several years to shift the balance noticeably toward "greener" vehicles. In the meantime, don't be surprised if a company tries to "upgrade" you into a less fuel-efficient car than you reserved. But stand your ground. If you insist, they'll accommodate you, if they can. On the other hand, you might want to take advantage of the fact that some companies now charge less for some larger gas-guzzlers than for some smaller, more efficient cars. This may be where you have leverage to get a great deal; just remember these gas guzzlers are not good for the planet.

At Hertz you'll pay $7 a day more to rent a Toyota Prius over a Ford Explorer. But you'll get more than double the gas mileage!

The Disappearing Grace Period

The car-rental companies didn't used to be sticklers about the rules. If your car was due back at noon on Tuesday and you didn't show up until 1:30 p.m., they'd usually turn a blind eye and not charge you extra. Nowadays, if you roll in more than 30 minutes past the scheduled return time, you shouldn't be surprised if you're charged for a full extra day.

Even more annoyingly, the companies have started enforcing fine-print rules about pick-up times. Since some discounted rates are based on what time you're picking up the car, if your flight is delayed, the rental company is technically entitled to cancel your discount and charge you more. They rarely used to do this, but with everyone in the industry now trying to squeeze out as much revenue as they can, if you give them an excuse to take back a discount, chances are that they will.

So before you rent, find out whether you will be subject to any penalty if your flight is late or if you have to cancel the reservation entirely. If you don't like the answer you get, switch to another company.

Unnecessary Options

Next to insurance, the car-rental companies' main source of additional profit are heavily promoted—and expensive—options like prepaid fuel, GPS devices, and satellite radios. While GPS devices, E-ZPass transmitters, satellite radios, and seat-back entertainment units are fun to play, they can add as much as 20% to the cost of renting a car.

Alamo, one of the smaller of the big eight rental companies, earned an extra US$30 million in North America from GPS devices alone in 2007—and that was when the trend was just getting started. As I shared earlier, I often get these extras for free just by asking nicely—so try asking; it can't hurt.

The prepaid fuel option is probably the trickiest of their tricks. The rental companies used to charge two or three times the going rate for gas. But with pump prices as high as they are, they can't get away with that sort of thing anymore. So they've come up with a new scam. What most of them do now is offer to sell you a full tank of gas at the beginning of the rental for a price just below what it would cost you at a gas station. The trick is that once you've bought the gas, it's yours—whether or not you use it all. There are no refunds, even if you bring the car back with a nearly full tank. So unless you know you're going to drive more than the 300 to 400 miles it takes to empty a modern gas tank, don't take the prepaid fuel option.

And if you're travelling with a small child, think about bringing along your own safety seat. Most airlines will not charge a fee to check a car seat—although be sure to double-check beforehand. The rental companies charge as much as $12 a day extra to provide them.

GO DIRECTLY TO SAVINGS

Cost of GPS per weekly rental:	$59.75
Cost of buying a map:	$2.95
You save:	**$56.80**

What to Do if Something Goes Wrong

In the event of a problem with a car-rental company, the best course of action is to deal with the manager at the car rental place you are renting from. She or he has the most power to fix your problem the fastest (while you are there). In my experience, these managers are overworked and stressed and most people are furious when they interact with them, so if you try a little kindness you have a better chance to get further faster. If you can't make progress with your problem or get it fixed on site then contact the company directly with an explanation of the problem. All of the major companies have customer service departments. You can find the necessary contact information on the company's web site.

If that doesn't help and you used a travel agency or some booking service, contact them to ask them to intervene on your behalf. And don't hesitate to complain to the Better Business Bureau (**www.ccbbb.ca**).

Also, if you are a member of the CAA or CARP, those organizations will act to help you if you aren't able to resolve any problems through other means.

Fight for Your Money Action Steps

- ☐ Shop around online. My favourite sites include:

  www.kayak.com **www.hotwire.com**
  www.sidestep.com **www.expedia.com**
  www.orbitz.com **www.travelocity.com**
  www.carrentals.com **www.carrentalexpress.com**

- ☐ Get your discounts! CARP, CAA, Costco, or Sam's Club member? Take advantage of the benefits! And check out consumer discount sites like **www.rentalcarmomma.com**.
- ☐ Don't rent at an airport if at all possible.
- ☐ Know what you're already insured for so you don't buy coverage you don't need.
- ☐ Read your contract and inspect the condition of the car *before* you drive off the lot.
- ☐ Fill up the tank before you return if you didn't prepay.

Car Repairs

Car repairs can be a financial disaster. Time and again, in doing money makeovers for people, I find out that it was car problems that first put them in debt. Often the story starts with someone taking their car in for what they think is a small problem only to be told it's actually a much, much bigger problem that will cost them thousands of dollars. The challenge is that most of us know little or nothing about how to fix an automobile, so it's really difficult to know if the advice we are being given is honest.

Just about everybody has a story about how a dishonest auto mechanic tried to rip them off. I remember my friend Allan telling me about how he brought his car into the service department at a big dealership a few years ago and was told that unless he spent $3,300 on a new exhaust system, he would definitely fail its smog test and probably ruin his engine. He almost fell for these scare tactics, but at the last minute he decided to have another garage take a look at the car. Sure enough, all it needed was a minor adjustment that cost him less than $75. He passed the smog test and drove the car problem-free for another five years.

I had a similar situation involving brake pads on my car. Every single time I brought the car in for service, I was told I needed new brake pads and an alignment—at a cost of $1,500 or more. Finally, I checked the owner's manual and discovered that there was no way the brake pads should need to be changed this often. I took the car to another mechanic, who told me that the pads my dealer had described as being shot and dangerous were actually fine.

It's rip-offs like these that can make car repairs cost us a fortune if we don't watch our mechanics—and fight for our money.

Not all auto mechanics are dishonest, but as a group they do not have a great reputation. Car repair shops consistently rank among the Better Business

> **The Automobile Protection Association found that as many as 51% of auto-repair charges are unnecessary.**

Bureau's Top 10 most complained about industries, and the Automobile Protection Association found that as many as 51% of all auto repair charges are unnecessary.

Finding a good mechanic has always been a challenge, but these days it's both tougher and more important than ever. Cars have gotten so technologically sophisticated that it practically takes a degree in computer science to understand what's going on under the hood. Forget about trying to figure out what's causing that strange rattle. You need a repair shop you can trust. Fortunately, there are some out there—and finding one isn't as hard as you might think.

How to Fight for Your Money

Do Your Homework

There are basically two ways to find a good mechanic: trial and error or old-fashioned research. The first can be expensive and painful, while the second requires just a little time and effort.

So let's focus on research. Word of mouth is usually the best place to start. This means soliciting suggestions from friends, relatives, and co-workers. And thanks to the Internet, you don't have to stop there.

Once you've gotten a few leads on good garages, you need to verify that they really are as good as they're cracked up to be. You can check with a website called Ripoff Report (**www.ripoffreport.com**) to see if the garage has been mentioned by a disgruntled customer, although this is a pretty hit-or-miss approach. A better way is by checking out whether the people who work at a place you're considering meet the standards of the National Institute for Automotive Service Excellence (ASE), a non-profit U.S. organization that tests and certifies auto mechanics in the United States and Canada in specialties ranging from engine repair to heating and air conditioning.

Garages that employ at least one ASE-certified mechanic generally display an ASE sticker in their window. Of course, all this means is that there's at least one mechanic on the floor who has passed at least one ASE test. It doesn't mean he's going to be working on your car. What you want is a garage where most of the mechanics are ASE-certified—and where at least a few hold ASE Master Technician certificates, meaning they have passed the exams in all eight automotive specialties. The ASE awards what it calls its Blue Seal of Excellence to garages where at least 75% of their service personnel are ASE-certified. At the time of writing, there are only seven garages in Canada, in British Columbia, Manitoba, and Ontario, that carry the Blue Seal, but we're sure there will be more as car owners become more demanding. (To find a Blue Seal garage near you, use the ASE's Blue Seal locator online at **http://locator.ase.com/blue/**.)

It's also a good idea to make sure a repair shop you're considering is endorsed by the Canadian Automobile Association. Garages that pass a strict CAA inspection, have at least one ASE Master Technician on the payroll, and earn a customer satisfaction rating of 90% or better are allowed to display the CAA's blue-and-red "Approved Auto Repair" sign.

Don't Wait Until the Last Minute

There's nothing like driving around town with black smoke pouring out of your exhaust frantically searching for a decent-looking service centre that's (1) open, and (2) capable of figuring out and fixing what's wrong. You want to establish a relationship with a good repair shop *before* you're in desperate need of their services. So start looking for one now, while your car is still problem-free.

Pick the Right Shop for the Right Job

There are three different kinds of auto-service facilities to choose from—dealerships, national chains like Sears, Midas, or Jiffy Lube, and independent garages. Which is best? Well, in fact, they all are . . . for different things.

It used to be that having your car serviced or repaired at a dealership was almost always a rip-off, since dealers' prices were generally much higher than those of independent shops. But that's not true anymore. With new-car sales no longer producing much if anything in the way of profits, the service business has become incredibly important to most dealerships. As a result, dealers have become more competitive with their shop rates, often offering special prices on oil changes, brake jobs, and the like.

Still, that doesn't mean you should bring your car to the dealer every time it needs servicing or repair work. For sure, you should always have any work covered by the manufacturer's warranty done by the dealer. If money is no object—and when the work is covered by the warranty, it's not—you don't need to worry about whether parts and labour might be cheaper somewhere else. The only thing that matters is the fact that dealers tend to have the most up-to-date equipment for your particular car and their mechanics are likely to have had the latest training in how to fix it.

For most routine work, however—things like changing a muffler, replacing a battery, or flushing a cooling system—you don't necessarily need an ASE-certified master technician. Depending on the nature of the job, one of the big national chains can probably do it much more cheaply than a dealership and, as long it's nothing out of the ordinary, every bit as well. Just don't get talked into having them do more than a basic job—and definitely not something outside their main specialty.

A good independent mechanic can be worth his weight in gold. He may charge more than the chains, but it's worth paying a little extra to have someone you trust handle the routine maintenance. Keep in mind that the law gives you the right to service your vehicle wherever you like without affecting your warranty. The only drawback is that, as cars have grown more sophisticated, it's become more difficult for independent garages to keep up with the latest technology and equipment. So the most complicated repairs are probably best left to a dealer—especially when they involve systems that are unique to your brand of car.

Follow the Manufacturer's Advice—Not the Garage's

Lots of mechanics, including those at dealerships, will tell you to ignore the owner's manual and instead take their advice on how often to change the oil and perform other routine maintenance. Amazingly enough, their advice almost always involves bringing in the car more often than the manual says or scheduling procedures like engine or transmission flushes that the manual doesn't call for (like having the brake pads changed every 15,000 miles!). This is almost always a rip-off. Remember, your owner's manual was written by the same company that built your car and backs your warranty. So trust what it says.

Always Get a Detailed Estimate— And Get It in Writing

Whether you're bringing your car in for a big repair job or a routine servicing, a good mechanic should be able to tell you in advance what it's going to cost. And he should be willing to put it in writing. As the saying goes, verbal estimates aren't worth the paper they're not printed on.

Never let anyone work on your car without first getting a written estimate that specifies exactly what all the parts and labour for your job are likely to cost. The estimate should also make it clear that the garage is not authorized to do any additional work without your approval. (This is why we have telephones—so the garage can call you if they discover some unanticipated problem once they've begun work on your vehicle.) Any garage that doesn't automatically give you a repair authorization form to sign before you leave your car with them is not a garage you can trust.

Get a Second Opinion

If your mechanic says your car needs major surgery, do the same thing you'd do if you got a similarly serious diagnosis from your doctor—get a second opinion. It's not simply that your mechanic may have a vested interest in persuading you that major work is necessary; it's also that everyone makes mistakes, even good mechanics.

If your mechanic really is honest, he won't mind your taking the car to a diagnostic centre for a backup check. Just tell the people at the second garage that you're interested only in a diagnosis—if they conclude that your car happens to need work, it will be done elsewhere. As long as you make this clear, they'll have no reason to recommend unnecessary repairs.

What to Watch Out For

The Old Bait-and-Switch

Local newspapers and pennysavers are constantly filled with ads from garages offering all sorts of bargains—oil changes for $19.99, free brake inspections, $95 tune-up specials. The idea, of course, is to get you in the door—and your car up on their lift. Once there, a dishonest mechanic will miraculously find all sorts of problems you need to take care of right away. And before you know it, your $95 tune-up will have turned into an $800 valve job.

Don't let them stampede you. If a garage tries too hard to sell you on anything beyond the deal that attracted you in the first place, tell them you appreciate their advice but you'd prefer to have the extra work done by your regular mechanic (even if you don't have one). Then get the heck out of there.

And be wary of those free brake inspections. No one I know has ever had a free inspection that didn't end with the mechanic saying they needed new pads, rotors, and calipers.

Mechanics Who Make Everything Sound Like an Emergency

Dishonest mechanics prey on ignorance and anxiety. They know that most of us don't really understand how our cars work, and they take advantage of that, painting all sorts of dire pictures about what might happen if we don't have the transmission flushed or the timing belt replaced RIGHT AWAY!

The worst of the scam artists actually try to *cause* problems—or at least the appearance of a problem. It's not unknown for gas station attendants to drip some oil under a car in an effort to convince the owner he's got a leak. Even worse, some may puncture water hoses or nick fan belts—which is why you should never let a mechanic you don't know look under your hood without you looking over his shoulder.

And don't think these sorts of things happen only at fly-by-night independent garages. It was just this sort of over-selling that eventually forced Sears in the United States to pay a $46-million settlement after it was sued for conning customers into unnecessary auto repairs and service in the 1990s.

Non-existent Replacement Parts

Another way dishonest repair shops take advantage of us is to insist we need to replace some supposedly broken part—say, a water pump—that's actually working just fine. They then do nothing—except charge us for the nonexistent new water pump and the nonexistent labour to install it, assuming we'll never be the wiser.

There's one way to prevent being ripped off in this way. Whenever you agree to have a part replaced, tell the mechanic you'll expect him to give you the old, damaged part when he's done. (In fact, some states have laws that require repair shops to do this.) Needless to say, an honest mechanic should not have any problem with this request.

Prices That Seem Unusually High

These days all repair prices seem high, but if what the garage is quoting you seems really astronomical, take the time to call a number of other garages and see what they would charge for the same job. A really good repair shop may well be more expensive than the average garage, but if your mechanic's prices are more than 20% or 30% higher than everybody else's, something may be wrong. Ask your guy why his prices are so out of line. If the answer is not convincing, find yourself a new mechanic.

Tax Confusion

Lazy or unscrupulous shops (which are often the same thing) may try to charge you sales tax on the total amount of your repair bill. In fact, you're supposed to pay tax only on the parts you purchased for the repair. So check your bill carefully.

What to Do if Something Goes Wrong

If you think you've been a victim of an auto-repair scam, there's a lot you can—and should—do.

If the work was done at a new-car dealership, you should begin by working your way up the chain of command, first bringing your complaint to the attention of the service manager, then to the dealership's general manager and owner, and then finally to the car company whose franchise they hold.

The process is similar if your problem is with a chain repair shop like Midas or Canadian Tire. If the local shop doesn't address your concerns, contact the customer service department at their national headquarters. You can find the necessary telephone numbers and email addresses on the chain's web site.

If none of this does any good—or if your problem is with an independent garage—report the shop to your consumer affairs office or local consumer protection agency. Some provinces used to have departments that specialized in combating auto repair fraud, but closed them down in the 1990s. The Automobile Protection Association, among others, says they should start them up again.

You should also file a complaint with the Better Business Bureau (www.ccbbb.ca) and, if you're a member, with your local branch of the CAA. Even if you're not a member, you should contact the CAA if the garage displays one of its CAA Approved Auto Repair signs. If your complaint is serious enough, the garage could lose its seal of approval.

Fight for Your Money Action Steps

- ☐ Find an ace mechanic you can trust before your car breaks down. Get a recommendation from a friend or neighbour and check the Ripoff Report website (www.ripoffreport.com). Look for ASE certification and CAA approval.

- ☐ Have all repairs covered by your warranty done by the dealership where you purchased your car.
- ☐ Always get a detailed estimate in writing before any work is done.
- ☐ For major repairs, get that second opinion!

Bank Accounts

The first thing you need to know about dealing with banks is that banking is a business—a *big* business. In all, Canadian banks employ more than 250,000 people and operate more than 8,000 branches. They generated more than $19 billion in net income in 2007 and manage more than C$2.7 trillion in assets.

By any measure, the banking industry is a crucial component of our economy. And as we are learning in the global banking crisis of 2008, which is going on as I write, we need our banks to be safe and strong. That said, it's not your job to personally make your bank rich. Unfortunately, if you handle your chequing and savings accounts like most people, chances are you are unwittingly making your bank richer at your expense.

In the old days, banks were a place simply to park your savings. In fact, for most of the 20th century that was pretty much all banks were good for. Then, with revisions to the Bank Act in 1954 and 1967, they began to expand into other areas like consumer and mortgage lending. Later revisions to the act allowed them to operate subsidiaries in the trust and securities industries.

Today, banks are truly full-service financial firms, offering everything from chequing and savings accounts to credit cards and mortgage lending to brokerage services, financial planning, and investment banking.

While banks used to make most of their money from lending, these days an increasing proportion of their profits come from getting customers to use as many of their products and services as possible. This one-stop financial shopping certainly can be incredibly convenient. But if you're not careful, it can also be very expensive.

Is Free Chequing Really Free? Probably Not!

In general, Canada's banking fees are lower than the fees applied by banks in the United States, but they still add up. In fact, Canadian banks now make more than half their income from fees. That amounts to about $9.5 billion. The other half of banks' profits comes from interest on loans.

Banks charge fees for everything from administering and selling mutual funds to processing derivatives transactions. As individual customers, some of these fees affect us more than others. In 2007, banks made about $3.7 billion from service fees charged to consumers for chequing accounts, ATM transactions, credit card processing, investment management services, and other activities conducted by people like you and me.

Penalty and service fees typically cost you around $120 a year.

You know the old saying, "There's no such thing as a free lunch"? Well, when it comes to banking, there's no such thing as free chequing. You may not be charged for each individual cheque you write, but whatever that giveaway costs the bank, you can be sure they are more than making up for it in penalty and service fees that typically run around $120 a year, according to the Canadian Bankers Association, although the CBA also says that one-third of consumers in Canada pay no bank service fees at all.

So when you're deciding where to do your banking, you need to consider not only what kind of interest rates they are offering to pay on your deposits, but also what sort of fees they are going to try to ding you with.

How to Fight for Your Money

The good news about dealing with banks is that they follow the rules. The bad news is that it's often hard to find out just what the rules are. So the most important thing to know about handling your bank accounts is that you have to be ready, willing, and able to ask a lot of questions. And if you don't get clear answers, you shouldn't hesitate to take your business elsewhere.

You'll never get the best out of a bank if it's not the right bank for you. So whether you are looking to open your first account or have been banking at the same place for years, consider *all* your options: online institutions, credit unions, trust companies, even branches of foreign banks.

Take a hard look at what you need, what your bank offers, and what it costs. Review your monthly statements. How much are you keeping in your accounts? What are you earning?

Which bank offers the best interest rates is only the first point of comparison. Just because an account pays a competitive rate doesn't mean it's a good deal. Does the account come with a free debit card, charge for cheques, pay bills, and otherwise manage the account online or over the phone? What kind of fees do they charge for bounced cheques, overdrafts, or using another bank's ATM, and how often are you likely to get hit?

Shop around. Compare a wide variety of accounts using The Cost of Banking Guide from the Financial Consumer Agency of Canada. The online guide compares about 100 account packages from major Canadian banks and other financial institutions in Canada. Only then will you have any idea if you're being well taken care of—or just being taken. (You can find the guide at **www.fcac.gc.ca**.)

Here are a few basic tips to keep in mind when selecting and using a bank.

Choosing a Bank

Unlike the United States, where more than 8,400 different banks compete for consumers' business, Canada has only six major banks and about 40 smaller financial institutions, and they're all well regulated. Canada also has one of the strongest banking systems in the world. In fact, the World Economic Forum rated Canada's banking system as the best in the world. While banks topple frequently in the United States, a bank hasn't gone out of business in Canada for years. Even in the Depression, when banks in the United States teetered on the brink of collapse, Canadian banks remained stable and operating.

So if there are relatively few banks in Canada, and they're all pretty strong, how do you choose the one that's right for you? My personal recommendation is that you go with the one where you get the best service. If you live in a city, talk to an account rep or branch manager at three or four different banks. If you live in a smaller community, you may still have a choice between a bank and a credit union. You'll notice that some of them treat you differently than others or that you feel more comfortable with one than another. If a financial institution doesn't treat you the way you think you should be treated, take your business to another one. (You might also consider banking over the Internet. We'll get to that in a moment.)

Even within the same bank, you might find that one branch treats you differently than another. Like real estate agents, good bankers are worth their weight in gold, no matter what company they work for. So if your account rep or branch manager moves to a different branch or a different bank, see if you can go with her or him.

Go Online for Higher Yields and Lower Fees

Online banking has come of age. According to a survey by the Canadian Bankers Association, 23% of Canadians did their banking through the Internet in 2004, and another 32% intended to bank online over the next couple of years. Maybe because you live in such a vast area or because you have one of the most advanced communications infrastructures in the world, Canadians have adopted to online banking more quickly than any other country.

We not only deal with our chequing and savings accounts online through our banks' websites, we also pay bills, invest in mutual funds, administer our retirement savings plans and a lot of other things, as well. We can even do all this through our cell phones and Blackberries.

It's not easy to compare fees charged by bricks-and-mortar banks with institutions that operate on the Internet. That's because all of them tend to charge for a range of services like chequing, bill payments, and transferring money. So even if you use one service but not the others, you pay for all of them.

At the low end of the scale, the biggest banks charge about $4 a month for a basic service of eight to 15 transactions, whether you're updating your passbook, withdrawing money from your account, or writing a cheque. That adds up to $48 a year, but even at that rate, the Bankers Association says you should shop around to make sure you're getting the best deal. The average Canadian pays much more than that, about $150 a year, in service fees. For them, it definitely pays to find the best value for the money.

An electronic bank like ING Direct (**www.ingdirect.ca**) may be one option, especially if, like a lot of Canadians, you seldom or never go inside your bank branch anymore. ING Direct doesn't have any branches, although it maintains four offices that you can visit if you really want to talk to a human being face to face. It also charges no fees and pays a higher rate of interest on savings and other accounts. This can add up if you leave your money in the account. But if you do that, you might as well invest it in a longer-term GIC or other type of financial instrument that pays even more interest.

Another option is a so-called discount bank like President's Choice Financial (**www.pcfinancial.ca**) or Canadian Tire Financial Services (**www.myctfs.com**). They offer high-interest savings accounts, as well. At PC Financial, you can deposit and withdraw money from an ATM without paying a fee, as long as you use one of their ATMs or the bank machines operated by CIBC, which is the big bank behind PC Financial. At Canadian Tire, you can use ATMs that are part of The Exchange Network, set up initially by credit unions in Canada. The network includes about 2,200 ATMs. By comparison, there are more than 50,000 ATMs in Canada operated by banks and other financial institutions.

Make Sure Your Deposits Are Insured

As I noted earlier, despite the recent world economic crisis, bank failures in Canada are extremely rare occurrences. Even though it's unlikely to happen, though, the government provides depositors with a safety net. It's called the Canada Deposit Insurance Corporation. CDIC covers deposits in all of Canada's major financial institutions, including Canadian Tire Financial Services and ING Direct, and most of the smaller ones, as well. Just in case, you can check to see if your financial institution is covered at CDIC's web site, www.cdic.ca.

CDIC covers all eligible deposits in savings and chequing accounts, as well as GICs with a term of five years or less, to a maximum of $100,000. That's the total coverage. If you keep more than $100,000 in different types of accounts and GICs at the same bank or financial institution, CDIC covers a maximum of $100,000. The rest isn't covered. It's important that you understand this, especially if you have more than $100,000 at the same institution. (Think about it: All you really need to reach that amount is a savings account with $5,000 in it and a few GICs and term deposits worth $95,000. Many people have that much on deposit with their bank.

If you're concerned about protecting your savings against the possibility of a bank failure, split your savings between two different banks or financial institutions. Keep a savings account at a branch of the Royal Bank, for example, and GICs at the Bank of Montreal. That way, your savings will be covered to a maximum of $100,000 at each institution.

You should also know that CDIC covers your eligible savings in an RRSP separately from your other savings on deposit with the same bank. So your RRSP holdings, if they qualify, are covered to a limit of $100,000, and your savings outside your RRSP are covered to the same limit, even if you keep everything with the same bank.

Check, also, to see that your savings are in a form that's eligible for CDIC coverage. Your saving and chequing accounts are covered, for example, as long as you hold your money in Canadian dollars. So are GICs with terms of less than five years. But CDIC does not cover mutual funds, stocks, bonds, or Treasury bills. (You can find a complete list of what's covered by CDIC and what's not at the CDIC web site.)

Finally, even if CDIC doesn't cover your particular financial institution, your savings might still be covered. The Deposit Insurance Corp. of Ontario (**www.dico.com**) covers credit union deposits in Ontario, for example, up to $100,000. And the Canadian Investor Protection Fund (**www.cipf.ca**) covers as much as $1 million in cash and securities held with investment dealer members of the Investment Industry Regulatory Organization of Canada.

Two Simple Tricks to Prevent Overdrafts

At most financial institutions in Canada, a bounced cheque will cost you $30 or more. The best way to avoid this charge is to get overdraft protection. Most banks and financial institutions provide it. It costs as little as $2 a month and covers overdrafts as high as $5,000.

An overdraft arrangement will also spare you the embarrassment—and damage to your credit history—of a bounced cheque.

If you don't have overdraft protection, use this old bookkeeping trick: record a $1,000 cheque to yourself, but never actually write it or cash it. Just like setting your watch ahead to keep you from being late to appointments, this will make it seem as if you have $1,000 less in your account than you really have—and make it all the more unlikely that you will ever incur an overdraft.

What to Watch Out For

There are lots of things banking customers should watch out for, but the biggest scams involve fees, bank policies on deposits, and old-fashioned con artists looking to rob you. Here are six of the most outrageous.

Unexpected Overdraft Fees

As I've said, it can cost as much as $30 to bounce a cheque, not to mention the embarrassment and hassle of making another payment.

There is one surefire way to avoid getting socked with a bounced cheque or overdraft fee: keep a close and constant eye on how much money you've got in the bank, and NEVER write a cheque or authorize a debit you can't cover. If you do overdraw your account, deposit enough money back into it as soon as possible to cover the shortfall plus any fees and daily charges your bank may have assessed. This won't undo the initial damage, but it will help you avoid additional overdrafts and fees.

Cheque-Processing Policies That Push You into Overdrawing

Some banks have cheque-processing policies that seem deliberately designed to maximize the number of bad cheques they can charge you for.

When several of your cheque arrive at the bank on the same day, the bank does not process them in the order in which you wrote them or even the order in which they arrived. What they sometimes do is process them in the order of size, starting with the largest dollar amount and working down to the smallest.

Say you have $100 in your chequing account and you write two cheques, one for $30 and one for $40. Then the next day, you have an emergency and you write a cheque for $75, figuring you can cover it with a deposit you're expecting to make. Worst case, you think, you may bounce the $75 cheque, but your other cheques should be fine. Wrong.

If all three cheques hit the bank on the same day, the bank would clear the $75 one first, leaving you with a balance of just $25—not enough to cover either of your other cheques. So even though you wrote those cheques first, the bank would bounce both of them—entitling it to charge you for two bounced cheques (around $30 each), instead of just one.

Once again, it's really important to monitor your account balances. Most banks let you do this both online and over the phone as well as through ATMs. Some banks will alert you by phone, email, or text message on your cell phone to let you know if your account balance drops below a certain level. They don't have to, though, so make sure you stay on good terms with your bank manager or account rep.

Record all chequing and electronic transactions when you make them.

In the meantime, record all chequing and electronic transactions when you make them, and, as boring as it may be, reconcile your cheque book with your monthly statements. Review those statements carefully, and notify your bank immediately if you see a transaction you did not authorize.

Unnecessary ATM Fees (That Earn Profits for White-Label ATM Operators)

Virtually every bank that has automatic teller machines charges a fee (ranging from $1.50 to $3) if you use a card from another bank to withdraw money. They sometimes apply that fee on top of the standard fee that they charge for an ATM transaction using their own network. The banks argue that they need to charge a fee to raise enough money to keep their own networks up to date. That may true.

But white-label ATMs—the ones that you find in convenience stores, bars, and gas stations—charge much more than banks do, and you can end up paying as much as $6 for a transaction. And they can't use the same excuse.

You've probably seen these ATMs. They've been around since 1997, when the government decided that the banks' ATMs needed some competition. Today, of the 51,000 bank machines in Canada, more than half are white-label units.

When you insert your card into one of these ATMs, the machine tells you upfront that you'll have to pay a fee. But by that time, you've usually run out of cash, and you have little choice but to go ahead with the transaction, no matter how much you get dinged for doing it.

The best way to avoid these fees is to make sure you have enough cash in your wallet or purse before you set out on your journey or hit the bar after your baseball game.

Deposit Holds—Know Your Rights!

Canada operates one of the most advanced clearing systems in the world. When you deposit money into an account in Halifax, you can make a withdrawal from that account on the same day from any bank branch or ATM in Canada.

But there's one sticking point to this otherwise excellent service: holds on cheques. Financial institutions can hold a cheque for a week before crediting your account. With changes in banking regulations and advances in technology for scanning cheques, the hold period will eventually be reduced to four days.

Once again, it helps if you're on good terms with your account manager. Banks will sometimes credit a deposited cheque to your account without holding it until it clears if you've dealt with your branch for a long time, you have enough money in your account to cover it if the cheque bounces, and if you've been a reliable customer of the bank.

Requests for Your Account Information

Here's a scary thought: anyone who knows your chequing account number and bank routing number can rob you blind. That's because this information is all that's needed to create a phony cheque or what's called a demand draft, which a bank will honour even though it does not bear the account holder's signature.

What makes this especially scary is that every cheque you write contains this information. It's those long strings of computerized digits printed at the bottom. This is one big reason that old-fashioned paper cheques are probably more risky to use than electronic transfers. As one expert puts it: "Paper inherently goes through a lot of hands. And every person who handles a cheque has the ability to commit cheque fraud."

This doesn't mean you should give up writing cheques. But be careful whom you write them to. And be *very* careful about giving out your account information to anyone.

One of the most popular bank-related swindles involves being conned into doing just that. Here's how it works. A guy calls you up and tells you that you've won a free prize or are eligible for a major credit card. At the end of the sales pitch, he adds you that in order to qualify for whatever it is he's offering you, he needs to know the numbers that appear at the bottom of your cheques. If you are foolish enough to let him have this information, he and his confederates will use it to send your bank a demand draft, ostensibly from you, ordering a transfer of funds—usually a *lot* of funds—to an account of theirs. You may not know any of this has occurred until you receive your next bank statement. At that point, it's usually way too late for any of the money to be recovered.

What to Do if Things Go Wrong

Banks are one of the most heavily regulated institutions around. So if you have a problem with one—and complaining directly to the bank's customer service department hasn't brought any relief—there are industry and government agencies that would love to hear about it. A list of the appropriate agencies is below. But before you call or write any of them directly, visit its web site to make sure it is the right one. Also make sure that the problem you think you have really *is* a problem—as opposed to your misunderstanding what the bank's obligations to you are.

The biggest potential problem banking customers face is getting hit with an erroneous or fraudulent charge. If you discover that any bank account of yours has been debited with any unauthorized payments, electronic transfers, or other charges (including unexplained penalty or service fees), you should notify the bank immediately. Were you charged the wrong amount on a debit transaction? Was there an error in a direct deposit? Do you see an ATM withdrawal or bank transfer that you did not authorize?

Under a voluntary code of conduct, banks have to show that you contributed to the unauthorized use of your card, and they cannot take longer than 10 business days to respond.

If you do discover that money's been taken from your account without your authorization, you should call or email your bank representative immediately and write a letter outlining your complaint and send it to the bank via certified mail. (You should be able to find the right mailing address by looking at your bank statement or on the bank's web site under "Customer Service.")

Depending on the nature of your complaint, the bank must initiate and complete an investigation within a specified period. If you are unhappy with the speed or nature of its response—or have any other issue with your bank—take your complaint to the bank's ombudsman, the CBA's Ombudsman for Banking Service and Investments (www.obsi.ca), the Office of the Superintendent of Financial Institutions Canada (www.osfi-bsif.gc.ca), your local MP, or, if you really want to make waves, a federal politician in the NDP party (www.ndp.ca).

The banks list their ombudsmen and describe their complain procedures on their websites. The CBA's ombudsman for Banking Services and Investments can be reached at:

Ombudsman for Banking Services and Investments
Tel: 1-888-451-4519/416-287-2877
Fax: 1-888-422-2865 or 416-225-4722
P.O. Box 896
Station Adelaide
Toronto, Ontario
M5C 2K3
ombudsman@obsi.ca / www.obsi.ca

Keep in mind that you have to try to resolve your complaint directly with your bank before you contact the CBA ombudsman.

Fight for Your Money Action Steps

- ☐ Shop around and switch banks if necessary. Compare a wide variety of chequing, savings, and money market accounts—be sure to compare fees as well. A great web site for this is the Financial Consumer of Canada (**www.fcac.gc.ca**).
- ☐ Read the fine print before selecting an account.
- ☐ Go with a bank that offers online savings accounts with the highest yields and lowest fees.
- ☐ Try to avoid white-label ATMs.

Debit Cards

As much as we Canadians love cash, we seem to love debit cards even more. Since 2001, Canadians have conducted transactions using their debit cards—which draw on an existing source of funds such as a chequing account—more often than they've used cash. We use debit cards at grocery stores, liquor stores, and drug stores. More recently, we use them to buy tickets to the movies. About half of all Canadians say they use a debit card most of the time compared to one-quarter of all Canadians who use cash.

It's easy to see why. Debit cards are simple to use and extremely convenient, and they can keep us from running up credit card balances.

In the United States, banks issue cards that can be used as either a credit card or a debit card. That's not the case in Canada, although Visa and MasterCard have both seen how much Canadians love their debit cards and would like to get a piece of the action.

At the moment, though, debit card transactions are cheap (about 6.5 cents apiece), easy, convenient, and popular.

How to Fight for Your Money

Your physical debit card doesn't need to be stolen out of your wallet or lost in the mall parking lot in order for your information to be compromised. You can lose that information without even knowing it if you use a machine equipped with a skimmer.

Criminals attach skimmers to the card-swiping devices at grocery stores, gas stations, and even banks. Undetected by consumers, these skimmers copy debit card numbers—including PINs—that are entered. Once the skimmer is retrieved by the criminal, the information is sold or used to create fake debit cards. (Actually, this scam applies to both credit and debit cards. However, thieves prefer to steal debit card information since credit cards are monitored more closely.)

So be on the lookout for physical tampering at your ATM or checkout line, which could indicate that a skimming device is present. Try to avoid white-label ATMs, as well—the kind you find in convenience stores or gas stations.

Also be aware of people lurking too closely at ATMs, or even for hidden cameras when you're entering your PIN. Use your hand to shield the numbers you're entering on the keypad.

Check Your Bank Statements Online Every Day

Does that sound extreme? Trust me, it's not. While you're online checking email every day, take two minutes to log on to your bank's web site (from a secure computer, of course) and pull up your current statement.

Glance over your recent transactions and make sure they're all legitimate. If you see anything suspicious, call your bank immediately. Don't wait for your paper statement in the mail. By then it might be too late.

Don't Let Your Debit Card Out of Your Sight

Make sure all your debit transactions are handled without the card being taken out of your line of sight. Once you take your eye off the card, anyone who handles it has the opportunity to steal the card information.

Don't Make It Easy to Steal Your Debit Card Password

To make sure they don't forget their password, some people write it down on the back of their debit card. That's just asking for trouble. Don't even carry it with you on a piece of paper. Instead, find a password that you can remember easily. Not your birthday or your postal code, which someone else could easily find out, but something more like the name of your pet rabbit or your high-school boyfriend's nickname.

Check Your Credit Report Regularly

If you suspect that your debit card information has been compromised, report it to the credit bureaus right away. Order a copy of your credit report and monitor it regularly.

As I mention in the credit-score section of this book, you should contact one of Canada's two credit bureaus, by mail, every 12 months, to receive a free copy of your credit report.

Cash or Debit?

Some people prefer to carry a debit card rather than cash. In fact, according to Interac, which administers the debit card system in Canada, people make more purchases with their debit cards than they do with cash. Unlike U.S. debit cards, Canadian debit cards do not allow you to withdraw more money from your account than you have. If you have an overdraft arrangement with your bank, you can withdraw money until you reach your limit. After that, Interac will refuse to complete your debit card transactions.

Unlike U.S. debit cards, Canadian debit cards do not allow you to withdraw more money than you have in your account.

What to Do if Things Go Wrong

Contact your bank immediately if your debit card is lost or stolen, or if you spot a fraud. And then monitor the situation closely.

If You Have a Complaint About Your Debit Card

If you think a bank or other financial institution has failed to fulfill its responsibilities to you, file a complaint with the Financial Consumer Agency of Canada (www.fcac.gc.ca). Again, you should do this only after you've contacted your branch manager and, if you receive no satisfaction there, your bank's head office.

She Fought for Her Money!

Here's a cautionary tale I heard from two different women, one a 53-year-old saleswoman named Jill in Tacoma, Washington, the other a 39-year-old teacher named Kathy in Winnipeg, Manitoba.

Right after Christmas a few years ago, Jill discovered that someone was using her debit card to make purchases online. First, it was a $9.75 charge for some cosmetics, then a $269 wire payment to Western Union. Jill immediately informed the bank that she hadn't authorized those charges and asked that her card be cancelled.

A few days later, she noticed another $150 in unauthorized charges—and when she called her bank's fraud department to report them, she learned that her debit card had not been cancelled as promised. Even worse, the bank told her they would not stop payment on these new charges. Rather, she would have to wait for the results of an investigation before she could get a credit. After countless phone calls, she finally got through to a supervisor who was willing to refund a portion of her money, but Jill was still out about $360. It took her another 10 days to get a credit for the full amount.

"My best advice is to take this very seriously and be persistent," Jill says. "The only reason I got my money back was because I wouldn't give up. I wouldn't let them toss me aside simply because they had more claims than employees. Lenders place the burden of proof on the customer and they have no guilt about freezing disputed funds. I was lucky. Unlike many people, I still had enough cash so this wasn't a real problem. But I can imagine how someone less secure could be placed in a real financial hardship by something like this."

Kathy went through a similar experience to Jill's when she discovered that someone had used her debit card to make a purchase for $85.43 in another part of the country, where she'd never been in her life. But unlike Jill, Kathy received immediate satisfaction from her bank when she reported the discrepancy.

Unlike banks in the United States, banks in Canada must prove that such discrepancies occur because of fraud or negligence on the part of the customer. Financial institutions adhere to a voluntary code that limits the amount of time they can freeze an account while they investigate a transaction, usually less than a week.

Fight for Your Money Action Steps

- ☐ Safeguard your PIN at all times.
- ☐ Never use your debit card at a machine with signs of physical tampering—or at an unbranded ATM.
- ☐ Check your bank statement online every day.
- ☐ Use your debit card only for small, immediate transactions.

CREDIT

Credit Cards

A few years ago, I appeared on Oprah Winfrey's "Debt Diet"—a series of TV shows on which we coached viewers on how to get out debt. The shows featured three couples battling to turn their finances around. The couple I coached, Dan and Sally Eggleston, had gone from a pleasant middle-class existence to a financial nightmare in just two years—mainly the result of overusing their credit cards when Dan quit his teaching job to go back to school. By the time I met them, they had maxed out a dozen credit card accounts and owed more than $72,000 in credit card debt. Struggling under the burden of interest rates as high as 29%, they found themselves getting dinged for $500 a month just in late fees and over-the-limit penalties.

Basically, they were drowning.

The sad fact is that there are thousands of people just like the Egglestons. As I write this in 2008, there are almost 65 million credit cards in circulation in Canada, about two for every Canadian. Most Canadians—about 75% of them—pay off their credit card balance every month. But the remaining 25% carry an outstanding balance. That means they're paying interest on the outstanding amount, sometimes at a rate as high as 20% or more. In fact, according to Statistics Canada, Canadians owe almost $26 billion on their credit cards. The median credit card debt in 2005 was $2,400, a rise of almost 60% from 1999. And most of the people who owe this money are young Canadians.

Fortunately for Dan and Sally, I was able to help them put together a plan to get them back on track. But it wasn't easy and it wasn't fast. Getting out of debt rarely is easy or fast. It can take decades—unless you have a smart plan and know how to FIGHT FOR YOUR MONEY.

Unfortunately for most of us, the credit card companies are experts at encouraging us to go into debt—and keeping us there as long as possible. In fact, keeping you in debt for as long as possible is how they make money.

And they make LOTS of money—most of it from the high interest rates we pay on our unpaid balances and the unfair penalty fees they trick us into incurring. In 2007 alone, those interest charges totalled $116 billion, while fees added another $23 billion to the industry's coffers.

How to Fight for Your Money

The fact is that when they're used responsibly, credit cards are a good deal. They free you from having to pay for everything in cash, which can be a huge convenience. They also allow you to borrow money interest-free—if you pay your bill before the grace period ends. But let's be honest. Some people don't do this, and even the ones who do sometimes miss a month every year or so.

To be smart with your credit cards, here is what you need to know—and do.

Pick the Right Card for You

There are hundreds of different credit cards to choose from these days: low-interest cards, rewards cards, balance transfer cards, airline cards, student cards, prepaid cards, business cards, cash-back cards—the list goes on and on. Are you a Montreal Canadiens fan? You can have a Montreal Canadiens credit card. Do you love your old university? You can get a loyalty card from your alma mater. You can even get one from World Championship Wrestling with Hulk Hogan's picture on it.

But is that the right card for you? How much is the annual fee? What's the interest rate? Who issued the credit card? What happens if you are late paying? How much is the penalty?

These are the type of questions you need to answer BEFORE you sign up for any credit card.

Some cards provide cardholders with elaborate concierge services, but they charge annual membership fees in the hundreds—and sometimes thousands—of dollars. Are these services worth that much to you? Other cards have no annual fee if you pay your balance in full every month. Are you going to carry a balance? If so, then you need a card with the lowest possible interest rate.

There are two easy ways to get a good sense of what's out there for you to choose from. First, simply hang on to all the junk mail you get this month. I promise you—there will be a few credit card offers in the pile. Simply spread them out on your kitchen table, side by side, and compare them.

The other way is to go online. You can find a list of credit card interest rates on the web site of The Financial Consumer Agency of Canada (www.fcac.gc.ca). The FCAC compares more than 200 cards issued by 26 Canadian issuers.

Read the Fine Print

I did a public television special a few years ago where I blew up a credit card agreement and pointed out all the legal tricks the credit card companies like to play. I had to blow it up because the fine print was so small. But these agreements are not simply hard to read. They are also hard to understand. All the same, you need to read them and do your best to understand what they say. At the very least, study the disclosure box that spells out the agreement's basic terms. These include:

- the annual percentage rates (APRs) you'll be charged if you carry over a balance, transfer a balance, or get a cash advance
- the minimum payment required and how long you can take to pay your bill in full before you get hit with a finance charge (known as the grace period)
- the method used to calculate your outstanding balance if you don't pay in full
- your credit limit and whether they can change it without notifying you
- what the penalty fee is if you exceed your credit limit
- the annual fee, if any
- when your payment is due—and when it is considered late
- what the penalty fee is for late payments, and whether paying late will trigger an increase in your interest rate

Using a credit card without knowing the terms of your account is simply dangerous. It can cost you hundreds if not thousands of dollars a year. To make sure you're not ripped off, you have to pay attention—you have to FIGHT.

Ask for a Lower Rate

Just because a credit card company sticks you with a high interest rate doesn't mean you have to accept it. This is especially true if you have decent credit, a record of paying on time, and haven't maxed out your card.

Here's what you do. First make sure you know the rate you're currently paying and the kind of rates other banks are offering. You can do this by checking your latest credit card statement and then going online to a site like the FCAC's, which posts comprehensive lists of what kind of interest virtually every credit card company in the country is charging. Then find the Customer Service phone number on your statement, call your credit card company, and ask to speak with a supervisor. Don't try to negotiate a lower rate with the first person who answers the phone. The people who answer the phones generally don't have the authority to approve changes, so you'd just be wasting your time.

When you are connected to the supervisor, tell him or her that a competing bank is offering you a much lower interest rate than the one you're currently paying—and that unless he can match or beat the competitor's rate, you intend to transfer your balance to that competitor. Don't be vague: tell the supervisor the name of the competing bank and the actual interest rate it is offering. Chances are that the supervisor will agree to lower your rate on the spot. This is particularly likely if your interest rate is, say, 20% and the average on cards at the time of your call is 12%.

If you are not that fortunate, don't give up. Just call back and speak to someone else.

Be aware that there are often many levels of supervisors. The departments that handle these calls have on average two to five levels of management. So if the supervisor you get the first time around doesn't give you what you want, ask to speak to that supervisor's manager. And if you don't like what he or she tells you, ask to speak to his or her superior.

The people who answer the phones generally don't have the authority to approve changes.

One other thing: make sure you write down the names of everyone you talk to. If you're told company policy forbids giving out last names, ask for an identification number. This will not only enable you to keep track of all the different supervisors and managers you're bound to wind up dealing with, but also make the customer service people wary of offending you. Generally speaking, as long as you are polite and reasonable, they will probably try their best to satisfy your request because ultimately they want to keep your business.

If They Won't Negotiate, Ask to Have the Account Closed

If they won't work with you, tell them you want to close your account. Often this will lead the person who took your call to transfer you to a new department—one whose job is to talk customers like you out of cancelling their cards. They will likely ask you why you are closing your account—at which point you can explain that it's because of the high interest rate you're being charged: their refusal to lower it gives you no choice but to transfer your balance to a competitor.

Time and time again this "close my account" approach gets cardholders a lower interest rate. (If it doesn't work, then you should transfer your balance to a competitor with better rates.)

Once your interest rate has been lowered, keep in mind that there's nothing preventing you from calling back and asking them to lower it AGAIN. In fact, I recommend you put a reminder in your calendar to call the credit card company 90 days after you get your rate lowered to see if they will lower it again. Often, they will—especially if you have paid your bills on time.

And don't give up. I have been in situations where it took as many as nine calls to get a rate lowered. Believe me—it's worth the effort. In total, those nine calls took a total of maybe two hours spread over a few weeks—and they resulted in thousands of dollars in lower interest payments in the first year alone.

Throw Out of Preapproved Solicitations

Credit card companies send out about 800 million such solicitations a year. The most dangerous of these are the pre-approved or pre-screened offers, where card issuers have checked out your credit history in advance. They not only pose a dangerous temptation, but also, if they fall into the wrong hands, expose you to the risk of identity theft. You should destroy them before you throw them out, so no one else can get hold of the information.

What to Watch Out For

The Minimum-Payment Trap

The dirty secret of the modern credit card industry is that the banks don't want you to pay off your balance. Their profits go up if you only make "minimum payments." And they're smart enough to know that if they ratchet the minimum payment down low enough (usually between 2% and 4% of your total balance), you'll keep spending money and they can make a fortune on you.

Not surprisingly, they don't want you to understand this. They don't want you to know that if you carry a $10,000 balance at an interest rate of 18% (which is typical of credit card users who don't pay off their bills in full each month) and make only a $200 minimum payment each month, it will take you *nearly 32 years* to get out of debt—and before you do, you will have forked over nearly $15,000 in interest charges. And that's assuming you never charge another dime on the card, never get hit with a late charge, are never billed for an annual service fee, and your interest rate never goes up.

WHAT HAPPENS WHEN YOU MAKE THE MINIMUM PAYMENT ON A $10,000 BALANCE

Interest Rate	How Long to Pay Off in Full	Total Interest Charges
8%	18 years, 5 months	$3,558
10%	20 years, 1 month	$4,888
12%	22 years, 1 month	$6,513
18%	31 years, 10 months	$14,615
20%	37 years, 8 months	$19,466
30%	50 years, 1 month	$150,250

The Old Switcheroo

Credit card issuers can change the terms of your account, hiking your interest rate, lowering your credit limit, and shortening your payment deadlines, any time they want for no particular reason. Generally speaking, the bank must notify you of any changes at least 30 days in advance and give you the chance to opt out if you don't like the new rules. (If you choose to opt out, they can close your account but you get to pay off your balance at the old terms.)

But don't expect the notification to be all that noticeable. The banks deliberately design these notices to look like junk mail so most people will throw them away without opening them.

The problem is that throwing out or otherwise ignoring the notice means you've accepted the new terms. You have to take action to opt out, either calling or writing to the bank.

There is one situation where the credit card company doesn't have to notify you of a change: when an increase in your interest rate is triggered by what's considered a *default* on your part—in other words, when you exceed your credit limit or make a late payment. Most credit card agreements entitle the issuer to charge interest on subsequent purchases over the next two months. If you make a late payment in September, for example, you'll see interest charged on your subsequent purchases in October and November.

The banks deliberately design change notifications to look like junk mail so most people will throw them away without opening them.

Some card issuers use this method, some don't. You can find out which ones do by checking the Financial Consumer Agency of Canada's web site (**www.fcac.gc.ca**).

Since the credit card companies are entitled to impose this kind of charge without warning, you should always scrutinize your statements, even if you don't think you've done anything wrong.

Be Wary of Balance Transfers

Credit card companies love to send you special cheques you can use to pay off other credit card bills by transferring the balance to their card—usually at a lower-than-normal rate (occasionally even at zero interest). Sometimes this can be a good deal for you, but most of the time it's not.

The interest rate may be low, but hidden in the fine print you'll often find a balance transfer fee that is usually around 3% of the total amount. This may not sound like much, but that 3% fee is really the equivalent of an additional 6% to 9% in annual interest, since most of these special balance transfer offers—and the low interest rates that go along with them—last for only four to six months. When you figure this in, those attractive special offers lose a lot of their appeal.

So before you take advantage of any special balance transfer offer, be sure to read the fine print and check out the terms. How long will the promotional interest rate last? How much is the balance transfer fee? And keep in mind that if you if miss the due date by even one day for just one payment, the special offer will likely be cancelled and your low promotional percentage will be replaced by a stratospheric penalty rate that might be retroactively applied to the entire amount you transferred—even if most of it has already been paid off!

Confusing Deadlines

The quickest way to make your interest rate skyrocket is to pay your credit card bill late. Needless to say, the banks love it when you do this because it adds to their profits. As a result, they do everything they can to make it difficult for you to pay on time.

When you're paying your taxes, all the Canada Revenue Agency (CRA) asks is that you get your payment in the mail by the deadline date. Visa and MasterCard are not so easygoing. If you mail in your payment, it needs to *arrive* at the bank by the due date; it's not enough for it to be postmarked by the due date. To make matters worse, many card issuers have a daily cutoff—often 3 p.m. Eastern Standard Time—after which they will no longer credit your payment that day. And many won't process payments made on a holiday or a weekend until the following business day.

So read your credit card agreement carefully and make sure you know what the cut-off deadline is. Ideally, you should pay your bill the same day you receive it, or at the very least four or five days before the due date.

Ideally, you should pay your bill the same day you receive it, or at the very least four or five days before the due date.

If you have trouble making your due date because it's out of sync with when you get paid, call your credit card company and ask them whether they can change your due date so it coincides with your payroll schedule. And to eliminate the risk of forgetting, consider arranging an automatic payment program for your credit card bills.

What to Do if Things Go Wrong

Under Canadian law, credit card issuers have to disclose the maximum liability that users incur if someone uses their card fraudulently. Some card issuers go even further.

Unauthorized Charges

Everyone knows that you should report a lost or stolen card immediately. That's because if you report the loss before the card is used, you can't be held responsible for any unauthorized charges. But even if you don't and a thief goes on a spending spree with it, your liability usually amounts to a maximum of $50. What's more, most of the major companies (including American Express, MasterCard, and Visa) have zero-liability policies that free you of any responsibility for the unauthorized use of a lost or stolen card regardless of when you report it.

Most issuers maintain a 24-hour toll-free "lost or stolen card" number for you to call when your card goes missing. You'll find it on your statement. It's a good idea to follow up your telephone report with a letter. Include your account number, the date you noticed your card missing, and the date you reported the loss.

Billing Errors

If your credit card statement includes a bill from a merchant who overcharged you, charged you for a product you never received, or sent you defective goods, you can and should dispute it. Provided you register your complaint in writing, credit card companies are obliged to look into the problem and cancel any improper charges.

To dispute an improper or erroneous charge, write to your credit card company at the address listed on your statement for "billing inquiries"—not the same address where you send payments. Send the letter by certified mail and request a return receipt. This is your proof that you responded. Include your name, address, account number, and a description of the billing error, including the amount and date of the error. (You'll find a sample letter you can use as a model on page 326 of the FFYM Toolkit.) Even if an identity thief changed the address on your account and you did not receive the bill, you still must dispute the charge promptly. So try to keep track of your billing statements and contact your card company if your bill doesn't arrive on time.

While you're disputing an error, you don't have to pay the disputed amount or any finance charges on it and your credit card company cannot report the nonpayment to a credit bureau as a delinquency. (Of course, a dispute doesn't get you off the hook from paying the rest of your credit card bill.) The credit card company must acknowledge your complaint in writing and the merchant must credit your account within two billing cycles.

Bad Products or Services

One of the advantages of using a credit card is that if you are not satisfied with the quality of the product or service you purchased with it, you can withhold payment. Before you do so, you must first make a good-faith effort to resolve the issue with the merchant.

If you and the merchant are unable to work things out relatively quickly, you should write to your credit card company and inform them you wish to withhold payment. But do this *only* if you have a valid complaint against the merchant. Simply changing your mind about a purchase you made isn't good enough. As with a disputed charge, once you inform the credit card company that you want to withhold payment, they can't report the amount as delinquent until the dispute is settled or a court judgment is issued against you.

Poor Treatment by the Credit Card Issuer

If your credit card company itself is the problem, you should obviously first try to work things out through its Customer Service department. But if they are unable or unwilling to help, there are a number of outside agencies you can turn to, including the Better Business Bureau (**www.ccbbb.ca**). You should also contact the Financial Consumer Agency of Canada (**www.fcac.gc.ca**). And if the case is particularly egregious, you might also want to complain to your local MP. (You can find his or her contact information by going online to **webinfo.parl.gc.ca**.)

Fight for Your Money Action Steps

- ☐ Go online to research credit cards with the best rates.
- ☐ Know your payment due dates. Set up an automatic payment program to avoid being late and incurring fees.
- ☐ Never pay only the minimum.
- ☐ Renegotiate your interest rates.

Free! My Gift to You

In *The Finish Rich Workbook*, I wrote a detailed chapter on credit card debt. If you feel you need help, visit my web site at **www.finishrich.com** to download this chapter for free.

Credit Scores

People get measured and tested in all sorts of ways these days, but of all the scores that are applied to you, probably none—not your IQ score, your SAT score, or your cholesterol score—has more immediate impact on how you live than your credit score. This three-digit figure pretty much determines whether you'll be able to get a credit card, a car loan, or a mortgage—and how much interest you'll have to pay if you do. It may even affect your insurance rates and your ability to get a job or rent an apartment. And in the aftermath of the 2008 U.S. mortgage meltdown, with the credit markets tighter and lenders more conservative, your credit score is more important today than ever.

So you need to know your credit score now. And if it's not so good, you need to know what you can do to improve it. The good news here is that no matter how irresponsible or unlucky you have been, you can fight your way back. The bad news is that there are no quick fixes or magic solutions. Unfortunately, this doesn't stop thousands of desperate people from paying millions of dollars each year to phony "credit repair" outfits that claim they can boost anyone's credit score, regardless of how bad their credit history might be.

How to Fight for Your Money

The most important thing you can do to help your credit score is understand what it is. To begin with, you should know that you don't have just one credit score—you have a bunch of them. That's because lenders, creditors, and the three national credit-reporting agencies (Equifax, TransUnion, and Northern Credit Bureaus) have their own particular methods and formulas for calculating what kind of a credit risk you are. They may also have different information about you.

The most widely used credit-scoring system was developed back in 1989 by a company called Fair Isaac Corp. The idea was to give lenders a quick and easy way to judge an individual's creditworthiness. Fair Isaac takes your credit history and runs it through a complicated series of calculations. The result is a number somewhere between 300 and 850. This is your FICO score. Anything over 700 is considered good. Score 750 or higher and most lenders will give you their best deals. On the other hand, a score below 500 means you will have trouble getting a loan no matter how high an interest rate you're willing to pay. As of 2008, the median FICO score was about 720—meaning that half of all Canadians scored higher than that and half scored lower.

The table below is similar to one you'll find on the FICO web site (**www.myfico.com**) that shows how differing FICO scores will affect the lending rates banks are willing to offer you.

HOW FICO SCORES AFFECT YOUR LOAN PAYMENTS

Score	Interest Rate	Monthly Payment
740–850	8.119%	$481
720–739	8.419%	$490
700–719	8.919%	$505
670–699	9.694%	$528
640–669	11.194%	$574
620–639	12.444%	$614

(based on a $50,000, 15-year, home equity loan, as of 11/22/08)

As you can see, a difference of just a few dozen points in your credit score can make a difference of hundreds of dollars in interest payments a year—and hundreds, if not thousands of dollars over the life of a loan. It makes an even bigger difference with mortgage payments.

WHAT YOU WILL PAY OVER 15 YEARS ON A $50,000 MORTGAGE	
With a 760 FICO Score:	$86,580
With a 650 FICO Score:	$103,320
Improve your credit score and you save:	**$16,740**

While FICO is the oldest and most popular credit-scoring system, it's not the only one. Since 2006, Equifax; Northern Credit Bureaus' parent company, Experian; and TransUnion have been pushing their own rating system, which they call VantageScore. Its gimmick is that its three-digit scores, which run from 501 to 990, translate into letter grades just like you got in elementary school. A score of 901 to 990 earns you an A, a score of 801 to 900 is worth a B—and so on, right down to a score of 501 to 600, which gets you an F.

Whether you're talking about FICO or VantageScore or some other system, the main factors that go into determining your credit score are all related to how you handle money in general and debt in particular. They include:

- your payment history (whether you pay your bills on time, how often you're late, and for how long)
- your utilization rate—how much of your total available credit you are using (the lower the better)
- how much you currently owe (less is better)
- whether you've gotten any new credit lately (this could lower your score)
- how far back your credit history goes (the longer your credit history, the better your score)

By changing these factors—say, by paying off a big chunk of what you owe—you can change your credit score.

Here are some basic tips for managing your credit score effectively.

Find Out How You Rate

The first thing you need to do is find out how you rate. The credit bureaus must provide every consumer who asks, by mail, with a free copy of their credit report, by mail. This can take weeks or months and sometimes the bureau will forget all about your letter and not respond at all.

For a better alternative, you can also get your credit report by going online to the web site of TransUnion, Northern Credit Bureaus, or Equifax—or all three.

As I indicated above, each credit bureau has its own records and issues its own reports, so you need to get a copy of what each of them is saying about you.

Keep in mind that your credit report is not your credit score.

Keep in mind that your credit report is not your credit score. Your score is based on your reports. Northern Credit Bureaus, Equifax, and TransUnion will send you your FICO score from Fair Isaac when you ask for your credit report.

Look for Errors—and Correct Them!

One of the most important reasons to get copies of your credit reports is so you can check them for accuracy. Having coached thousands of people on the process of both pulling and fixing their credit scores, I can tell you from personal experience that you will probably find they contain some incorrect information about you or your credit history. In the U.S., surveys have shown that no less than one of every four credit reports contains at least one mistake serious enough to keep you from getting a loan, a credit card, and in some cases a job. It's probably no different in Canada.

Given what's at stake, it's vitally important that you check out your credit reports and get any errors corrected as quickly as possible. Fortunately, it's not very difficult to do this. Credit-reporting agencies will investigate inaccurate or incomplete information in your report when it's pointed out to them and make the correction when it's called for.

So if you find any inaccuracies, point them out! You can do this by sending the credit agency a letter sent by certified mail that explains what information was inaccurate, including copies of documents (such as bank records or mortgage statements) that verify what you're saying, along with a copy of your credit report with the disputed information circled in red. There's a sample letter you can use as a model in the FFYM Toolkit on page 327. Here's contact information for the three national companies.

Equifax Canada Inc.
Consumer Relations Department
Box 190 Jean Talon Station
Montreal, Quebec
H1S 2Z2
Toll-free: 1-800-465-7166 between 8:00 a.m. and 5:00 p.m. ET
www.equifax.com/home/en_ca

Northern Credit Bureaus Inc.
336 Rideau Boulevard
Rouyn-Noranda, Quebec
J9X 1P2
Toll-free: 1-800-646-5876
www.creditbureau.ca

TransUnion Canada
All provinces except Quebec
TransUnion Consumer Relations Department
P.O. Box 338, LCD1
Hamilton, Ontario
L8L 7W2
Toll-free: 1-800-663-9980
Quebec residents
Centre De Relations Aux Consommateurs TransUnion
1 Place Laval Ouest
Suite 370
Laval, Quebec
H7N 1A1
Toll-free: 1-877-713-3393
www.transunion.ca

Raise Your Score by Paying Down High Balances

There are lots of myths about things you can do to improve your credit score. In fact, there really isn't any mystery about it. On its web site, Fair Isaac spells out how it weighs the various factors that go into calculating your score: payment history counts for 35%, amount owed (which includes both the dollar amount and your utilization rate) is 30%, length of credit history is 15%, how many new accounts you've opened is 10%, and types of credit used is 10%. The question is, if you want to raise your score, which of these factors can you affect? And how long will it take?

Obviously, there's not a lot you can do about the most important factor, your payment history. It is what it is. If you have a habit of making late payments, you should certainly try to do better. But even if you never miss a payment deadline again, it will take several years for this to be reflected in your credit score. When negative information in your report is accurate, only the passage of time can assure its removal. A consumer reporting company can report most accurate negative information for seven years and bankruptcy information for 10 years.

On the other hand, the second most important factor, amounts owed, is something you can change. Indeed, there is nothing you can do that will have a positive impact on your credit score more quickly than reducing the amount you owe.

She Fought for Her Money!

What if your credit is terrible? The fact is, you can turn an awful credit score into a great one. It just takes time and discipline. I know a woman, a real estate agent and mother of two named Susan, who managed to raise her credit score by 186 points—from 582 to 768—in three years. She did it by setting a goal and sticking to it.

The first step was to get her whole family to make a commitment to becoming debt-free. "It's important to involve the whole family or it won't work right," Susan says. "Don't make it like a fad diet that makes you feel like you are neglecting yourself or that life is all of a sudden plain and boring because, if you do that, you'll wind up going back to old habits."

Once her family was on board, Susan cut up her credit cards and started paying off the balances, one by one. The family lived frugally on a strict budget that eliminated all unnecessary spending. They cancelled premium cable and movie download services, and cut back on family vacations.

Susan first paid off the credit cards with the lowest balances, so she could enjoy some small successes. She kept track of her debts on a computer spreadsheet, and each time she zeroed one out, it gave her additional motivation to keep going.

Thirty days after she paid off each credit card, Susan would check her credit report and credit score to make sure her accomplishment had been accurately reported to the credit reporting agencies. At the same time, she was careful not to add on any new debt, never to miss a payment deadline, and to refrain from opening any new accounts.

Today, her credit is excellent. But that doesn't mean she's easing up. Her goal now is to see her score crack 800.

Closing Old Acccounts Doesn't Help—It Hurts

One of the myths about credit scores is that you can improve your numbers by closing down old credit card accounts that you no longer use. In fact, the opposite is true. Closing down old accounts generally hurts your credit score.

Not only does it shorten your credit history, which accounts for 15% of your FICO score, but it also can increase your credit utilization rate, which is an even more important factor.

Here's how that works. Let's say you have two credit cards, a Visa and a MasterCard, each with a $5,000 credit limit, but you use only the Visa card. If you are carrying a $2,500 balance on your Visa account, your credit utilization rate would be 25%, since your total available credit from both cards is $10,000. However, if you closed the MasterCard account, your total available credit would drop to $5,000, which would raise your credit utilization rate to 50%—and that would hurt your credit score.

Closing down old accounts generally hurts your credit score.

That's not to say you shouldn't close some accounts if you think doing so will help you manage credit more wisely and prevent you from racking up too much debt. But don't do it because you think it might help your credit score.

Watch Those Inquiries

Too many credit inquiries can hurt your credit score. You may think there's no harm in having an auto dealership or mortgage broker run your credit, but to the credit-rating companies, a sudden surge in inquiries is a sign that you may be in danger of overextending yourself. That may sound silly, but according to Fair Isaac, people with six or more inquiries on their credit report are up to eight times more likely to declare bankruptcy than people with none. So don't let merchants or financial institutions run your credit unless it's absolutely necessary. (This isn't the case when you check your own credit score.)

What to Watch Out For

Credit-Repair Firms That Promise to "Clean Up" Your Credit Report

"Increase your credit score by 61 points in 30 days!"

"We can erase your bad credit—100% guaranteed!"

"We can remove bankruptcies, judgments, liens, and bad loans from your credit file forever!"

The come-ons can be hard to resist, especially if you've got real credit problems.

Too bad it's all bunk. The fact is that when it comes to credit repair there are no magic bullets.

There isn't anything that a credit-repair company can do for you legally that you can't do for yourself—and probably for free.

Certainly, there is no legal way to rid a credit report of negative information that is accurate and timely. Nor is it really possible, as some of these outfits claim, to take advantage of the 30-day investigation deadline by swamping the credit bureaus with baseless error disputes.

The bottom line is that there isn't anything that a credit repair company can do for you legally that you can't do for yourself—and probably for free.

As Ontario's Ministry of Small Business and Consumer Affairs says on its web site: "Be wary of advertisements promising to "fix" bad credit. Credit repair companies may claim to improve consumers' poor credit ratings, but, in reality, no credit repairer has the power to change or erase accurate information in a consumer's file."

There are three big tip-offs that a credit-repair offer is not to be trusted.

- THEY GUARANTEE AMAZING RESULTS UPFRONT. Legitimate credit counsellors don't give guarantees—and certainly not before they know your situation.
- THEY ASK FOR PAYMENT IN ADVANCE TO REMOVE BANKRUPTCY AND DEFAULT JUDGMENT INFORMATION FROM YOUR RECORD. This is impossible under the law. By law, this information must remain in a credit report for a specified period.
- THEY ADVISE YOU NOT TO CONTACT A CREDIT BUREAU DIRECTLY. Usually, this is so they can get you to pay them to file a dispute that you could easily file yourself for free.

Credit-repair outfits are sometimes confused with credit counselling services, which are usually nonprofit entities that help people figure out how to pay off their debts. If your situation is so bad that you're tempted to try a credit-repair service, try a credit counsellor instead. Sadly, some credit counselling services have earned a bad reputation for charging high fees. So before signing up with one, always check them out with the Better Business Bureau first.

One of the better bets is a local outlet of Credit Counselling Canada. You can find an office in your area by checking CCC's web site at **www.creditcounsellingcanada.ca**.

Make Sure Your "Free" Credit Report Really Is Free and Not a Membership

If you watch television, you are bound to see commercials offering a "free credit report." These ads will push you to web sites that promote the importance of getting your free credit report, and having your credit regularly monitored. But before you sign up for anything, READ THE FINE PRINT! A lot of these offers really aren't free. For example, Experian sponsors a web site called **FreeCreditReport.com** through which you can order a supposedly "free" credit report. But as the site points out (in hard-to-read type), there's a catch: "When you order your free report here, you will begin your free trial membership in Triple AdvantageSM Credit Monitoring. If you don't cancel your membership within the 7-day trial period, you will be billed $14.95 for each month that you continue your membership." As I mentioned earlier, the way to get a really free credit report is by submitting your request in writing to one of the three credit-reporting agencies.

Outdated Information on Your Credit Report

There is one foolproof way to get accurate negative information removed from your credit report, and that's to be patient. Most bad marks are supposed to stay in your file for only seven years; the main exceptions are bankruptcies (which stick around for ten years) and criminal convictions (which never come off).

That said, don't expect the credit bureau to automatically clean up your report without your requesting it. So when you're going over your credit report, keep an eye out not only for errors but also for negative information that should have already dropped off but hasn't. If you find any, file a dispute report.

What to Do if Things Go Wrong

The dispute-resolution process with the credit-rating companies is strictly regulated, and while it's not foolproof, it is chock-full of protections for the consumer.

Specifically, you have the right to dispute any information in your credit report that you regard as incomplete or inaccurate—and unless your dispute is frivolous, the credit agency must investigate it. Moreover, if it turns out you're right, the credit agency must correct or delete the bad information (though they can continue to report information they have verified as being accurate). And even if your complaint is rejected by the credit agency, you have the right to insist that a statement of the dispute be included in your file and in all future reports. You can even make the company send your dispute statement to anyone who received a copy of your report in the recent past (though you may have to pay a fee for this).

Still, no process is perfect, and if you have a complaint with any of the credit-rating agencies—or with a credit-repair outfit—you should report it to the Financial Consumer Agency of Canada (**www.fcac.gc.ca**), if you can't get your complaint resolved by the credit reporting agency itself.

Financial Consumer Agency of Canada
427 Laurier Avenue West, 6th Floor
Ottawa, Ontario
K1R 1B9

Fight for Your Money Action Steps

- ☐ Find out your credit score today and get a free copy of your credit report from Equifax, TransUnion, or Northern Credit Bureaus.
- ☐ Review your credit report for mistakes. Report any inaccuracies right away, and follow up to be sure they've been corrected.
- ☐ Work on paying off your balances in order to raise your credit score.
- ☐ Have patience *and* persistence. Set a goal and stick to it—and watch your credit score improve.

Payday Loans

Not too long ago, I got a letter from a reader that told me everything I needed to know about payday loans. Alicia was a 64-year-old retail clerk with a problem. Christmas was approaching and she didn't have enough money in her chequing account to be able to buy her grandchildren gifts *and* pay her utility bills. So she did what about 350,000 or so other Canadians do every year. She went to one of those stores with a sign in the window saying "Get Cash Now! Bad Credit OK!" and took out a payday loan.

The result was a financial nightmare. Alicia originally borrowed $400 for what was supposed to be two weeks, but when the due date came around, she didn't have the $460 she now owed (for the principal plus a $60 loan fee). Because the lender wouldn't take a partial payment, she had no choice but to take out a new loan with a new higher fee to pay back the old one. Before she knew it, she was caught in a vicious cycle. Every other Friday, she would get up early in the morning, use her paycheque to pay off one loan and immediately turn around and take out another one. "It was like a merry-go-round," Alicia wrote me. "I was a wreck."

By the time she managed to get off the treadmill, she had forked out $1,780 to repay a $400 loan.

Payday lending is a booming business. With upward of 1,200 outlets across the country—about the same number as McDonald's—payday lenders claim they are helping out cash-strapped wage earners by providing as much as $1 billion a year in short-term loans. In fact, they make their money by charging INSANELY HIGH FEES that end up trapping people in a never-ending cycle of two-week cash advances that they are unable to pay off. Because the lenders don't accept instalment payments, payday borrowers who can't come up with the entire amount they owe have to keep "flipping" their loans—and each time they do, a new, higher loan fee is added to the total.

Payday loans are used most by people who can least afford them. A study by Statistics Canada shows that young families are three times more likely to have used payday loans than people over 35.

"Families with little savings or no credit cards, particularly those who had been refused, were significantly more likely to have used payday loans," the report says. "Without these options and faced with financial shortfall, these families may have turned to payday loans in an effort to bridge the gap between paycheques."

Of course, what the lenders call fees are really exorbitant interest charges, typically with APRs as high as 400%—and sometimes more than 1,000%. In the United States, according to figures compiled by the Center for Responsible Lending in 2006, even though the average payday loan customer borrows only $325, he winds up paying back $793. In Canada, studies have shown that the fees charged by payday lenders amount to an annual interest rate of more than 1,200%.

The bottom line about payday loans is: YOU MUST KNOW THE FACTS AND THE COSTS. It is truly in your financial self-interest to do just about anything else you can before you turn to this as a solution.

How to Fight for Your Money

There's no question that payday loans can be tempting if you're short of cash. It doesn't matter how bad your credit is. As long as you have a chequing account and can produce a payroll stub showing that you receive a regular paycheque, a payday lender will be happy to take care of you.

What they do is have you write them a postdated cheque for the amount you want to borrow plus fees. The lender holds your cheque until your next payday, at which point he either deposits your cheque or you come in with the cash and take back your cheque.

If you don't have the money to cover your cheque, the lender will be happy to roll over your loan—that is, make you a new loan to pay off the old one. Of course, the new loan will be bigger than what you initially borrowed, since you now owe not only the original principal but also the fee they charged you. And that means the fee for the new loan will be larger too.

Do You Really Want to Pay 1,564% Interest?

Typically, payday lenders charge around $12.50 for every $100 you borrow, including interest and fees. On a 17-day loan, this is the equivalent of an annual interest rate of 1,242%!

ANYTHING IS BETTER THAN THIS

Average interest rate on a credit card:	12%
Average interest rate on a payday loan:	426%

Say you're borrowing $100. To begin with, you write the lender a postdated cheque for $117.50. If you can't cover that cheque when the loan comes due, the only way to get him to rip it up is for you to take out a new loan covering the $100 you borrowed and the $17.50 you were charged. But the amount of the new loan won't be $117.50. It will be $138.06—the $117.50 you failed to pay plus a new fee of $20.56 for this new loan. So now you write the lender a postdated cheque for $138.06. If you can't cover this when it comes due, your third loan will be even bigger—the $138.06 you already owe plus another new fee of $24.16, for a grand total of $162.22. By the time you get to your third flip, you will owe more than $191—or nearly twice what you borrowed in the first place. And on and on it goes.

Anything Is Better Than This

Those numbers add up to a royal rip-off. That's why six provinces have passed legislation to regulate the payday lending industry. However, federal law regulates lending and interest charged on loans, and the provinces have yet to coordinate their legislation with Ottawa's.

As Alicia, the grandmother, wrote me: "These gifts that I bought, they were long gone and half of them were destroyed, and I was still paying for them. At the time, you think there's no other way, and you're desperate, and they make it so easy. You think, 'Well, I could do this and I can pay it back.' If you're desperate, go to your family or a close friend, or try to deal with your problem. Talk to your creditors and try to set up some kind of arrangement. Or go to your church to ask for help."

A Sign That Something Is Amiss?

Payday loans are used by young families and others who can least afford them.
Anything is better than a payday loan.

Alicia is right. No matter how desperate you are, there are plenty of alternatives to borrowing from a payday lender. To begin with, ask your boss if you can get an advance on your paycheque. If you're a reliable worker, he may well say yes—and not even charge you any interest.

If that's not an option, check with your credit union, bank, or local community-based organization to see if they offer short-term loans at more reasonable rates. And contact your creditors to ask for more time to pay your bills or negotiate a payment plan.

Take it from Alicia—anything is better than a payday loan. "You feel like it's a quick fix," she said. "You think you're going to be paying back just what you borrow. But it's just an endless merry-go-round. You feel like you're never going to get off. People can justify it all that they want. I've got the scars."

What to Do if Things Go Wrong

If you're trapped in the revolving door of payday loans, there are many non-profit credit-counselling services that will give you good advice for littleor no cost. Some may even provide emergency assistance, including help with paying essential bills. Contact Credit Counselling Canada at www.creditcounsellingcanada.ca.

If you believe you've been treated unfairly or victimized by deceptive practices (which is practically a given with many payday lenders), contact your local MP. You should also complain to the Financial Consumer Agency of Canada through its web site at www.fcac.gc.ca or by contacting them at:

Financial Consumer Agency of Canada
427 Laurier Avenue West, 6th Floor
Ottawa, Ontario
K1R 1B9
Toll-free: 1-888-461-3222

You might also contact the Canadian Payday Loan Association (www.cpla-acps.ca), the trade association for the payday-loan industry. (It represents

20 companies, representing roughly half of the nation's 1,200 payday loan outlets.) The CPLA promotes responsible use of payday loans and "best practices" among payday lenders. Of course, its mission is to promote more business for its members, but the CPLA does understand the value of good PR, and if you've got a problem with a payday lender, it could be helpful in working it out. You reach them at:

The Canadian Payday Loan Association
25 Main Street West, Suite 2010
Hamilton, Ontario
L8P 1H1
Tel: 905-522-2752
Fax: 905-522-2310

Fight for Your Money Action Steps

- ☐ Avoid taking out a payday loan at all costs.
- ☐ Explore all alternatives—talk to your employer, church, credit union, bank, or local nonprofit community organization that might be able to offer a short-term loan at a reasonable rate.
- ☐ Contact your creditors to negotiate a payment plan on outstanding bills.
- ☐ Never roll over a payday loan.
- ☐ To get help if you are in debt, contact a nationally accredited consumer counselling agency in your area by visiting **www.creditcounsellingcanada.ca.**

Identity Theft

Identity theft ranks among the most prevalent of consumer complaints in Canada. The Better Business Bureau estimates that Canadians lose more than $2.3 billion a year to the crime. The RCMP and provincial police agencies receive more than 7,800 calls a year about identity theft on their PhoneBusters anti-fraud hotline and say that number represents only 5% of all victims of identity theft. That means more than 150,000 people a year have their identities stolen every year in Canada. The good news is that you don't have to be one of them.

Identity theft is an absolute nightmare for its victims. Your personal data—Social Insurance Number, credit card numbers, and bank account numbers—can all be stolen by a thief posing as you, and who uses this information to spend thousands of dollars or more. You may not even have a clue that anything is wrong until your application for a mortgage is rejected or you are contacted by a collection agency over a debt you never heard of.

The damage goes way beyond money too. Identity theft can have a devastating impact on your entire life—destroying your credit score and taking you months or even years to recover from the damage. Identity theft is truly the epitome of needing to learn to fight for your money.

How to Fight for Your Money

You might think that identity theft occurs most frequently online, when people submit credit card numbers and other information electronically to pay for things they buy from retail web sites. But a study conducted in the United States by Javelin Strategy & Research says that, in cases where victims knew how their data was stolen, online identity theft methods (like phishing, hacking, and spyware) represented only 12% of fraud cases. The vast majority of known identity-theft cases—almost 80% of them—occur through traditional methods, when a criminal makes direct contact with the consumer's personal identification—including stolen or lost wallets, chequebooks, or credit cards, shoulder surfing (when someone looks over your shoulder at the ATM or cash register), and stolen mail from unlocked mailboxes. And still another 17% report friendly theft—when friends, family, or in-home employees steal your personal data.

Some studies show that friendly theft is thought to be even more prevalent. In a submission in 2007 to a Parliamentary committee on information, privacy, and ethics, Canada's Privacy Commissioner said that there's no authoritative data to show how people's identities are stolen. Some studies say that at least half the cases of identity theft involve family members, friends, and co-workers. Another study shows that 70% of the cases of identity theft occur when employees steal confidential information from a business. And no matter how it happens, many people don't bother to report incidents of identity theft.

Regardless of how it happens or who tries to steal your identity, here's how to protect yourself.

Safeguard Your Personal Information

Sounds obvious enough, right? But you would be surprised how easily people are tricked into providing their private information to complete strangers, let alone their friends and relatives.

You're probably already familiar with online phishing scams where a fraudulent email asking you to resolve an account problem will redirect you to a bogus web site. Well, a scam dubbed "vishing" is even less sophisticated and low-tech. Here's how it works, as described by the Javelin study mentioned above. In one version, you get an email that appears to be from your bank, like a traditional phishing scam. Instead of being directed to a fake web site, you are given a number to call where you'll then be asked or prompted for your personal information. In the second variation, you are contacted over the phone, either by a real person or a recorded message requesting that you solve a problem with your account.

Vishers often use VOIP (Voice Over Internet Protocol) to autodial credit card or bank customers with a security warning about possible fraudulent activity on your accounts. Customers are asked to call the bank back, and when you do, you're told to input your account numbers and other private information.

Here's the bottom line: Never provide personal information over the phone, unless you have initiated the call to a verified phone number. Do not click on a web site when responding to emails or text messages. Do not respond to automated phone messages or emails prompting you to call a number to resolve a bank account issue. Instead, only use contact addresses, sites, or phone numbers that you have verified are legitimate.

Also, make it a habit not to leave things lying around at home or in the office—specifically your wallet, chequebook, or anything else containing private or financial information.

Buy a Shredder—and Use It

You might not think you have any top-secret documents worth shredding, but bank and credit card statements, utility bills, cancelled cheques, and the like all contain exactly the kind of personal information that ID thieves need. So before you throw out these sorts of documents, shred them. ID thieves have no compunctions about dumpster diving—and they count on the fact that most people think shredding documents is silly or paranoid. This isn't new advice, but I'd be remiss not to mention it.

Clean Out Your Mailbox

You probably regard those credit card offers that come in the mail all the time as a nuisance, but ID thieves love them. That's because they're easy to steal and they often contain useful personal information. So tell the banks to stop sending them to you.

You can also opt out of receiving direct-mail solicitations, at least from companies that belong to the Canadian Marketing Association (www.the-cma.org). The CMA administers a Do Not Contact service, which tells its members that you don't want to receive their direct-mail material. You can sign up for it on the CMA's website.

You can reduce the junk mail that arrives in your mailbox, including unsolicited credit card offers, by attaching a sign on or near your mailbox that says No Junk Mail. Canada Post employees respect these signs, although third-party delivery agencies often ignore them. You can also send a letter to your local postal outlet. If, after opting out, you still receive unaddressed mail, you should contact Canada Post by calling 1-866-607-6301.

You might want to sign up to receive the electronic newsletter of the Red Dot Campaign (www.reddot.ca). You'll find more tips on reducing junk mail and electronic communications, often associated with identity theft, while reducing your carbon footprint, as well.

The point is that you want to do as much as you can to keep sensitive information *out* of your mailbox. So in addition to opting out of unsolicited credit offers, you should also take advantage of any invitations you get from your bank, credit card companies, and utilities to start receiving your statements and bills online instead of through the mail. (This is not only more secure; it's also better for the environment.) By the same token, when ordering new cheques, don't have them mailed to your home. Instead, arrange to pick them up at the bank.

When Asked for Your Social Insurance Number—Just Say "No"

Your Social Insurance Number (SIN) is the key to everything. So guard it carefully. Don't carry your SIN card in your wallet and don't give out your number to businesses that have no need for it, such as a local gym or retail store. It's entirely proper for a new employer or a bank or credit card company with whom you're opening an account to ask for your SIN. The same is true of businesses that need to run a credit check on you, such as a cell-phone provider. But businesses and government agencies should give you a clear reason for requesting it and tell you whether disclosure is mandatory or voluntary, what they'll use the information for, and the consequences, if any, if you refuse to provide it.

Everyone seems to want your SIN, from the video store to the health club to the dentist.

Why do so many businesses and organizations request this private data? Simple—because "it's on the form." But just because you're asked for the information doesn't mean you have to give it.

Who does have the right to it? Your employer, the drivers licence office, welfare and tax departments, and institutions that handle transactions involving your taxes, like your bank. If you're unsure, you should pose the following questions of anyone asking for your SIN:

- Why is my number needed?
- How will my number be used?
- What happens if I refuse to give my number?
- What law requires me to give the number?

How Accessible Is Your SIN?

There are many ways to obtain personal information about anyone, even a complete stranger. For example, a journalist was able to get the telephone records of Jennifer Stoddart, Canada's privacy commissioner, without her knowledge or consent, from an offshore company that solicited her phone records under false pretences.

Right now anyone who knows your name can log on to various web sites and access your SIN in a matter of seconds. Don't believe me? Check out the NetDetective.com web site. For $29, an identity thief can use it to pull up not only your SIN and date of birth, but also your employer's name, salary, and the name of your spouse! Chilling.

Check Your Statements Weekly

You may want to consider opting for online statements. You're more likely to have personal information stolen from your mail than from the Internet.

One of the great things about online banking is that you can log on and check your account at any time. Make a point of checking your bank statement weekly to be sure there aren't any red flags.

That said, be sure to always use a secure computer. Using a public computer, like one at your local library, is risky due to tracking software that thieves can use to steal your passwords.

Beware of Wireless Computer Connections

Even though a relatively small percentage of identity theft occurs online, you should still take necessary precautions.

In addition to being careful about surfing the web on public computers, you should also be aware of the risks involved when using a wireless connection. Wi-Fi and Bluetooth are becoming increasingly popular, and as a result there's bound to be an increase in wireless hacking.

Wireless connectivity is the perfect platform for thieves to get your personal data. If you have a wireless network at home or work, make sure you're incorporating password protection and encryption. When accessing public hotspots, use a personal firewall.

Also, keep your computer safe by updating your antivirus and anti-spyware programs regularly. Use passwords so that others can't log on to your computer, laptop, or even your PDA, and be sure to change your passwords often.

Make Sure Deleted Data Is Really Deleted!

The Washington Post recently ran an article on cell phones—specifically, "smartphones" like the Palm Treo and BlackBerry—that was quite an eye-opener.

According to the story, resetting your phone to wipe out personal data doesn't exactly delete information. It turns out that your phone's operating system never actually deletes data, only the pointers to where the data is located. Once you sell or discard it, anyone with the right software can recover information that was stored on your phone.

Contact the device manufacturer for complete instructions on what to do to wipe your data clean. You can also visit **www.WirelessRecycling.com** for instructions. Click on "Online Tools/Cell Phone Data Eraser." And think twice about what information you store on your device in case it's ever lost or stolen.

Opt Out Wherever and Whenever Possible

The fine print—it'll get you every time. Whether you're completing an application for a new bank account, credit card, or sweepstakes, you need to read the fine print carefully to find out how to opt out, which means your personal information won't be shared.

It may seem perfectly harmless to provide your personal information without getting a guarantee that it won't be sold or shared. But when this happens, your information enters the public domain and becomes part of the ever-expanding information industry. You just have no way of knowing what's in these information files, which soon become permanent.

So try this. Log on to your bank's web site. Chances are that if you scroll all the way to the bottom you'll see a "Privacy" or "Privacy Statement" link. Click it and read what your bank's privacy policy is. It should provide instructions on how to choose not to have your personal information shared—that is, to opt out. If so, protect your privacy and opt out today.

Monitor Your Credit Report for Unusual Activity

Once ID thieves have your SIN, date of birth, and other crucial information, they typically use the data to open bank and credit accounts in your name but with a different home address. As a result, you never get any bills and statements from these accounts—and you never have any idea that they exist. Until, of course, it's too late.

Fortunately, there is an easy way to make sure no one is using your identity to open any bogus accounts. The credit reports generated by the three big credit-reporting agencies—Equifax, TransUnion, and Northern Credit Bureaus—list every bank and credit account that exists in your name. So as long as you keep checking your credit reports regularly—through each one of the three credit bureaus—you should be able to spot any fraudulent accounts. Go to page 91 to learn how to monitor your credit report throughout the year for free.

Identity-Theft Protection and Monitoring Services—Do They Really Work?

It may sound like a no-brainer to monitor your credit report automatically by subscribing to a credit-monitoring service. However, *Consumer Reports* ran an article last year that says these services "are often overrated, oversold, and overpriced."

There are over 24 million customers in North America who subscribe to credit monitoring through services like those offered by Equifax, TransUnion, or Northern Credit Bureaus—paying as much as $180 a year for the peace of mind they may offer. The problem is that many credit monitoring services pull from only one credit bureau, not all three.

Many credit-monitoring services pull from only one credit bureau, not all three.

If you're going to purchase one of these services, make sure it monitors all three credit bureaus and be sure you understand what kind of credit-report activity will trigger an alert and how quickly you will be notified. As *Consumer Reports* points out, some products don't alert you to sudden activity in dormant accounts, unexpected increases in balance levels, changes in existing accounts, or the appearance of a negative public record.

The Next Generation of Credit-Monitoring Services

You've probably seen the ads for LifeLock (**www.lifelock.com**), a company that professes to provide *proactive* identity-theft protection (unlike monitoring services, which are more *reactive*) by placing fraud alerts with the three major credit bureaus in addition to reducing junk mail and credit card offers—all with a $1 million service guarantee.

The CEO, Todd Davis, runs full-page ads with his Social Security Number as well as posting it on the web site, to prove just how ironclad his company is in preventing identity theft.

As a customer, you'll end up paying $110 a year for LifeLock's service. But as the U.S. Federal Trade Commission warns, before you pay for an identity-theft prevention product or service, make sure you understand *exactly* what you're paying for. You may be paying to protect your identity and recover from identity theft when you can do the same thing for free.

So the bottom line here is to get a service like LifeLock if you want to pay for the convenience. But remember that you can also provide the same protection for free by placing a fraud alert on your own, although you will need to remember to renew it every three months. You can also easily reduce your junk mail in the ways I've mentioned earlier.

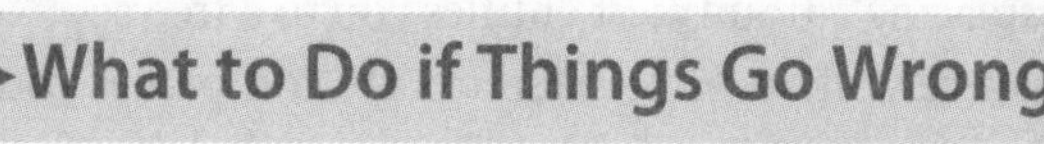

What to Do if Things Go Wrong

The moment you suspect you may be the victim of identity theft, ask the credit agencies to place a fraud alert on your credit file. A fraud alert requires creditors to verify your identity before issuing any credit in your name. Like all your interactions with a credit bureau, it's a laborious process. It will take you hours on the phone, mailing letters and sending emails, and, unlike U.S. residents, Canadians have to notify each of Canada's three credit agencies. But it can make it difficult for thieves who are trying to use your name to obtain new credit, without affecting your existing accounts.

To request a fraud alert, contact each of the credit agencies listed below.

Equifax Canada Inc.
Consumer Relations Department
Box 190 Jean Talon Station
Montreal, Quebec
H1S 2Z2
Toll-free: 1-800-465-7166 between 8:00 a.m. and 5:00 p.m. ET
www.equifax.com/home/en_ca

Northern Credit Bureaus Inc.
336 Rideau Boulevard
Rouyn-Noranda, Quebec
J9X 1P2
Toll-free: 1-800-646-5876
www.creditbureau.ca

TransUnion Canada
All provinces except Quebec
TransUnion Consumer Relations Department
P.O. Box 338, LCD1
Hamilton, Ontario
L8L 7W2
Toll-free: 1-800-663-9980
Quebec residents
Centre De Relations Aux Consommateurs TransUnion
1 Place Laval Ouest, Suite 370
Laval, Quebec
H7N 1A1
Toll-free: 1-877-713-3393
www.transunion.ca

Among other things, placing a fraud alert entitles you to a free copy of your credit report. When you receive it, look for references to companies you never contacted, accounts you didn't open, and debts you can't explain. If you find any inaccurate information, contact the credit agency to correct the errors. (For details on how to do this, see page 94 in the section CREDIT SCORES.)

As soon as you know that someone has opened a fraudulent account in your name or otherwise appropriated your identity, call the police either where you live or where you believe the theft took place. Get a copy of the identity-theft report that results from your complaint and make multiple copies. You want the actual report, not just a case number. You will need it in order to prove that you were the victim of a crime and not a scam artist yourself.

Another reason you want a police report confirming that you've been a victim of identity theft is that providing one to a credit-reporting agency entitles you to an extended fraud alert, which lasts for six years.

You should also file an identity-theft report with Phone Busters (**www.phonebusters.com**), operated by the RCMP and provincial police authorities, by email at info@phonebusters.com or by calling 1-888-495-8501.

You should report the loss of personal information to Reporting Economic Crime Online (RECOL), a partnership involving international, federal, and provincial law enforcement agencies. **www.recol.ca**.

In some cases, you should also contact Canada's Competition Bureau (**www.cb-bc.gc.ca**) at 1-800-348-5358 or by email at compbureau@cb-bc.gc.ca.

As the Phone Busters web site says, if you suspect that you may be a target of fraud, or if you have already sent funds, don't be embarrassed—you're not alone.

Close Any Unauthorized Accounts Immediately

If you discover that any bank, credit, or other business accounts have been opened or accessed without your permission, contact the appropriate company's fraud department and ask to have the accounts closed immediately. Follow up in writing. Be sure to keep copies and send all letters by certified mail with a return receipt requested.

You should also inform the credit-reporting agencies of any fraudulent accounts you've discovered and request that they remove all information regarding these accounts from your credit report. This will help protect your credit score and prevent a company from hiring a debt collector to go after you.

In addition, if you suspect that an identity thief has submitted a change-of-address form with Canada Post to redirect your mail or has used the mail to commit frauds involving your identity, contact Canada Post (**www.canadapost.ca**). In the meantime, If you are going away or are unable to pick up your mail for any reason, have it collected by a trusted neighbour or go to your local post office or online at www.canadapost.ca and file a Hold Mail Request. If you haven't received any mail for an unusual period of time based on your normal delivery patterns, contact Canada Post Customer Service at 1-800-267-1177.

Know Your Rights

If you are the victim of identity theft, there are certain rights that you are entitled to:

- rights to document and report the theft
- rights involving dealing with the credit-reporting companies
- rights when it comes to dealing with creditors, debt collectors, and merchants
- rights around limiting your losses

Canada's Privacy Commissioner operates a useful web site for victims of identity theft at www.privcom.gc.ca.

Fight for Your Money Action Steps

- ☐ Visit Canada's credit-reporting agencies today and start requesting your credit report on a regular basis.
- ☐ Shred your documents and mail instead of just tossing them in the trash.
- ☐ Opt out of unsolicited credit card offers through the Canadian Marketing Association (www.the-cma.org).
- ☐ Check your bank and credit card statements weekly at the very least.
- ☐ Use password protection and encryption if you have wireless Internet access.
- ☐ Stop giving out your Social Insurance Number unless the law requires it.
- ☐ Visit www.privcom.gc.ca and explore the identity-theft resources there.

Divorce

Nothing causes more trouble in marriage than arguments over money. And what's true for marriage tends to be true for divorce. Next to child custody, money is generally *the* major issue during the divorce process.

The fact is, whatever else it does to you, a divorce will put your finances through the wringer. Think about these statistics. The average woman experiences a 45% decrease in her standard of living after going through a divorce. And while the average man experiences a 15% improvement in his standard of living, that boost is just temporary. Over the long term, a divorce reduces the average man's ability to earn a living as much as 40% below his married counterparts.

The point is that divorce can be a financial nightmare in which no one comes out ahead, except maybe the lawyers. But it doesn't have to be that way.

How to Fight for Your Money

There are many financial traps on the road to divorce and many people—including your estranged spouse—who may try to take advantage of you. But you can get through it all by being smart and disciplined. The main thing to keep in mind is that your real adversary isn't your spouse, but rather an expensive system that encourages the two of you to run up huge bills by declaring war on each other.

Here's how to make sure that instead of ruining your life, your divorce frees you to restart it.

Consider the Alternatives to All-Out War

Regardless of why you're getting divorced, if you really want to get through it without having your life destroyed (financially and otherwise), you should do everything you can to avoid an all-out war. A contested divorce, involving lawyers and judges, is not only unpleasant but also expensive. In Canada, a contested divorce can cost each party $20,000 or more in legal fees alone. So if circumstances permit (meaning you're still speaking to each other), try really hard to agree on taking a less confrontational path.

No matter how you do it, a Canadian couple has to separate before they can divorce. That means you have to live apart for a specified period, usually a year, before you can divorce. You don't have to have a separation agreement for this to happen. You just have to agree on the date when you began living apart. Legal separation is governed by provincial law; divorce is governed by federal law.

Your separation agreement covers all the messy details like custody, spousal support, the division of assets, responsibility for debts, and issues related to pensions and RRSPs. Because couples often disagree about some or all of these issues, they often hire a lawyer to help them to draft the agreement. A separation agreement can take months or even years to finalize, especially if one person is stubborn or wants to antagonize the other (not uncommon in these situations).

Once you've completed the requirements of the separation agreement, and if you don't have children and a lot of assets, perhaps you could manage a no-lawyer uncontested divorce (also called a *pro se* divorce) in which you and your partner work out the terms on your own. For as little as $25, you can purchase a divorce kit (there are dozens available online) that contains all the necessary legal forms along with instructions on how to complete them. You file the finished documents with the court and, if your spouse doesn't contest the application, you get your divorce within about four months.

If you are not the do-it-yourself type or your situation is a bit more complicated but still amicable, you might consider hiring a lawyer to take care of all the paperwork. This shouldn't cost you more than a few hundred dollars.

Another alternative to contested divorce is divorce mediation. Rather than have your respective lawyers go at each other like cats and dogs, you and your partner sit down with a neutral mediator, who helps you work through all the issues you need to resolve before you can go your separate ways. (You can find lots of information on mediation on the Internet.) Using a mediator not only saves you money on legal fees, but also can (and usually does) lead to a better understanding of the financial realities you are both going to face as newly single people.

Once you've settled on a general course, if you're not going the *pro se* or mediator routes, you should interview a number of divorce or family law lawyers. Be sure to have a frank discussion about payment before signing on as a client. Don't be afraid to ask about payment caps and other strategies that can be used to ensure you don't break the bank.

How to Hire a Divorce Lawyer

Hiring a divorce lawyer is like hiring any other professional. You need to check credentials and ask a lot of questions. Here's a quick how-to.

ASK AROUND. Without a doubt the best way to find a great lawyer is by getting a recommendation from someone you know who has gone through a difficult divorce but speaks highly of their lawyer. So if you are facing a divorce, think about who you may know who has gotten divorced in your city or town in the last few years. You may not know this person well, but don't be afraid to ask. Tell them the truth: "I'm going through a divorce and I recall that you recently went through one too. Were you happy with your divorce lawyer and, if so, why? Would you mind referring me?" If you don't know anyone—or if the divorcees you do know didn't like their lawyers—check a referral website in your area such as www.canlaw.com. You should also look in the Yellow Pages.

SCHEDULE A CONSULTATION. After you've put together a list of several prospects, call their offices to schedule a consultation. Most divorce lawyers don't charge for a consultation meeting, but some do. So before you go, make sure to ask if there is a cost for the consultation. There is nothing wrong with paying for a consultation, but you want to know upfront what it costs. It's usually the lawyer's hourly rate, which can range from a few hundred dollars to $700 for a top practitioner.

ASK LOTS OF QUESTIONS. The job your divorce lawyer will be doing is way too crucial for you to take anything about him or her on faith. So don't be shy about peppering him or her with questions. The most important include:

- How long have you been practising law?
- Have you always specialized in family law?
- What do you charge? How is it billed and when will I be expected to pay? When all is said and done, how much do you think it will cost me?

- Who else might be working on my case with you and what would their role be? What are their credentials and how do you charge for their time?
- Can you give me an idea of how the process works and how long it will take?
- Are most of your cases settled out of court? What percentage wind up going to trial?

ASK WHAT THEY WOULD DO IF THEY REPRESENTED THE OTHER SIDE. One of the most important questions you can ask a lawyer you are interviewing is what they would do if they represented your spouse. How would they handle your opponent's case? What would they accuse you of? How much money would they try to get out of you? This will give you real insight into the potential downside—both financial and emotional—that you are facing.

MAKE SURE YOU UNDERSTAND WHAT IT WILL COST. Don't be shy about asking how much this will cost you. A lawyer who is not willing to discuss financial terms clearly and straightforwardly is not a lawyer you want to hire. In addition to finding out exactly how much a prospective lawyer charges—and how billing is handled—you also should ask about their retainer policy. A retainer is a deposit you pay in advance against future billable hours. Depending on the nature of your case, a retainer can run anywhere from a few thousand dollars to as much as $50,000. But retainers are almost always negotiable. Make sure you get in writing what happens if the full retainer is not used, including exactly when you can expect to get the unused portion refunded.

TRUST YOUR INSTINCTS. You and your divorce lawyer are going to be discussing the most intimate and painful details of your life, so you need someone you not only can trust but also feel completely comfortable with. No matter how impressive his or her credentials may be, if there is *anything* about a prospective lawyer's manner that puts you off—if you feel at all intimidated or patronized—scratch him or her off your list.

TEST THEM. The single biggest complaint that clients often have about their divorce lawyers is they can't get them on the phone. It is very difficult if not impossible to test a lawyer on this upfront. But what you can test for is how fast they respond to your initial request for a consultation and how professional their support staff is. If a lawyer doesn't get back to you the same day you make your initial call, it's more than likely they won't get back to you quickly once you've hired them. Keep in mind that the service you receive while they are selling you on using them is bound to be as good as it's ever going to get. So if it's bad upfront, expect it will be much worse down the road—and look for someone else. Also, if you find during your initial consultation that a lawyer is willing to share lots of "private, off-the-record" information about other clients, assume he or she will do the same with your information, and move on.

SHOP AROUND. I strongly recommend that you meet with at least three to five divorce lawyers before you hire one. You need to see who's out there and whom you feel most comfortable with. Remember, you may be working with this person for at least a year—and in many cases, as long as two or three years.

Consult a Financial Planner

A lawyer is not the only professional you should consult. You should also think about hiring a financial planner with expertise in divorce-related issues. When you're facing divorce, it's essential to have a clear picture of your family's finances and what they are likely to look like post-divorce. Among other things, this means running your credit report, gathering a list of assets, computing your net worth, and making copies of bank and investment statements. Particularly if you've left the bookkeeping and bill paying to your partner, having a professional who can help you with all this is a huge advantage.

You can find financial planners who specialize in divorce matters on the Internet. The web site of *Divorce Magazine* (**www.divorcemag.com**) lists some Canadian planners, and so does the web site of the Academy of Financial Divorce Specialists (**www.afds.ca**).

If you'd rather not spend the money on a financial consultant, there are many organizations with web sites that offer guidance and tools to assist prospective divorcees to take control of their finances. Your local library will also have a number of books on the topic.

Create a Budget

In addition to helping you assess your current financial condition, one of the most important things these sites or a financial planner can do for you is help you create a budget for your new life as a single person.

Whatever else it may be, life after divorce is generally more expensive than life before. Some of the additional expenses are obvious and predictable (like the cost of new furniture and housewares). But a lot aren't. For example, there's the cost of individual insurance for an ex no longer eligible for their partner's company plan. If you have kids and are going to be sharing custody, a second set of toys may have to be purchased. (After all, little Johnny can't be expected to lug his bicycle or PlayStation every time he shuttles back and forth between Mom's house and Dad's.)

It's during this budgeting process that you can come to grips with what kind of lifestyle you are going to be able to afford in your post-divorce life.

They Fought for Their Money!

Janice and Fred are a divorcing couple who started out agreeing that Janice should keep the family's $1 million home in order to lessen the disruption on their 10-year-old son Jake. With the help of a financial planner, they developed a detailed budget—and in the process realized that with all the new expenses that single life would entail for both of them, Janice simply couldn't afford to continue living in such an expensive house. As a result, they decided to sell the house immediately, which provided the cash she needed to support herself while she adjusted to her single life.

Untangle Your Finances

This may seem obvious, but many divorcing couples forget how legally and financially tangled up their lives have become—and as a result, they fail to cut all the ties that bind them together.

One common mistake is neglecting to take your name off the deed to your house if it goes to your ex in the settlement. If your name is still on the deed, you could find yourself on the hook in the event your former spouse fails to keep up the mortgage payments. The same goes for credit card accounts. It may not seem fair, but divorce decrees don't carry much weight with credit card companies and mortgage lenders.

Divorce decrees don't carry much weight with credit card companies and mortgage lenders.

That shouldn't be surprising. A divorce decree is simply an agreement between the divorcing spouses; it does not relieve either of them of any financial obligations they may have to outside parties.

So make sure you close all your joint credit accounts, including overdraft protection on your chequing account. Do it in writing, especially if your spouse's spending is out of control. If you're not yet legally divorced, notify your spouse in writing of your intent to close these accounts at least 10 days before you do so. If your spouse won't cooperate—or if the credit card companies involved won't close the account on your word alone—simply report the card lost or stolen. This will force the companies to close the account.

At the same time, be sure to establish credit in your own name. This is especially important for women who have left the banking and credit arrangements largely to their husbands—with the result that they have no real credit history of their own. If you lack a credit history, for this or any reason, act quickly to establish one: open a chequing account in your own name and apply for a credit card *before* your divorce goes through.

Pay Attention to Retirement Assets

Although most married people plan for their retirement as a couple, the fact is that one of them usually has a better paying job and a more substantial nest egg than the other. This imbalance is generally not an issue—until the couple gets divorced. Then, the spouse whose name is on the RRSP accounts may insist that they belong to him or her alone (usually, it's him). But this is not necessarily the case. Just because one spouse's name happens to be on the retirement accounts that doesn't mean the other spouse isn't entitled to a share of the proceeds. Simple fairness (not to mention community property laws) generally dictate a 50-50 split of at least the retirement assets that were accumulated during the course of the marriage.

All too often, when both sides are working out the settlement, the spouse in the weaker financial position will underestimate the importance of retirement savings, telling the lawyer that he or she would rather get an asset that seems more real (like the house). Don't make this mistake. Real assets like houses or cars cost money to maintain; retirement savings don't. And retirement benefits, on the other hand, grow tax-deferred.

And don't forget that even though you're divorced, you may still be eligible for Canada Pension Plan (CPP) spousal benefits. CPP credits built up by a couple during the time they lived together are considered to be assets. When a relationship ends, the credits can be divided equally in the same way as other assets through a procedure called credit splitting.

As the government's web site says, "If you are the lower wage earner or if you were not employed during the time you lived together, credit splitting could increase the amount of your CPP benefits or make you eligible for CPP benefits for which you might not otherwise qualify. If you are the high wage earner, the amount of your credits will decrease and so will your CPP benefit amount."

For more information about CPP benefits for divorced individuals, check the web site of Service Canada at **www.servicecanada.gc.ca**.

Safeguard Your Cheque

If you are going to depend on child support or alimony to make ends meet, be sure your settlement includes the purchase of a life insurance policy on the breadwinner—in an amount high enough to cover the value of their lifetime contribution. Consider disability insurance as well.

And make sure you are either the owner or the irrevocable beneficiary of the policy. If you're neither, your ex could stop paying premiums without your knowledge. The policy could thus be cancelled without your ever having a clue—until after the breadwinner dies and you file a claim, at which point you are told that the policy lapsed many years earlier. If you are the owner or irrevocable beneficiary, they have to let you know immediately if there are any problems with the policy, such as premiums not being paid.

Don't Stop Before the Work Is Finished

When the divorce is final, your work has really just begun. The divorce process is draining—physically, emotionally, and financially. This causes many people to shut down before they've finished the job. They don't bother to rewrite their will, change names on accounts, revise beneficiaries on life insurance policies and retirement plans, and roll retirement money into an RRSP.

Remember—the secret to surviving a divorce financially is the same as the key to surviving it emotionally. You need to stop dwelling on the past and start focusing on the future.

What to Do if Things Go Wrong

For the most part, there is relatively little you can do if you come to regret having agreed to any (or all) of the terms of your settlement. You can always ask your ex if he or she would consider renegotiating, but if the answer is no, your options are limited.

If your economic circumstances change, you can ask the court to modify child support and other child-related arrangements until your youngest child turns 18 or finishes high school. Spousal maintenance can often be reconsidered as well. However, if you belatedly realize that you should have sold the house or divided the assets differently, you're out of luck. Judges generally won't set aside property settlements unless you can prove that the agreement was fundamentally unfair or that your ex committed fraud (such as hiding assets) during the negotiations. Just changing your mind or deciding it was a bad deal isn't enough.

If your divorce went to trial and you are unhappy with the divorce judgment you received, you generally have 30 days to appeal. After that, the judgment is final. Keep in mind that you can appeal only if the judge made an error of law or abused his or her discretion. Moreover, if an issue wasn't raised in the trial, you generally can't raise it in an appeal. In any case, discuss your specific concerns with a divorce lawyer. And prepare to pay; appeals can be expensive.

Fight for Your Money Action Steps

- ☐ Try to avoid litigation. Explore cooperative alternatives such as mediation.
- ☐ If you must hire a lawyer, get a referral from someone who's been through a divorce and interview several candidates to find one who's right for you.
- ☐ Consult a financial planner to help you sort through your family's finances and to get you on track going forward as a single person.
- ☐ Close all joint accounts in writing—and don't forget to take your name off the deed if your home goes to your ex in the settlement.
- ☐ Establish your own credit.
- ☐ Revise your will and update beneficiaries on insurance policies and retirement plans.

Life Insurance

As a financial advisor, I have reviewed hundreds of my clients' insurance policies and for the most part what I have seen firsthand is that most people and most families are actually underinsured. With a total of $2.9 trillion of life insurance, Canadians tend to be better insured than Americans, although even that enormous sum works out to only $148,000 in coverage per insured individual, which isn't really a lot of money when you consider the repercussions of the death of a family's breadwinner. In most cases your beneficiaries are going to need that money to cover the cost of your funeral, pay off the mortgage and other debts, replace your lost income, and perhaps send the kids to university. In my experience most people have purchased an insurance policy through work and at best it's somewhere between one to three times their annual income—which again for most people is not enough to cover expenses for an extended period if they have dependants. On the other hand, I have also seen that many single people who don't have dependants are over-insured. So the first key to insurance is determining what you really need as far as amount and type of insurance—we'll cover that in a moment—and then what is the smartest way to buy it.

Most people with dependants are underinsured. Most people without dependants are over-insured.

How to Fight for Your Money

When it comes to life insurance, knowing what you don't need is as important as knowing what you do. Here are some basic guidelines.

Term vs. Permanent

There are basically two kinds of life insurance. There's term insurance, where you pay a premium and in return get a set amount of protection for a set period. And there's permanent insurance, where you pay the same premium over the lifetime of the policy even though the risk of death increases with age. Most Canadians choose permanent policies, even though consumer advocates agree that term policies make more sense for most people. Permanent policies generally cost five to ten times more than term policies—meaning insurance agents make a lot more commissions selling them—which is why your friend in the insurance business will gladly come to your home at night to discuss it.

Make Sure You Really Need It

If you are single, buying life insurance makes sense only if you are concerned about paying for your funeral expenses and maybe settling some debts that might otherwise fall on your parents or siblings, for example if you had a joint credit card account or had someone co-sign a loan for you. Life insurance for children may make sense if your child is likely to develop health problems. Purchasing a life insurance policy for him now will protect him against the possibility that he won't be able to qualify for one in the future. But for most people, buying insurance for a child shouldn't be a priority. You can save for a child's education, for example, through a Registered Educational Savings Plan (RESP) rather than a life insurance policy.

Shop Around

There are three main factors to consider when you're deciding which insurer to buy your policy from—how stable the company is, how well it takes care of policyholders, and how cheap its rates are.

To get an idea of how strong a company's finances are and whether you can count on it to be around for the long haul, check with one of the firms that rates life insurers. The best known in Canada is Dominion Bond Rating Service (**www.dbrs.com**). You can also check with U.S. agencies that rate Canadian companies, such as A.M. Best (**www.ambest.com**) and Standard & Poor's (**www.standardandpoors.com**).

As far as customer service goes, it's not as easy in Canada as it is in the U.S. to get information about the way a life insurance company treats its customers. You can find case studies on the website of the General Insurance Ombud-Service (**www.giocanada.org**). And you can find other anecdotal information on the Internet. But word of mouth provides the best source of information. If you know anyone who has dealt with a life-insurance company, ask about the service they received and how the company treated them.

Once you've satisfied yourself on these two counts, you should look for the best price. The most efficient way to do this is through an online broker such as Life Insurance Canada (**www.insurecan.com**), YourInsuranceBrokers.com, and Insurance Direct (**www.lifeinsurancequote.com**). If you prefer to work through an agent, find an independent one who's not tied to just one company.

Buy the Right Amount

Some financial planners will tell you that the size of your life insurance policy should be anywhere from five to 10 times your annual salary. In fact, no simple rule of thumb can possibly take into account all the variables that must be considered when you're trying to decide how big a policy you need. Life insurance is all about protecting your family against financial hardship in the event you die. So you need to base the size of your policy on one of two things: either what your potential earnings would have been if you hadn't died or how much money your family will need in order to stay afloat after you're gone.

To estimate the value of your lost earnings if you were to die, you can use a "Human Life Value" calculator. There are a number of them on the Internet operated by financial publishers like CCH (**www.finance.cch.com**). Others calculate how much your family will likely need. You can find one of these calculators at Insurance Direct (**www.lifeinsurancequote.com**).

Buy the Policy That's Best for You—Not Your Agent

The kind of life insurance that's best for you may not be what's best for your insurance agent—at least not when it comes to his or her commission. So take your agent's advice with a large grain of salt.

The best deal for most people is what's called level term insurance.

In general, the best deal for most people is what's called level term insurance—in which you're guaranteed that your premium will stay the same for a period of time you select when you sign up (usually anywhere from five to 30 years). If you die during that period, your beneficiaries collect the death benefit. If you outlive the policy or cancel it at any point, no one gets anything. The policy has no cash value, but neither is it particularly expensive.

In general, the older you are, the more expensive term insurance is. And the longer the term, the more expensive it is. The idea is that you pick a term that covers a period of your life in which your family will need a replacement for your income if you die—say, until your kids are out of university. When your term insurance expires, you will presumably be very old, with fewer (if any) family obligations and no longer generating income that needs replacing.

Most insurance agents will talk up the benefits of permanent policies, which are expensive but do have a cash value, as a great way to build a nest egg. (Given how expensive these policies are compared to term insurance, they are certainly good for the agent's nest egg.) There are two basic variations: Whole Life and Universal Life. They are called permanent because they stay in effect as long as you keep paying the premiums.

WHOLE LIFE. Imagine paying for term insurance but adding a 50% surcharge to the cost of the annual premium and having some of that extra money invested where it can grow tax-deferred into a little nest egg for your old age. That's what whole life is. It's a term policy with a little cash-value basket added onto it. The problem is that you don't have much or any control over where the money is invested. Also, the money is invested so conservatively that the policy's cash value grows too slowly to really amount to anything. Whole life is no longer as common as it used to be in Canada, for good reason.

UNIVERSAL LIFE. After decades of being sold on whole life insurance, people began to wake up and realize that it was not the great retirement vehicle they had been told it was. So the insurance industry came up with a new angle. "Instead of just investing your extra premium money conservatively," the industry told potential customers, "we will invest it more aggressively and pay you a great rate." Insurance agents sold these policies on the promise that policyholders could earn as much as 11% a year. They would flash fancy illustrations showing that if you earned 11% percent a year, your cash value would be just enormous in 20 years. These illustrations always looked really impressive. The problem was they were just illustrations, not guarantees.

If it's structured properly, a Universal Life Policy can provide tax-free retirement income. That's because the policy includes a tax-sheltered cash value fund. This fund can't exceed the policy's face value, so people tend to buy large policies. The deposits you make into the policy go partly to fund the life insurance and partly to investments—usually mutual funds—that grow tax-sheltered inside the policy. To accumulate enough money for retirement, your deposits must be far more than the cost of the underlying insurance. When you retire, you can draw on the accumulated capital in your policy by using it as collateral for bank loans. Your estate repays the loans after you die, with the tax-free death benefit, and any remaining funds are paid out tax-free to named beneficiaries.

Universal life works great when the insurance company invests well and when you can afford to pay the premiums, which tend to be quite high. But it can be a disaster when the company doesn't invest well or when you have difficulty meeting the premium payments.

Advocates of permanent life insurance tout its tax advantages and the fact that you can borrow against it. But the fact is that permanent policies cost a lot and contain many hidden fees, including management fees of mutual funds that are sometimes higher than the norm.

If you buy a permanent policy, you have a legal right to understand the detailed costs and commission. Ask your insurance agent to provide you, in writing, what the commission on the policy is, even if you are not paying it upfront and the insurance company is paying it. The truth is you are always paying the commission in costs that are added to the policy or penalties if you terminate the policy or stop funding it early. In most cases you will find that the entire first-year premiums are a commission to the insurance agent selling it to you. There is nothing wrong with an insurance agent earning a living, but you DESERVE to know the truth of the costs you are paying. This cost may impact you financially later on and it may also help you determine if the advice you are being given feels unbiased or self-serving.

You should use permanent insurance as an investment only after you have maxed out your RRSP contributions.

Bottom line—if you're looking for an investment vehicle, you'd probably do better to buy a term policy and invest the money you save in a no-load mutual fund. At the very least, you should use permanent insurance as an investment only after you have maxed out your RRSP contributions.

Don't Forget Your Company Benefits

Many employers offer *free* life insurance coverage that can be worth as much as, if not more than, your annual salary. So when you're figuring how much insurance you need, don't forget to factor in your workplace benefits.

Keep in mind, too, that some companies also allow employees to purchase additional life insurance through the company's group plan. There are tremendous advantages to this—not least that a doctor's exam is usually NOT required, a huge benefit for workers with medical conditions that could make acquiring insurance on their own difficult or expensive. Additionally, group insurance policies offered through your employer can be significantly cheaper than if you bought one directly and can usually be paid on a pre-tax basis. If you are young and healthy, however, do a comparison between your employer's group rate and what it would cost you for an individual policy. Because a group policy covers both healthy and unhealthy workers alike, your company's policy could end up being more expensive than an individual policy for a healthy person in the open market.

Make Sure Your Employer Plan Is "Portable"

The most important advice I can give you regarding a group employer policy is to make sure the plan is portable. This means, should you leave your employer, you can take the insurance policy with you (and fund it yourself). The advantage is that you won't have to requalify for the policy and you should be able to keep the group rate that you were paying—which can save you a lot of money.

Look for Premium Discounts

Sometimes buying more insurance can actually cost you less. Most companies offer rate discounts when you surpass certain benchmark amounts. For example, you might actually pay a smaller premium for $500,000 of life insurance than you would for $450,000, because a discount kicks in at the higher insurance amount.

Don't Overlook Your "Free Look" Period

When you're buying life insurance, keep in mind that most companies allow you to cancel within 30 days if you evaluate a newly issued insurance policy and then decide it's not the right product for you. The company will then give you a full refund. Check with your insurance company to see how long it allows for cancellation.

Don't Forget to Update Your Beneficiaries—or to Name One in the First Place

When your life changes, your life insurance should change with it. If you have a new child—or get a new spouse—don't forget to update the beneficiary designations on your life insurance policies. There's nothing wrong with leaving an ex-spouse as a beneficiary, if that's what you want to do (or because a judge ordered you to as part of a divorce settlement). But don't do it by accident.

And don't just name a primary beneficiary. You should also list a contingent or secondary beneficiary in the event you outlive your primary beneficiary. Also, don't name your estate as a beneficiary because if you do, the death benefit will have to go through probate, meaning your heirs won't be able to access the money quickly and probate fees will apply.

See if Your Old Policy Can Be Improved

If you already have life insurance, now is as good a time as any to see if you can increase the death benefit at no additional cost. This is probably the MOST important advice I can give you today. As I write this in 2008, the cost of life insurance has dropped significantly. Why? Because we're living longer. Since 2000, term life insurance premiums have dropped and are as much as 50 percent lower than they were a decade ago. In many cases today you can double your death benefit with a new policy at the exact same price you are currently paying provided you are still healthy. Or you can cut your annual premiums in half!

Since 2000, term life insurance premiums have dropped. You can cut your annual premiums in half!

Stop Smoking—Live Longer and Save a Fortune!

I pulled some online quotes through **www.accuquote.com** for a 20-year term life insurance policy with a face amount of $500,000. For a healthy 43-year-old male, the lowest quote for a nonsmoker was $495 per year. For someone smoking more than a pack a day, the lowest price more than quadrupled to $2,065 per year. That is simply amazing. So quit now—and you'll already be on your way to saving money on life insurance.

You save $1,570!

What to Do if Things Go Wrong

If you have any kind of a problem with a life insurance company, you should file a complaint with your province's insurance regulator. You can find a list of these provincial organizations and a contact at each one on the web site of the Canadian Council of Insurance Regulators (**www.ccir-ccrra.org**).

Fight for Your Money Action Steps

- ☐ Check with your human resources department at work to see how much life insurance you currently have and what the premium is costing you, if anything.
- ☐ Calculate how much money your dependants will need to pay your debts and replace your income after you die.
- ☐ Decide whether to go with a term or permanent policy.
- ☐ Request quotes online or work through a recommended agent.
- ☐ Name your beneficiaries, and keep your insurance records up to date.
- ☐ If you have a term policy, call your provider to request a lower premium that reflects today's lower rates.

Estate Planning

Thousands of Canadians pass away each year without a will, leaving behind no legally binding instructions about what should be done with their property, not to mention their remains. What they do leave behind instead is a legacy of problems and heartache for their loved ones, along with a big stack of legal and tax bills.

No one likes to think about this stuff. I know I don't. But if you have people and things in your life that you care about, you need to do some estate planning.

And don't assume your estate won't be worth bothering about. Most people have more assets than they realize—what with even modest homes in some places still going for upward of half a million dollars and lots of companies offering both free life insurance and RRSP contributions to their employees. More assets generally mean more hassle and, in some cases, higher costs of probate, capital gains taxes, and administering the estate, which could easily have been avoided.

Anyway, even if your estate isn't worth all that much, do you really want to leave it to the government to divide up your things and decide who gets what? That's what happens when you die intestate, which is the legal term for not having a will.

What's more, smart estate planning can protect your family from the risk and expense of probate. Generally speaking, when someone dies, you're not allowed to distribute their property until the validity of their will has been confirmed and any claims against their estate have been resolved. The process of doing this is known as probate. In essence, it involves an appointed person notifying your heirs and creditors that you're dead, taking an inventory of your estate, paying any outstanding debts and taxes, and then distributing what's left to your heirs.

Probate is something to avoid if you can. For one thing, it opens all your private affairs to public disclosure. For another, even if things go smoothly, probate is likely to cost your heirs tens of thousands of dollars in legal fees—on average, between 4% and 7% of your estate's total value. Just hope no one contests the will, because if they do, the sky is the limit.

The good news is that it's not hard to avoid this kind of misery. All it takes is a little planning.

How to Fight for Your Money

No matter how much or how little money you think you have, most people need a will. That's because, from a practical point of view, a will enables the division of your assets in a reasonable way, according to your wishes.

You probably have more than you think. When you add in the value of a house, the death benefit from a decent-sized life insurance policy, and the proceeds from brokerage and retirement accounts—all of which count when you're calculating the value of an estate—there are a surprising number of middle-class people whose estates could easily be worth more than $3.5 million.

Anyway, estate planning isn't just about money. It's also about specifying the kind of medical treatment you'll get at the end of your life, picking someone to make decisions about you and your affairs in the event you're incapacitated, and figuring out what's going to happen to your kids.

There are a surprising number of middle-class people whose estates could easily be worth more than $3.5 million.

This is particularly crucial for unmarried couples, whether gay or straight. Without the right documents, your unmarried partner has zero rights in the event of your incapacity or death. The good news is that unmarried partners can enjoy virtually all the protections available to married couples—*if* they plan properly.

So here is what you need to keep in mind.

Think Hard About Setting Up a Living Trust

A living trust is basically a legal document that does two things. First, it allows you to transfer the ownership of any of your assets (your house, your car, your retirement accounts, whatever you like) to a trust while you are still alive. Second, it designates who should be given those assets after you die. By naming yourself the trustee of your trust, and naming someone else as the beneficiary, you can continue to control your assets—which means that as long as you live, the transfer of ownership will have no practical impact on your ability to enjoy and manage your property.

The main advantage a living trust has over a simple will is that if you create a living trust properly and fund it correctly, the assets in it won't have to go through probate when you die.

There are different kinds of trusts, although people in the United States use them in their estate planning most commonly to avoid estate taxes. Since Canada doesn't tax people's estates when they die, Canadians don't use trusts as often as Americans, although they may be useful for minimizing capital gains taxes payable when the estate cashes investments that have gained value.

If you create a living trust properly and fund it correctly, the assets in it won't have to go through probate when you die.

Canadians who set up a trust in their will use a testamentary trust. Testamentary trusts are used for many purposes: to hold property for the benefit of minor children or children with special needs, for example, or to postpone the transfer of property from an estate until children or other beneficiaries have reached a specified age.

Whatever Else You Do, You Always Need a Will

Even if you've got a fancy trust, you still need a will. That's because you probably have some assets (such as art or antiques) that you couldn't put in the trust or that you forgot to retitle. Even more importantly, if you have minor children, you also need to name a guardian who will take care of them in case your death leaves them orphaned.

You Also Need a Durable Power of Attorney

With a document called a power of attorney, you can appoint someone you trust to handle your finances in the event you become incapacitated. A lawyer will generally prepare one when he or she drafts your will, but there are also standard forms that enable you to do it yourself. Giving someone this sort of power over you may be a little scary, but the alternative to a power of attorney is not pretty. If you're incapable of carrying out some essential transaction, your family might have to ask a judge to declare you incompetent and appoint a guardian to take over your affairs.

And You Need a Health Care Directive

In addition to specifying how you want your assets to be treated, you need to specify how you want yourself to be treated. You can do this with two documents that every adult should have: a *health care directive* (also known as a living will) and a *health care power of attorney*. The directive sets out what kind of medical treatment you're going to want at the end of your life (e.g., whether you want to be hooked up to machines if that's what it takes to keep you breathing). The power of attorney appoints someone to make health care decisions for you if you are incapacitated (e.g., when, if ever, they should pull the plug).

These documents come in many varieties, but it's best to use standard forms that were specifically developed to match the laws of your province. You can usually get them free of charge from provincial government offices, health care providers, and agencies that serve the elderly. If what you want to specify is more complicated than the standard form can accommodate, you can have a lawyer draw up a directive that explains your precise wishes in as much detail as you need.

If you're wondering how necessary these documents really are, think back to the heart-rending (and well-publicized) case of Terri Schiavo. Schiavo was only 26 when she suffered irreversible brain damage and lapsed into a coma in 1990. She spent the next 15 years in what doctors called a persistent vegetative state. Unfortunately, because she never signed a health care directive or power of attorney, her husband and her parents spent the last seven of those years fighting bitterly over her care, what her wishes would have been had she written them down, and who should have the right to make decisions for her. Ultimately, the courts granted her husband's request to have her feeding tube removed, but in the process her family was torn apart.

The Canadian Bar Association discusses living wills and health care powers of attorney on its web site (**www.cba.org/cba**). In addition, you should always consult a lawyer about a living will and a health care power of attorney to make sure the documents achieve what you want them to. In many cases, they don't.

As the CBA warns, "Living wills have very limited legal effect in Canada. There are two main problems: First, the living will may have been made many years before the time comes to use it, so it may not reflect the adult's current wishes. Second, if the living will sets out specific treatments or conditions for which the adult does or does not wish to be treated, changing medical technology may radically alter the effectiveness of the living will."

Doing It Yourself Is Better Than Not Doing It at All

As a rule, you want your estate documents drawn up by a lawyer who specializes in wills and trusts. That said, the fact is that many people may feel they can't afford the $500 or so a lawyer may charge to draft a basic will or the $2,500 or more it can cost to set up a trust. I would argue that it's a matter of priorities. Maybe before you buy a new flat-screen television, you should consider getting your estate in order. It's certainly not cheap—but believe me, it's worth it.

In the meantime, if you can't afford to get it done professionally, then do some estate planning yourself as soon as possible. There are plenty of online resources that can explain the fundamentals. You can find them by typing "wills" and the name of your province into a search engine like Google. For about $10, you can also buy a kit like the Wills Guide for Ontario, written by a lawyer, that shows you how to prepare your own will. You can download a Power of Attorney kit from the Office of the Public Guardian and Trustee in Ontario (**www.attorneygeneral.jus.gov.on.ca**). Although it's an Ontario document, it will generally be applicable in other jurisdictions in Canada, although you should check with the appropriate ministry in your province. The British Columbia branch of the Canadian Bar Association (**www.cba.org**) administers a useful web site, as well, where you'll find information on estate planning, wills, trusts, and powers of attorney.

Help Yourself by Giving Some Assets Away

If you are lucky enough to have more than you need, consider reducing the size of your estate by giving part of it away while you are still alive. You can receive a credit for as much as 75% of net income if you structure your charitable donations properly. Planned giving of this type has become increasingly popular in recent years, and there are a number of organizations that can help you do it properly. In addition, beneficiaries of planned giving will help you to set up your estate so that some of your assets are directed toward them. The Canadian Cancer Society, the Heart and Stroke Foundation, and many universities in Canada all have planned-giving specialists on staff.

Giving while you are still alive offers more than just financial benefits. You get the satisfaction of seeing your bequests put to use and receiving the thanks of those who benefit from your gifts. You also get an income tax deduction for charitable gifts, although deductions for very large gifts may have to be spread over several years.

What to Watch Out For

Obsolete Beneficiaries

If you get married, get divorced, or your spouse dies, don't forget to update the beneficiary designations on your life insurance policies as well as on all your retirement, brokerage, and bank accounts, not to mention your will and trusts. There's nothing wrong with leaving an ex-spouse as a beneficiary, if that's what you want to do (or because a judge ordered you to as part of a divorce settlement). But don't do it by accident.

Don't Forget to Fund Your Trust

Trusts can't protect your assets if you don't put any assets in them. So if you have a living trust, don't forget to "retitle" your assets. This means that if you buy a house you should make sure it's deeded not to you as an individual but to your trust. The same thing goes for your car, your bank and brokerage accounts, and any other assets you may own—*except* qualified retirement accounts like life insurance policies or RRSPs (because with these you designate a beneficiary, so they don't go through probate hence there's no need to put them in a trust).

Pay Attention to the Tax Consequences

Say you have an investment account and an RRSP, both of which are worth about $400,000. If you leave the investment account to your son and the RRSP to your daughter, have you treated them the same? Not by a long shot.

This is because when you leave someone an investment account, your beneficiary pays tax on the capital gain. The recipient of the RRSP, on the other hand, will have to pay income tax on the contents of the plan, and the tax rate is different than the rate applied to capital gains. The unintended inequality can lead to hurt feelings.

From a beneficiary's point of view, the best items to inherit are ones with no built-in tax liability, such as a house.

The point is that you have to be careful about the tax consequences of what you're leaving to your heirs. From a beneficiary's point of view, the best items to inherit are ones with no built-in tax liability, such as a house. Assets like traditional stocks, annuities, and savings bonds all carry tax liabilities and are thus less desirable.

With this in mind, if you want to leave something to a CRA-recognized charity, try to leave them one of these tax-burdened assets. Since charities aren't taxed, they'll get to enjoy the asset's full value. Save your assets that don't carry any tax liabilities for your family or friends, who do have to pay taxes. But consult a lawyer who specializes in wills and estates to make sure you do this properly.

What to Do if Things Go Wrong

If you have problems with a trust lawyer, you should first try to reach a satisfactory arrangement with the lawyer directly. If that doesn't work, you can file a complaint with your province's law society. You'll find a list of provincial law societies on the web site of the Canadian Bar Association (www.cba.org).

You should also visit the Canadian Bar Association's web site to find information on living wills, medical powers of attorney, and the legal implications of these documents.

Fight for Your Money Action Steps

- ☐ Set up a trust to avoid having your assets go through probate when you die as well as to save your heirs a lot of money.
- ☐ Once it's set up, retitle your assets to put them in the trust.
- ☐ Hire a lawyer to draw up a will, a power of lawyer, and a health care directive.
- ☐ If you can't afford a lawyer, download the proper forms or obtain one of the books available to assist you in preparing your own will.

Saving for Post-Secondary Education

Think getting into university is tough? Try scraping up the money to pay for it. The cost of a post-secondary education has never been higher—and it's growing more expensive with every passing year. According to government figures, full-time students in Canada pay more than $14,500 on average to cover a year of post-secondary expenses. That's almost $60,000 for a four-year program. Tuition alone has risen to as much as $8,000 a year from about $1,200 in 1988. Add on books, room and board, Internet access, and a couple of pairs of jeans, and the cost keeps rising.

For most of us, the only way to make sure there will be enough money to send our kids to university is to start saving for it as early as possible. The good news is that there are programs designed to make this easier. The best known is the Registered Education Savings Plan (RESP) program, which allows you to put away as much as $50,000 on a tax-deferred basis. These plans have become very popular among Canadian parents. On average, Canadian families have saved more than $10,000 in an RESP for their child's education, with some families aiming to save the maximum $50,000. At the beginning of 2008, parents of univeristy-bound kids had invested nearly $109 billion in them—and the numbers are expected to keep rising.

Depending on your income, you can also get a federal grant of $100 to $200 a year, to a maximum of $7,200, to put toward your child's post-secondary education. Lower-income families can get Canada Learning Bonds worth as much as $2,000 plus interest for their children's education after high school.

There are also loan, grant, and scholarship programs available for students attending Canadian post-secondary institutions, including universities, community colleges, and trade schools. And in some cases, your employer might operate a program that covers a portion of the costs of sending employee's children to university. But you have to know where to find all these programs, and in the meantime you should start saving as soon as you can.

Your children's education is a good investment. Studies have shown that the annual return on an investment in post-secondary education in Canada can amount to 10% or more. That's $100 for every $1,000 spent on tuition, room and board, books, and other expenses, every year after the child graduates from university or a post-secondary institution. You'd have a hard time achieving that rate of return on most other investments, and it's far more than you'd get if you just spent the money.

How to Fight for Your Money

If you're going to be able to afford to send your kids to school after they leave high school, you're going to need a plan. Exactly what kind of plan is right for you depends on a lot of variables—like how old your kids are, what kind of post-secondary institution they have in mind, where tuition levels are likely to be by the time they are ready to go, and what kind of return you can reasonably expect to earn on your savings.

Fortunately, there are lots of great tools for figuring all this out. One of the best ones is the Government of Canada's website called CanLearn (**www.canlearn.ca**). You can find all sorts of information on this site, including online tools and calculators that cover everything from budgeting to borrowing to the contributions that parents and their children can expect to make to the children's post-secondary education.

What you will learn from these various resources is that there are different ways you can prepare for your children's education after high school. But there is one basic approach that everyone should consider: the RESP.

The Biggest and Best Savings Program—Registered Education Savings Plans

The best way to save for a child's post-secondary education is to start investing as early as possible in a Registered Education Savings Plan (RESP).

You can invest as much as you want in an RESP, to a maximum of $50,000. For example, if you inherit $10,000 this year, you can put it all into an RESP. If you have only $1,000 to spare next year, you can invest that amount.

Money invested in an RESP grows tax-free until the child starts to withdraw it to pay for tuition and other education-related expenses after high school. You can't deduct your contributions from your annual income, but you can contribute as much or as little as you want to an RESP over the course of a year.

Once you open an RESP, you can receive additional money from the federal government in the form of a Canada Education Savings Grant and, for qualified low-income earners, a Canada Learning Bond. In addition, if you live in Alberta, you may qualify for a grant from the Alberta Centennial Education Savings Plan. (You'll find more information about that program at **www.advanceducation.gov.ab.ca**.)

The details of an RESP such as the minimum deposit, the frequency of deposits, and the types of investments that you can make within an RESP usually depend on the service provider. In most cases, you can invest in stocks, bonds, and GICs, or keep the money in a savings account. Since you're planning for the future and you've already invested in your retirement plan (as we'll discuss in a moment) you can probably afford to take a little more risk with your RESP investments. Your financial institution or RESP provider can give you more advice about your investment options.

You can't deduct the money that you contribute to an RESP from your taxable income, but it grows within the RESP tax-free. When your children need the money, they withdraw it from the RESP in their name and pay the deferred taxes. But since children don't earn much income at this stage in their lives, they're in a very low tax bracket, so they end up paying little or no tax.

You can open an RESP, usually for a small administration fee, at any financial institution in Canada, including a bank, credit union, or caisse populaire.

There are three types of RESP: family, individual, and group. With a family plan, you have to be related to the child or children who will be the plan's beneficiaries. With an individual plan, you can save money for any individual, whether or not the person is related to you. Group plans are administered by group plan dealers, usually for a number of parents with school-age children. These plans come in different shapes and sizes, so you should get specific details from the dealer.

Anyone can open an individual RESP for a child's future education. And anyone can make a contribution to an RESP, including grandparents, relatives, friends, and neighbours. In fact, an RESP is a great way to solve the problem of what to give your future Rhodes Scholar for her birthday or Junior for his public-school graduation.

There's More! Canada Education Savings Grants

Once you open an RESP and invest $500, the federal government will kick in as much as $200 in the form of a grant.

Every child in Canada is eligible to receive the grant up to the age of 17 as long as they're a Canadian resident and an RESP has been opened in their name. The government makes additional grants that vary with your family income, to a maximum of $7,200.

You can get more details about the Canada Education Savings Grant at the Can Learn web site (**www.canlearn.ca**).

What to Watch Out For

Putting Your Kids First

The single biggest mistake most parents make when it comes to post-secondary savings is making Junior's university funding too much of a priority. Saving for your kids' education is important, but you should *not* put it ahead of your own retirement needs. Your security comes first. You shouldn't even consider putting aside money for your kids' education costs unless you are already putting at least 10% of your income into a pretax retirement account.

The right order of savings is to fund retirement first, then post-secondary education. Even paying off high-interest debt should get priority over post-secondary education savings.

Why? Because you can borrow for university but you can't borrow for retirement.

The greatest gift you can give your children is to ensure that you won't be a financial burden to them. If money is tight, your kids can always get part-time jobs when they're in high school and start putting aside their own money for education after that. There are also countless scholarship and loan programs for deserving students. (And there's absolutely nothing wrong with asking for help: a majority of all full-time undergraduates get some sort of financial aid.)

It can be tough for good parents to put their own needs ahead of the kids'—especially when tuition bills are looming and your retirement is still a long way off. But the right order of savings is to fund retirement first, then university. Even paying off high-interest debt should get priority over post-secondary savings.

Not Starting Early Enough

Obviously, the longer you wait to start building your education fund, the more you will have to save each month to reach your goal. What you may not realize is that waiting just a little can cost you a lot. If you don't start saving until your child is 12, you'll have to put aside twice as much each month as you would if you'd started when your child was eight. Time really *is* money.

Investing Your RESP Too Conservatively

Surveys show that nearly a third of all parents would prefer not to take any risk at all with their kids' post-secondary education money. That's understandable, but being overly cautious is not necessarily the best plan—especially if your kids aren't yet in their teens. To reach the same financial goal, a family that puts its RESP investments in a super-safe savings account that pays annual interest of around 2% has to put roughly twice as many dollars aside for post-secondary education as one that invests in a mix of stocks and bonds that earns about 8% a year.

If your kids are at least five years away from leaving high school, you should be willing to tolerate a little risk for the sake of a better return—for example, investing your RESP savings in a good mutual fund and then gradually shifting into safer fixed-income investments as Junior's freshman year approaches. Playing it too safe can actually wind up hurting you.

What to Do if Things Go Wrong

If you've spent years saving for your kids' post-secondary education only to discover that they don't plan to go any further after high school, don't despair. You can keep money in an RESP for as long as 36 years. Even the most stubborn children sometimes change their minds before that. You can also transfer the money to another child's RESP, as long as there's still room left to contribute.

Since you haven't taken a tax deduction for your contributions to the RESP, you may also transfer the money into a Registered Retirement Savings

Plan. Or you can simply withdraw your contributions. In any case, you should talk to your advisor or RESP specialist at the bank where you opened the plan to determine the best way to proceed.

If things go really wrong or if you have any complaints about the way your RESP is being handled, the Financial Consumer Agency of Canada (**www.fcac.gc.ca**) oversees the proper administration of RESPs by banks and other financial institutions to make sure you get what you expect from the program.

You can get more information about RESPs and banking by phone at: 1-866-461-3222 or by email at: info@fcac.gc.ca.

Fight for Your Money Action Steps

- ☐ Start saving for college early. Get online and start your "homework" at **www.canlearn.ca**.
- ☐ Find an RESP that's right for you. Talk to your bank, credit union, or financial advisor.
- ☐ Remember the best order for savings: Fund retirement first, pay off high-interest debt, *then* save for post-secondary education.

Health Insurance

Unlike the United States, where millions of people live without health insurance of any kind, Canadians don't face the harsh realities of paying for their own health care. With Canada's universal coverage, everyone's covered, although, at a cost of more than $170 billion in 2008, some Canadians might wish the coverage were a bit more extensive and a lot more convenient. In both countries, it sometimes seems as if the health care industry, whether private or public, has found it more profitable to work against their customers than with them.

While all Canadians have access to medical services in any part of the country, universal health insurance doesn't cover everything. That's why some Canadians pay an additional amount for extended health insurance coverage, which pays for treatments and services that the government plan doesn't cover.

Coverage for long-term care, for example, is becoming more popular as Canada's population grows older. By 2021, Statistics Canada says 7 million seniors in the country—19% of Canada's total population—will place increasing demands on our health care system. If they require long-term care, many people say they would use their retirement savings or rely on government programs to pay for it. But as one long-term-care insurer, Manulife Financial, points out, "A long term care facility costing $4,000 per month over 10 years adds up to nearly $500,000. When care needs for an elderly couple are considered, asset depletion can become even more rapid."

Most Canadians who have extended insurance coverage obtain it through group policies provided by their employer. The problem is that with private insurance costs skyrocketing, a growing number of employers can no longer afford to offer such extensive health benefits as they once did. As a result, many are forcing employees to pay more of the costs themselves—if they're not eliminating the benefit entirely.

The bottom line is that you need to be prepared to fight for what you're entitled to. That's because the insurance companies make money by saying no, even when the answer should be yes.

How Extensive is Extended Coverage?

In Canada, private health insurance usually covers things that the government-run health plans don't include, such as prescription drugs and semi-private hospital rooms. Some plans cover dental care and eye examinations and glasses. (Government health care plans in some provinces cover dental care for children up to 14).

Certain plans also cover the cost of full-time care in a nursing home, medical aids such as artificial limbs, wheelchairs, and crutches, and even the cost of travelling to and from a medical facility for treatment.

If You're On Your Own, Do Your Homework

About 65% of Canadians have supplementary private health coverage, and most of them receive it through their employers. Individuals can obtain extended coverage, as well, if they're willing to pay for it. Companies like Blue Cross, Sun Life and Manulife sell extended health coverage for a premium that ranges from about $300 a year and up.

These plans cover such things as hearing aids, nursing specialists, semi-private hospital accommodation, drugs up to $10,000 a year, and dental services such as cleaning, fillings, and root canals.

If you're not a group member, you should decide if you really need individual extended health coverage or whether you can afford the additional health care costs that aren't covered by Canada's government-funded health program. After all, Canadians spend an average of only $900 a year on extended health care services, dental and eye care, and drugs. Some insurance companies charge this much for extended coverage.

How to Fight for Your Money

As more and more of us become self-employed or work on contract, we have to arrange our own extended health coverage if we want it. Before you surrender to the Wild West of the independent insurance market, see if there is any professional or social organization you belong to—or could join—that offers members a group health plan. If not, it's time to do some homework.

Your university alumni association, for example, may offer an extended health care and dental plan. Professional organizations and trade associations sometimes offer similar programs. If you don't belong to one of these groups, you might consider joining just for the insurance coverage.

If you are struggling to make ends meet, are over the age of 65, or have small children, visit the Public Health Agency of Canada web site at **www.phac-aspc.gc.ca** and check the list of provincial health care ministries to see what government programs you may be eligible for and what options you may have in your province. Seniors should check their provincial health ministry web site and the federal government's Seniors Canada web site at **www.seniors.gc.ca**.

Hospital Bills

The biggest complaint that Canadians make about health care is the amount of time they have to wait to see a doctor or to receive treatment if they go to a hospital's emergency ward.

Studies have shown that one-quarter of all Canadians who visit an emergency room wait for four hours or more compared to 12% in the United States Half of us wait four weeks or more to see a specialist compared to 23% of Americans.

And yet, once Canadians receive treatment at a hospital, they don't have to go bankrupt when they pay for it. In the United States, some 700,000 families are forced into bankruptcy because of health-care costs, while another 80 million or so Americans struggle with medical bills they can't afford to pay. So perhaps the waiting is worth it.

Know What's in Your Contract—and What Isn't

Not every health insurance plan covers every ailment or therapy. Obesity treatments, acupuncture, cosmetic surgery, and mental health care are often excluded from many plans. So read your health plan contract carefully—particularly the sections that explain exactly what's covered and what's not, as well as how much you will have to pay when you need health care.

Many insurance companies and almost all employer-sponsored health plans provide policyholders with a Summary Plan Description that lays all this out in plain English. The problem is that this summary is not legally binding. The document you want to read is called the "Evidence of Coverage" or "Certificate of Insurance." If you have your own independent health coverage, you should have gotten it when you bought the policy. If you have company coverage, ask your HR department for a copy.

Use Your Plan to Its Fullest

The great truth about health insurance is that many of us don't actually use all the health insurance we have, whether it's publicly or privately funded. In health care, as in many other aspects of our lives, the 80-20 rule applies: 20% of the population uses 80% of the resources. That may sound unfair, unless you're one of the 20%, and sooner or later, we all will be.

In any case, to get the most out of your extended health insurance, you need to take the time to read the plan documents—and ask questions if you don't understand what it says (which is more than likely, because it's so complicated).

Virtually every plan has complicated rules about what's covered and what's not covered. A lot of these rules may strike you as bureaucratic nonsense. And a lot of them are. But you need to know them and play by them if you want to get the best medical coverage possible and have your claims paid.

Should You Consider a Health Savings Account?

Unlike the United States, Canada doesn't encourage people to pay for health care by giving them tax breaks on health care accounts. Some banks like HSBC advertise health savings accounts, but they're really no different than other savings accounts where you save money for a rainy day.

That's not to say you shouldn't put some money aside for medical expenses. It just means that you won't get any tax breaks if you do.

What to Watch Out For

How to Locate the Plan For You

If you decide to get extended health coverage and you need help in finding an insurance company that will give you reasonable coverage at a reasonable cost, you may try to narrow your search with the help of an online service. These services sounds like independent agencies that will help you find the best deal on health coverage to suit your needs. But they're usually run by insurance agents, who operate in the same way as the agent in the office down the street or on the next block. So don't be fooled.

What to Do if Things Go Wrong

If you have a complaint about your life or health insurance, contact the Canadian Life and Health Insurance OmbudService (CLHIO). CLHIO is an independent service to help consumers with complaints that they are not able to resolve by dealing directly with their insurance company. For more information, visit www.clhio.ca.

Fight for Your Money Action Steps

- ☐ If your employer offers group health coverage, make sure you use it if you need medical and health care services.
- ☐ If your employer doesn't offer health insurance or you are self-employed, check with organizations like your university alumni association to see if they provide extended health care coverage.
- ☐ Read your policy carefully and understand the rules that govern it, so you can get maximum value out of your coverage.

Health-Club Memberships

When it comes to high-pressure sales, health clubs, particularly the big national chains, can be surprisingly adept at separating you from your money. The come-ons are always so attractive—huge discounts off the normal enrollment fee, personalized evaluations, free guest passes. It sounds like such a good deal. And when you walk into the place, there's always some incredibly buff guy or really cute girl who seems happy to show you around, tells you how there's never a wait for any of the machines, and reassures you that it's no hassle to quit if you ever change your mind. Before you know it, they've persuaded you to sign a contract that commits you for at least a year to two years and allows them to take their monthly dues directly from your chequing account. Worse, many of these contracts have penalty fees should you terminate early or require a few months notice before termination (otherwise the membership is automatically renewed).

With tactics like these, it's no wonder the health club industry in Canada rakes in revenues of close to $2 billion a year. Nor is it surprising that the Better Business Bureau reports that complaints about health clubs have nearly doubled in recent years.

How to Fight for Your Money

There's no question that among the roughly 5,000 health clubs in Canada today, there are many terrific gyms offering really good deals on really good services. But there are also plenty of rip-offs. The good news is that if you know what to look for, it's not too difficult to separate the good from the bad. Here's how.

Shop Around—and Don't Be Rushed

Start your search by checking with your employer—and your insurance company, too. Many employers now offer group discounts at certain health clubs. Be aware of what benefits you're entitled to. Additionally check with your credit card company, which may have special offers for its members, and with membership retailers like Costco.

The fitness business is an incredibly competitive one. Most areas are home to a wide range of workout places—from big chains like GoodLife and Premier, which offer lots of amenities, to community centres like the YMCA and JCC that have fewer bells and whistles but generally lower costs. There are also small, independent clubs and if you live near a university campus, you may have access to school facilities (possibly even for free, if you're an alumnus).

Having all these choices gives consumers more control. So don't be afraid to push for a good deal. Don't feel you have to sign up for a long-term commitment or pay an initiation fee. If one gym in town is offering a really attractive promotional offer, bring their flyer to another gym you like (or already belong to) and ask them to match it. Check for new membership specials, or refer-a-friend specials—or anything coming up. Most clubs offer a new promotion each month.

Above all, don't let anyone (no matter how cute they may be) twist your arm to join. Never sign a contract on your first visit to a gym. Instead, take it home, where you can read the fine print without anyone rushing you. And check with your local Better Business Bureau (**www.ccbbb.ca**) to see whether a gym you're considering joining has been the subject of many complaints.

If a sales rep gives you a hard time about doing any of this, it's a sure sign you should find another gym.

Be Wary of Automatic Billing

As anyone who's read my bestseller *The Automatic Millionaire* will know, I am a great believer in automating your finances. But I don't recommend the kind of automatic bill paying most health clubs try to impose on customers.

A lot of gyms include in their contracts a provision that allows them to arrange a credit card charge or an electronic funds transfer that takes your monthly payment out of your chequing account and automatically sends it to them.

The idea that anybody besides you should have the right to take money out of your account is bad enough. But to give that power to an outfit as untrustworthy as a health club is downright outrageous. Consider this story, which I was told by a young woman named Donna.

About two years ago, Donna signed up at a local health club for a tanning package that she thought was for one month only. What she didn't realize was that it was an ongoing package that automatically renewed each month—and that the club had the right to take each month's payment directly out of her chequing account.

Now, at the time, Donna was living paycheque to paycheque, and before she realized what was happening, the health club's automatic withdrawals had drained her account. As a result, in addition to the unexpected tanning charges, she also got hit with bank overdraft penalties.

When she explained the problem to her bank, they agreed to cancel the overdraft fees. But the gym was not nearly so nice. It refused to release her from her contract unless she agreed to pay it off in full. Feeling she had no choice, she did.

Nonetheless, the health club continued to take money out of Donna's chequing account. Finally, she got her bank to place a "stop payment" on her account so that the gym could no longer withdraw money from it. But they keep trying to this day.

For all her trouble, Donna learned two valuable lessons: from now on, any time she's in a dispute with a company, she'll keep a written record of everyone she speaks to and what they promised. And most important, she will never again sign a contract that gives any business the right to pull money directly from her account.

Sadly, Donna's situation is not unusual, and her advice is worth following. If a gym is not willing to trust you to pay your monthly dues on your own, why should you trust them with the keys to your bank account? Given how competitive the fitness industry is, a reputable gym should be willing to waive the electronic funds transfer requirement and invoice you like any other business. If they're not, find another place to work out. And if you feel you MUST join this gym and they require automatic withdrawal then do it with your credit card, not your bank account which can be harder to stop and/or recover if you are debited twice by accident (which happens all the time).

Make Sure It's All in Writing—and Give Yourself an Out

Make sure you read and understand exactly when your contract expires. Health club salespeople will promise you the moon—especially when it comes to how easy it supposedly is to transfer or cancel your membership. In fact, their promises mean nothing unless they are written into the contract.

When you're dealing with a chain, you should make sure you understand what the contract says about using your membership at different outlets. For instance, a Fitness Plus membership at GoodLife Fitness allows you to use most of their branches in Canada, but not all of them. And if you're thinking about taking out a long-term membership, pay special attention to the cancellation rules. Don't assume you can get a refund if you decide you don't like the place. It's hard enough getting out of a health-club contract if you get injured or have to move.

In fact, some clubs will allow you to temporarily freeze your membership in the event you're laid up due to illness, injury, or pregnancy, as long as your account is in good standing. But cancelling a long-term health club membership for good—no matter how legitimate the reason—can be horrendously difficult.

As a result, it's probably a good idea to avoid signing up for a long-term membership at a club you're joining for the first time. A short-term trial membership may be a little more expensive on a monthly basis, but the extra cost will be more than worth it if your circumstances change or the gym doesn't live up to your expectations. And again, read the small print that explains what it takes to cancel your membership. Many contracts require written notice of cancellation—and have a specific day of the month written notice must be received by or you are billed for the entire month.

Avoid the "Platinum Membership" or Bells and Whistles

Many salespeople will first sell you on the idea of a membership and then as soon as you are ready to sign—push to sell you the higher-end membership. Usually the Platinum or Gold membership will give you access to more clubs depending on the club. In reality most people have a hard enough time going to the gym that's a mile from their house. The extra ten to twenty bucks a month you may spend to get this added benefit in most cases won't be worth it. And in truth, your club may offer free passes you can use later at a club in another city (ask them for a few guest or free passes before you sign on the dotted line). Lastly, before you sign up for, say, the gym locker membership that allows you to leave your clothes in the locker and even get them washed, ask yourself is it really worth it? It's not just ten dollars a month more—it's $120 dollars more a year or $240 more if it's a two-year contract. Think about the added costs in annual or two-year time frames and you may rethink adding the extras and save yourself a fortune.

Negotiate Hard Against the New-Membership Fee

Most clubs push for a new membership fee or a special one-time initiation fee—which in some clubs could run over $100. This fee is a huge profit centre for the club—and in almost every case it is negotiable and different depending on the time of the year. Most clubs will offer specials at certain times of the year when the initiation fee is waived. January seems to be peak time for deals like this since all the gyms are competing for all those New Year's Resolution makers.

Don't Forget Your Cooling-off Period

By law, consumers are entitled to a cooling-off period, during which they have the right to cancel a health-club contract they've just signed. So don't panic if you've gotten talked into signing a health-club contract that you can't afford or otherwise isn't right for you.

In most provinces, you have ten days to change your mind. You should check with your province's consumer affairs department to get more information about consumers' rights and protections.

What to Watch Out For

Bills That Don't Stop Coming

It's illegal in many jurisdictions in Canada for a fitness club to sell lifetime memberships. Most clubs sell memberships for a period of one or two years, although ending a health-club membership might sometimes seem to take a lifetime, and getting them to stop billing you can be even harder. The Better Business Bureau reports that fully one-quarter of all the billing complaints they get regarding health clubs come from people who continued to have money taken out of their chequing accounts even after they felt their contracts had expired or been cancelled.

So even though you may be convinced that you no longer belong to a gym, don't assume they feel the same way. Even if they're not pulling money out of your chequing account, that doesn't mean you're in the clear. It's entirely possible that your membership wasn't properly terminated, in which case the club may decide that you've skipped out on them and so turn over your account to a collection agency.

Even though you may be convinced that you no longer belong to a gym, don't assume they feel the same way.

To guard against this happening, double-check with the club that your account is closed. And then, just to be triple sure, check your credit report after a few months to make sure they haven't reported you as a delinquent account. If they have, you will need to dispute the report with the credit agency (see the section CREDIT SCORES on page 94 to learn how) and then straighten things out with the club.

Annual Increase in Fees

Many gyms are now raising their rates, especially as times get tough. You may even receive a written notice of a rate increase. The nice letter lets you know you don't have to do anything. The truth is that one thing you can do is go back into your membership office and find out if they are offering any new specials, where the monthly fee is lower than the one you signed up for. Some contracts may have guaranteed rates as well, in which case the gym isn't technically allowed to raise your rate during the contract period—so be sure to check. Lastly, you can always threaten to close your account, and when they ask why explain because the fee is being raised and you can't afford it. You may be surprised to find out they will let you keep your current membership fee for an additional year.

Keep an Eye on Your Valuables

Even at the most upscale places, health-club locker rooms are prime targets for petty thieves. Wallets, credit cards, laptops, cell phones, watches are all at risk, and the club is not liable for items that are stolen. So when you go to the gym, it's best to bring as few valuables with you as possible. What you can't leave at home, carry with you in a fanny pack. And if you must leave valuable items in a locker, take inventory before you leave the gym. That way, if something is missing, you'll know right away and be able to notify the club and the police immediately.

What to Do if Things Go Wrong

Always start by putting your complaint in writing and addressing it to the head manager of the club where you had the problem. At the same time, copy the CEO of the gym. More than likely the founder can be found on their web site as can the company headquarters. Then follow up the letter with a call or meeting with the manager. By starting a paper trail, and copying the founder or CEO of the national company, you will find that you are instantly taken more seriously and they may be more motivated to help you quickly resolve the problem. If you find yourself in a dispute with a health club that you haven't been able to resolve with them directly, your best bet is to file complaints with both the Better Business Bureau (**www.ccbbb.ca**) and your province's consumer affairs department. A call to your local newspaper may generate some unwanted publicity for the club, as well.

Fight for Your Money Action Steps

- ☐ Shop around for the best deals in your area—and check with your membership organizations, employer, and insurance company for special discounts and reimbursements.
- ☐ Read the fine print—know for sure when your contract expires and how to cancel.
- ☐ If you absolutely must enroll in automatic payments, charge the fee to a credit card. Do not give your new gym the right to pull money directly from your bank account.
- ☐ Take advantage of the cooling-off period if you sign a contract you immediately regret.

Buying a Home

As I write this at the end of 2008, the United States is experiencing the most difficult real estate market in over 20 years, and Canada's real estate market is having difficulties as well. Housing sales in Canada, particularly in major markets like Toronto, fell by 14% in October from the previous month, the biggest decline since 1994, and the amount of money paid for these houses fell by more than 17%. The number of houses sold was lower than it had been since 2002.

Mortgage and real estate markets operate under far different rules and standards in Canada than they do in the United States, where as many as 1 million homes were lost to foreclosure in 2008. Canada's economic conditions are different, as well, and Canada has weathered the turbulence in financial markets far more successfully than the United States.

Having said this, the usual conditions continue to apply in Canada's relationship with the United States. When the United States sneezes, Canada catches a cold. While we may not go through the same crises to the same degree as they do, Canadians will still face some tough times in our economy, including our housing markets.

This isn't entirely bad news. Real estate has always been a cyclical business and market. And with all down and difficult markets comes real opportunity. Home prices right now are falling across the country, making homes more affordable in most cities. According to the Canadian Real Estate Association (CREA), the national median existing-home price was $288,133 in October 2008, down 9.9% from a year ago.

The bottom line for home buying is that buying a home is more than just an investment; it is in fact *your home,* where you live, love, and have a life. The good news for most people is that buying a home will ultimately be the best investment you make over your lifetime because over the long term, real estate values increase. Simply buying a home and paying down the mortgage can provide you with financial security for life.

The other reality is that recent conditions have created what is arguably the best BUYERS MARKET for real estate in years.

But even with this buyers market, buying a home can be complicated and expensive if you do it incorrectly. Whether it's a buyer's market or a seller's market, the fundamental issue for people looking to buy a house is always the same: how can you find a place you love at a price you can afford? And how do you borrow responsibly to make this purchase something you can hold on to? (Be sure to read the next section on mortgages.)What complicates matters is that in even the simplest real estate transactions there are so many issues and so much money involved. As a result, unless you're very careful, you can get taken to the cleaners—not only by the folks you're buying from but also by the very people whose job it is to help you make a deal.

How to Fight for Your Money

Realistically, buying a home is probably the biggest purchase you'll ever make. It's also likely to be the most confusing. Here's how to go about it without getting ripped off.

Hire a Great Real Estate Agent

With all the real estate web sites available on the Internet these days, it's possible for anyone with a computer to do a lot of the stuff that only a real estate agent used to be able to do. Certainly, you don't need a professional in order to locate homes for sale in a particular area or to get a good sense of where prices are in the category that interests you. But this kind of research may be the least important thing a great real estate agent can do for you. (By the way, we're supposed to call them salespeople or representatives, not agents, according to the latest federal law. But I still think of them as agents, and so do most people).

I've been a real estate agent myself (specializing in commercial properties) and I've worked with real estate agents on all of my own real estate transactions. I know from personal experience how much they can help you.

But I also know that not all real estate agents are created equal. There's a constant stream of newcomers into the field.

As of this writing, there are roughly 97,000 real estate agents in Canada. Many—but not all— of them are great. So how do you find the one who can guide you through the process intelligently and help you close a great deal? Here's a list of things you should look for.

- A GREAT REAL ESTATE AGENT WILL LISTEN TO YOU CAREFULLY. Great agents are great listeners. They have to be in order to really help you. When a great agent meets you for the first time, he or she will pepper you with questions to find out what you're looking for, what you really want, why you want it, and most importantly, what you think you can afford.
- A GREAT REAL ESTATE AGENT WILL HELP YOU FIGURE OUT WHAT YOU REALLY *CAN* AFFORD. The first thing a top-notch agent will do is run your numbers and give you a ballpark estimate of what your price range should be. A great agent will also provide you with referrals to lenders that can help you get pre-approved for a mortgage.
- A GREAT REAL ESTATE AGENT WILL SAVE YOU TIME BY NARROWING YOUR SEARCH. A great agent won't run you ragged (and waste your time) by dragging you around to countless properties. Rather, the agent will help you figure out what you are looking for, show you a selection online, and allow you to narrow your choices before you actually hit the streets. He or she will then "tour you" to ones you've chosen—and keep track of what you like.
- A GREAT REAL ESTATE AGENT WILL EDUCATE YOU ABOUT THE MARKET. Great real estate agents know more than simply what's for sale in a particular neighbourhood. They know the neighbourhood. They can tell you all about an area's history, what makes it special, and where they see the market there going. If you're looking at a new development, the agent will know the developer's track record and plans for the future.
- A GREAT REAL ESTATE AGENT WILL SHOW YOU WAYS TO GET MORE VALUE FROM THE PROPERTY. From the moment a great real estate agent first sees a house, he or she is thinking about what could be done to increase its value. Install new kitchen cabinets, redo the floors, knock out the back bedroom and add a master bath—great agents will look at houses and immediately begin suggesting ways you could make it more valuable.

- A GREAT REAL ESTATE AGENT WILL HOLD YOUR HAND AT CLOSING. The closing of a home purchase at the title office can be a scary few hours. Great agents will go over the paperwork with you and your lawyer, checking it for errors. They will also work closely with you and your mortgage banker or broker to make sure everything is as it should be.

How to Find a Great Agent

Finding an agent who is ready, willing, and able to do all these things is not as hard as you might think. You should start by asking trusted friends and colleagues for recommendations. If one name keeps cropping up, that's a good sign. Make a note if you see a particular agent's name repeatedly on For Sale signs in the neighbourhood where you want to buy. You can also collect business cards from agents you meet at open houses.

As your list of prospective agents begins to take shape, do an Internet search on all the candidates you're considering. Look for articles, chat room or blog posts, and personal web sites to get a feel for their work, their style, their values, and how they market themselves.

Don't Be Afraid to Ask Tough Questions

When you've narrowed your list to three to five prospects, schedule a meeting with each—and treat your meeting like an actual interview. I recommend that you ask the following questions:

- How long have you been in business?
- How long have you worked in this particular market?
- How many listings (properties for sale where you represent the seller) do you have?
- How many clients are you currently working with?
- How many deals did you do last year in the area I'm interested in?
- Why should I work with you rather than one of your competitors?
- What makes you a good real estate agent?
- What is your process—how do you work with your clients?
- Do you have a team or an assistant? Will I be working with them or you?
- Can you give me the names of three clients you've worked with whose situation was similar to mine?

My Free Gift to You!

Visit my web site at **www.finishrich.com** to listen to my free audio on how to hire a real estate agent.

Based on their responses, ask yourself how you think it would be to work closely with each of them. Does your gut say this person is trustworthy? The only correct answer is whether the agent feels right for you. It's all about chemistry.

Before you commit to a particular agent, check them out with your province's real estate association. (You'll find a list of every province's real estate association at CREA's web site, www.crea.ca.) You want to verify that your choice is not only licensed but also that his or her license is in good standing, meaning that the agent has kept current with all educational requirements. You also want to find out whether he or she has any record of complaints or disciplinary actions.

Pick an Area Where You Want to Live and Start Looking

Before you can buy a house, you have to find a house. And the sooner you start looking, the sooner you'll finish. So don't feel you need to wait until you've hired a real estate agent. Get started right away. Just draw a circle on a map that covers an area within five miles of where you want to live. Somewhere within that circle you are going to find a home you like in your price range.

The place to begin your search is the Internet. In fact, that's where about four in five prospective home buyers start. Given the terrific real estate resources available online, it's not hard to see why. In just a couple of hours at your computer, you can gather information about what's available where and for how much that would have taken you months to assemble ten years ago.

The best place to start is the website of the Multiple Listing Service (www.mls.ca). You just identify the location in Canada where you want to start looking, type in the details about the home you're looking for—two-storey, detached, three-bedroom, for example—and start searching. You can also find homes listed on other websites like RealEstate.ca and on the web sites of individual real estate companies like Century 21 and RE/MAX in your area.

Of course, Internet research goes only so far. For all the convenience of online house hunting, nothing beats firsthand experience. So be sure to check the open-house listings in a local newspaper. Some local real estate boards list open houses on their web sites. Make a list of the ones in your price range, and then get in your car and go look at them. In a matter of hours, you'll be able to see as many as a dozen properties and get a real sense of what's out there that you can afford.

Run the Comps and Make a Realistic Offer

Once you find a house you love (or at least one you like enough to want to buy), you're going to have to make an offer. As a rule, houses don't have set prices. What they have is an asking price. It's up to you to respond with an offer, which can be more or less or the same as the asking price.

How do you know how much to offer? This is where a great real estate agent comes in handy. He or she will help you figure out whether to go high or low, and by how much. Agents do this by assessing how much demand there is for the property, how eager the owner is to sell, and most of all by running comps—providing you with an analysis of what comparable properties in the area have been selling for. Your real estate agent will be able to do this for you at no cost. You can also check out the sites of your local real estate board.

Most experts recommend that you look back between 90 to 180 days. But it really depends on the market. Real estate is local. Some markets are so hot that you need to gauge the most recent comps possible. Other areas are so slow that you may have to research property sales going back more than a year to get a feeling for the market.

You should run the comps even if you know the neighbourhood. Thinking you know what prices are and actually knowing them are two different things. Your purchase decision should be based on hard facts, not hunches.

Knowledge Without Offers Costs Money

If you're not scared when you make an offer on a home, you are definitely the exception, not the rule. Most people get really nervous when they make an offer on a property. There are so many factors to consider—and so much money at stake—that pulling the trigger can be downright nerve wracking.

Having purchased half a dozen properties in the last ten years, I can tell you that while it does get easier the more you do it, it's never really easy. And I certainly understand what it is like to freeze up and not be able to make a decision. Back in the mid-1990s, I found myself unable to pull the trigger for nearly four years!

As a result, I wound up paying $640,000 for a two-bedroom condo that I probably could have bought for about $300,000 when I first started looking.

Learn from my lesson. Spend as long as it takes to find a place that you like. But once you do, STOP LOOKING AND MAKE AN OFFER.

Protect Yourself with a Well-Drafted Purchase Agreement

When you make that offer on a house and then get the great news that it's been accepted, don't think you're done. You still have to close on the purchase, and this can be a complicated process that takes weeks, if not months.

The first step in the closing process is to sign an agreement of purchase and sale and put down a deposit. You'll need to hire a good real estate lawyer to review your purchase and sale agreement. (They often work for a set price.) The purchase and sale agreement commits you to buying the house at a specified price, subject to various contingencies such as your being able to get a mortgage. One thing you should insist on is that the purchase agreement include language that gives you the right to have some or all of your deposit returned in full if the conditions aren't met or you change your mind about buying the house. Given all the uncertainties that go along with buying a house, you want to give yourself maximum flexibility.

Have the House Inspected by a Professional

Unless you are purchasing a new, custom-built property, you should never close on a house without having it first checked out by a professional home inspector. Some people balk at the cost, which can run anywhere from $250 to $1,000 or more, but that doesn't make sense. Considering how much the house is going to cost you, the inspection fee is a small price to pay to ensure that the biggest purchase of your life doesn't turn out to be a lemon.

A properly performed home inspection will uncover any serious problems involving structural issues, leaks, faulty appliances, electrical and plumbing woes, possible health hazards like lead and so on. (You might also consider ordering up a termite inspection and, if the property has water tanks or a well, a water inspection, too.) Although a professional inspector will provide you with a written report of his findings, don't just wait for him to submit it. Show up at the house and personally watch him conduct the inspection. Chances are that he will do a better job if he knows you are looking over his shoulder.

You should be able to get a referral for a good inspector from your real estate agent or your mortgage lender—preferably from both. And make sure he is a member of the Canadian Association of Home and Property Inspectors (**www.cahi.ca**). You want someone who really knows what he's doing.

You can get more good information on home inspections from the Canada Mortgage and Housing Corporation (**www.cmhc-schl.gc.ca**).

If You Get a Warranty, Make Sure You Know What It Says

In every Canadian province, newly built houses and condos come with one- and two-year warranties that guarantee against defects in materials and workmanship, and longer warranties against major structural defects. You can get more information about your province's new-home warranty program by checking the web site of Canadians for Properly Built Homes (**www.canadiansforproperlybuilthomes.com**).

What to Watch Out For

Conflicts of Interest

In most cases, the agent you choose to help you find a home will work exclusively for you. But sometimes the agent will also represent the seller of a home that you're looking at. This is called dual agency, and the agent must tell you when this situation arises.

The problem with dual agency is that it's just not realistic to expect one agent (or real estate firm) to do the best possible job getting the lowest price for a buyer at the same time that it's trying to get the highest price for the seller. Even with the most ethical of agents, there are bound to be problems. At the very least, once you express interest in a house that your agent represents, you will probably find him or her becoming a bit more distant and less willing to advise you candidly on what the seller might or might not accept.

If you do end up working with an agent or firm that also represents sellers, avoid sharing crucial details—such as your bottom-line position in negotiations.

The fact is, you need to know that your agent is representing you and you alone. One way to do this is use a buyer's agent who works in an office representing only buyers. In most provinces, if an agent is showing you homes, she is regarded automatically as your agent. But make sure you discuss this with your agent at the outset and even get it in writing that the agent works exclusively for you, the buyer. In fact, agents are required to do this under the CREA code of ethics.

If you do end up working with an agent or firm that also represents sellers, always keep in mind that even though you may really like your agent personally, he or she may not have your interests at heart. So avoid sharing crucial details—such as your bottom-line position in negotiations. You don't want to put your agent in the awkward position of knowing your spending limit when he or she is discussing strategy with the seller.

Rebates, Referral Fees, and Kickbacks

CREA's Code of Ethics also requires agents to disclose any financial arrangements such as referral fees or rebates that they might have negotiated with other parties. Make sure you ask about these, as well.

What to Do if Things Go Wrong

Problems with a Real Estate Agent

If you feel your real estate agent has acted unethically or otherwise shortchanged you, complain *in writing* to the agent's supervisor. List specifics. Tell exactly what happened, when it happened, and who was involved. Keep a copy for yourself, and send the letter by certified mail, return receipt requested, to provide you with a record of when and to whom you filed your complaint.

If that doesn't resolve the problem, complain to your province's real estate association. As I noted earlier, you can find contact information for every provincial association at CREA's web site (www.crea.ca). When you contact the association, look for the procedure for filing a complaint, what steps the agency will take to investigate and handle the complaint, how long it will take, and how you will be notified of progress and decisions.

If an ethics issue is involved, you should complain to your local real estate agents' association, with a copy to your the provincial association.

Defective Construction and Warranty Problems

If you buy a newly built home and then discover it has construction defects, your best bet may be to consult Canadians for Properly Built Homes (www.canadiansforproperlybuilthomes.com), an advocacy group that helps home buyers understand their rights and pursue remedies. Although CPBH does not investigate complaints or bring legal action of any kind, it is allied with Industry Canada's Canadian Consumer Information Gateway. Its web site is also a treasure trove of valuable information, including ongoing issues involving new-home warranty programs and inadequate building codes.

Fight for Your Money Action Steps

- ☐ Make a commitment to find yourself a great real estate agent. Schedule interviews with your top three to five prospects and make a decision.
- ☐ Figure out what kind of home you want to buy and where.
- ☐ Run the comps and make a realistic offer.
- ☐ Hire a great real estate lawyer to look out for your best interests, from the purchase agreement all the way through the closing.
- ☐ Order a complete home inspection.
- ☐ Read more about the home-buying process in the next chapter, HOME MORTGAGES.
- ☐ Read *The Automatic Millionaire Homeowner* to create a truly powerful lifetime plan to finish rich as a homeowner.

Home Mortgages

The most important truth I can share with you on this subject is that you need to understand your mortgage BEFORE you sign on the dotted line and close on a home. And if you are already in a home and have a mortgage, you need to understand NOW what type of mortgage you have and how it truly works.

Unfortunately, a stunning number of homeowners simply do not understand how mortgages work, much less what they currently have. According to a recent U.S. study by BankRate.com, one in four people do not know what type of mortgage they have. Canadians are probably in a similar position, although mortgages in this country are a lot less confusing, since there aren't as many variations as there are in the United States.

Considering that for most people, home mortgage payments make up more than 30% of their spending, it's utterly stunning that thousands of us simply have no clue as to how our homes are being financed. You cannot let yourself be one of these people.

For years I have stood by one very simple axiom about real estate that is very different from other experts':

I believe the old saying that the secret to real estate is "location, location, location" is wrong. The secret to real estate is "FINANCING, FINANCING, FINANCING."

If you get the financing of your home wrong, you may well wind up losing the property entirely.

How to Fight for Your Money

Basically, a home mortgage is a loan you take out to buy a house, the collateral for which is the house itself. (This means that if you fall behind on the payments, the lender can seize your house and kick you out.) In its simplest version, a mortgage loan is repaid over a set period of time (usually 15 to 25 years) with a series of regular payments, part of which go to pay the interest charges and part of which go to pay down the principle. Early in the life of a mortgage, when the loan balance is high, most of the payment goes to pay interest. But as time goes on and the loan balance diminishes, the interest charge declines along with it and more and more of the payment goes to pay down the principle. By the time you get to your last payment, virtually all the money is applied to the principle. This process is known as amortization.

As a borrower you shouldn't expect a mortgage lender to look out for your interests. You've got to do that for yourself. Here's how.

Figure Out How Much You Can Afford

When it comes to buying a place to live, the bottom line isn't how much houses or condos cost; it's how much you can afford to spend.

So how much home can you afford?

The most sensible rule of thumb is probably the one recommended by most banks and other mortgage lenders. They say that your monthly housing costs such as mortgage payments, taxes, heating expenses, and a portion of condo fees should not amount to more than 32% of your gross monthly household income. And your entire monthly debt load including housing costs, car payments, personal loans, and credit card payments should not exceed 40% of your gross monthly income.

WHAT MORTGAGE MONTHLY PAYMENT IS RIGHT FOR YOU

Annual Gross Income	Monthly Gross	32% of Gross	40% of Gross
$20,000	$1,667	$533	$667
$30,000	$2,500	$800	$1,000
$40,000	$3,333	$1067	$1,333
$50,000	$4,176	$1,336	$1,670
$60,000	$5,000	$1,600	$2,000

$70,000	$5,833	$1,867	$2,333
$80,000	$6,667	$2,133	$2,667
$90,000	$7,500	$2,400	$3,000
$100,000	$8,333	$2,667	$3,333

As the table indicates, if you have a household income of $80,000 a year, you should be able to afford to spend somewhere between $2,133 and $2,667 a month on mortgage payments. Whether you should be on the high side or the low side of this range depends on how much debt you are already carrying, what other financial goals or commitments you have (like retirement savings or special medical expenses), how secure your job is, and what your future prospects are. Obviously, if you have little or no debt, few other commitments, and are looking forward to a series of promotions at work, you can comfortably bump up against the 40% ceiling. If things are a little tight, you'll want to stay closer to the 32% floor.

The next table shows what the monthly payments are for different-sized 30-year-mortgages at different interest rates—in other words, how much house you can get for a monthly payment you can afford.

MONTHLY PAYMENT TABLE PER $1,000 OF MORTGAGE
(SEMI-ANNUAL COMPOUNDING AND 25-YEAR AMORTIZATION

%	$	%	$	%	$
6.00%	$6.40	8.25%	$7.79	10.50%	$9.29
6.25%	$6.55	8.50%	$7.95	10.75%	$9.46
6.50%	$6.70	8.75%	$8.12	1100%	$9.63
6.75%	$6.85	9.00%	$8.28	11.25%	$9.80
7.00%	$7.00	9.25%	$8.44	11.50%	$9.98
7.25%	$7.16	9.50%	$8.61	11.75%	$10.15
7.50%	$7.32	9.75%	$8.78	12.00%	$10.32
7.75%	$7.47	10.00%	$8.95	12.25%	$10.50
8.00%	$7.63	10.25%	$9.12	12.50%	$10.68

For example, if you borrow a mortgage of $100,000 at an interest rate of 6.5%, you should multiply $6.70 by 100. Your monthly payments would be $670.

Figuring an interest rate of around 6%, what the table says is that someone who can afford to spend between $2,133 and $2,667 a month on housing—that is, someone who earns $80,000 a year—could easily carry a $350,000 mortgage. In most parts of the country, that's still more than enough to buy a pretty decent home

Clean Up Your Credit *Before* You Start Shopping for a Mortgage

The single most important factor in whether you will qualify for the best possible and least expensive mortgage is your credit score—the three-digit number, based on your credit history, that essentially summarizes what kind of credit risk you are. Credit scores range from 300 to 850. A difference of just 50 points can cost you thousands of dollars over the life of your mortgage, and a 100 or more points can be worth tens of thousands to you to lose or keep. So your credit score is truly critical and if it's not ideal, now is the time to fix it. Ideally, you should start working on your score at least a year before you start shopping for a mortgage, but the good news is you really can raise your score in six months. The section CREDIT SCORES on page 91 explains how credit scores are calculated and what it takes to raise one.

When you're finally ready to start applying for a mortgage, make sure you concentrate all your applications and inquiries into one 30-day period. You need to do this because every time you ask a bank or broker about the possibility of getting a mortgage, they're going to check your credit—and every time someone checks your credit, a few points get shaved off your credit score. Fortunately, the credit-rating agencies that set your credit score don't want to penalize consumers for shopping around for a mortgage, so they count all credit inquiries received from mortgage lenders within the same 30-day period as just one inquiry.

Shop for Your Mortgage Before You Start Shopping for Your House

There's nothing worse than finding the house of your dreams—and not knowing if you'll be able to get the money it's going to take to buy it. Actually, there may be one thing worse: finding the house of your dreams and then making a hasty, ill-informed decision about a mortgage because you're excited and want to close the deal as quickly as you can.

Mortgages are complicated, and you want to make your choice calmly and deliberately, not when you're keyed up, stressed, and in a hurry. This is why you should get an ADVANCE COMMITMENT from a lender *before* you start looking at houses.

You should get an ADVANCE COMMITMENT from a lender before you start looking at houses.

Basically, a pre-approval is a solid commitment from a particular lender to give you a particular mortgage at a particular rate, subject only to your finding a suitable house. You shouldn't confuse this with a pre-qualification, which doesn't really commit anyone to anything.

When you ask a lender to pre-approve you for a mortgage, you are asking him to formally review your financial situation, decide whether you are creditworthy, and then, assuming you are, commit to lending you a certain amount of money on particular terms, subject only to your finding an appropriate property. To do all this, the lender will pull your credit report and score and study your credit history to see whether you can be trusted to pay your bills on time. In addition, the lender will want to verify both your current income and your income history. He will probably want to see copies of your tax returns for the last three years, especially if you are self-employed, and he will want to see a verified list of all your assets and liabilities.

Because this review is so thorough it may take several days to complete. But once it's done, you'll have a real commitment that you can literally bank on.

Knowing in advance exactly what kind of mortgage you can get will not only make the whole home-buying process more enjoyable, but also could get you a better deal, since sellers are generally more willing to talk turkey with buyers who have solid financing.

Getting Preapproved: Whom to Ask and Where to Go

So how do you decide who to ask for a pre-approval? Finding a mortgage lender is mainly a matter of shopping around. You should start by meeting with your current bank. Banks in Canada account for the majority of mortgages that people use to buy a home. You should also get recommendations from your real estate agent. And, of course, ask people you trust who have mortgages themselves as well as financial professionals you deal with, such as your accountant or financial advisor. Whittle the list down to a half-dozen or so banks, finance companies, and mortgage brokers, and then start making the rounds.

With a good idea of how much you want to borrow, visit each of the candidates, either in person or online. There are four basic questions you should ask them:

- WHAT'S THE PROCESS LIKE? Applying for a mortgage is a lot like applying to university. There are all kinds of forms to fill out, scores to worry about, and choices to make. Ask the banker or broker to spell out the process he or she will go through to help you do all these things. You should also make sure they can help you get pre-approved. If the answer is, "No, but I can get you pre-qualified," this is not a broker or banker you want to work with.
- WHAT KIND OF EXPERIENCE DO YOU HAVE? You want someone who's been in the business for a while with plenty of experience handling what you're looking for. If you are buying your first home and the lender's experience is mainly with refinancing, he or she may not be the right one for you.
- WHAT KIND OF LOANS DO YOU GENERALLY RECOMMEND? Every mortgage lender will tell you that the answer depends on the client's particular needs and situation. So ask which kinds of mortgages he or she favours and why. If you're not comfortable with what you hear, find someone else. And be wary of anyone who talks up exotic products that you don't understand.
- DO YOU SPECIALIZE IN A CERTAIN KIND OF CLIENT OR PRODUCT? Some mortgage professionals welcome first-time homebuyers. Others work mainly with sophisticated investors. You want someone who works with the type of borrower you happen to be.

The answers you get to these questions should give you a sense of whether the mortgage professional you're talking to is the right one for you. Chemistry should count for something, too. You're going to be discussing a lot of sensitive personal information, so if you don't feel comfortable, the relationship is not going to work.

If you're satisfied by the answers you get, ask the candidate for a ballpark estimate of the kind of rate and terms her institution would be willing to give you. And don't be shy about pressing for details. Ask all the questions listed above.

This shopping process is a good way to screen out sleazy lenders and abusive loans. Good lenders will give you clear explanations. Predators, on the other hand, never answer your questions clearly. So if you come away from a meeting feeling confused, even if you really like the lender or mortgage broker, don't do business with that lender—keep shopping.

Most likely, each lender will present his proposals in a slightly different way. As a result, you may find it hard to compare competing mortgage offers. One way is to match up each mortgage's interest rate, fees, and closing costs. A better way is to use a mortgage calculator such as the one on the CMHC's web site (**www.cmhc-schl.gc.ca**) to see how much you can afford, on what terms, and then ask each lender to match them.

Once you've figured out which lender's offer is the best, ask that lender for a pre-approval. If, after going through the rigorous pre-approval process, you're told that you don't qualify for the mortgage originally offered, continue to shop around before you accept one with less favourable terms.

Don't Buy a Loan You Don't Understand

As I said earlier, one-quarter of all homeowners don't understand what type of mortgages they have. They can easily change this.

What you need to know to really understand your mortgage is NOT COMPLICATED. It's just been made more confusing than it needs to be—so much so that even financially sophisticated people have been taken in.

Questions to Ask a Mortgage Lender Before You Sign on the Dotted Line

- What type of mortgage is it? Is it a fixed rate or floating rate?
- If it's floating, does it have a variable rate?
- How long is the term of the loan?
- What is the amortization schedule?
- Is it open or closed? In other words, can you pay off part or all of the mortgage at any time (open) or do you have to pay a penalty (closed)?
- If the lender charges you a penalty fee, how much is it?
- What happens if I rent out the property, as opposed to living there myself? Do I have to let you know, and is there a penalty fee or interest rate adjustment?
- What is the cost of the loan? Are there origination fees (for preparing loan documents, making credit checks, and appraising the property)? If so, how much is the fee?
- If the down payment is less than 25% of the purchase price, how much will I have to pay for CMHC Mortgage Insurance or similar coverage provided by Genworth, a private company? And once my equity in the house reaches 25%, how can I get my mortgage insurance obligation waived?

If you insist on getting answers to these questions, you will learn more than most people ever do when they get a mortgage—and as a result, you will be prepared to make an educated decision.

If there's anything in your mortgage agreement that doesn't make sense to you—or doesn't seem to reflect what you were promised—demand an explanation. And don't believe the banker or broker who tells you, "Don't worry—we'll fix it later." The fact is, later never comes. As one consumer advocate says, "I've never met anyone who actually got the better loan later."

Take a Homeowner Class—Get More Financial Education

I wrote an entire book on homeownership called *The Automatic Millionaire Homeowner*. This book is a true "Homeownership 101" course, and you can find out all about it at my web site at **www.finishrich.com**. Whether you buy *The Automatic Millionaire Homeowner* or check it out of the library, you should read a book like it, especially if you are a first-time homeowner.

Remember: no matter how nice they may seem, most bankers, mortgage brokers, and real estate agents are paid by commission and earn money when you close the transaction. While most mortgage advisors are honest, it takes only one bad apple to destroy your life financially. So you MUST educate yourself and make sure the advice you get is objective and honest.

Don't Overreach

As I said earlier, the key to real estate is "financing, financing, financing." It's not enough to be able to pay for your home in the beginning—you have to be able to pay for your mortgage for as long as you own it (which may be much longer than you think). In the United States, part of what went wrong during the sub-prime mess was that irresponsible lenders persuaded people to take on mortgages they simply could not afford. They did this because banks don't keep most of the mortgages they make. Rather, they repackage them into what are called mortgage-backed securities, which are sold to institutional investors around the world. As a result, it wasn't their problem if the borrower couldn't make the payments.

Just because a bank or other financial institution might be willing to lend you a certain amount of money doesn't mean you should take it all.

The point is that just because a bank or other financial institution might be willing to lend you a certain amount of money doesn't mean you should take it all. Buying a house almost always costs more than you think it will. Not only are there taxes and insurance premiums on top of the mortgage payment—not to mention closing costs—but also there are the costs of moving and decorating. And when you stretch to buy the biggest house you can possibly afford, it's easy to forget that in addition to the higher mortgage payments, you're also going to have to cope with higher maintenance costs, higher utility bills, a higher property-tax assessment—pretty much higher everything.

There are a number of calculators available online to help you come up with a realistic estimate; two good ones are www.cmhc-schl.gc.ca and www.mortgagecalculator.org. Whatever you do, don't let a real estate agent or mortgage broker convince you to take on bigger payments than you can feel comfortable with. Use the chart on page 171 to guide you instead.

What to Watch Out For

Unsolicited Offers

Predatory lending is not as prevalent in Canada as it is in the United States. When it occurs, predatory lenders in Canada traditionally target older homeowners who are looking to refinance an existing mortgage to get more equity from their home after it has increased in value. If you receive an unsolicited offer to refinance your mortgage, look at it carefully and NEVER respond without advice from a lawyer or financial advisor.

Because all mortgages are publicly recorded, it's easy for unscrupulous lenders to find out your current interest rate. They can then phone you or show up on your doorstep claiming that you're paying too much and that they can get you a better deal. This in itself is a giveaway. As a rule, you should never do business with a mortgage lender who approaches you with an unsolicited offer—whether in person, by phone, or via email.

Private Mortgage Insurance

Private mortgage insurance (PMI) is a policy that ensures your lender will get paid if you cannot make your mortgage payments. Most lenders require you to buy it if the size of your mortgage exceeds 75% of the value of your house.

The cost of PMI varies, depending on the size of your down payment and the nature of your mortgage, but it's not cheap. The extra costs could range as high as 2.5 percent of the mortgage, plus an application fee of as much as $235. All these costs are incorporated into your mortgage payments, so you can pay them off over a period of years.

Given that PMI doesn't help you—just the bank—it's something you want to get rid of as soon as possible. So you should keep a sharp eye on the value of your house and the outstanding balance of your mortgage. The moment your loan-to-value ratio reaches 75%, ask your lender to cancel your policy.

Property Title Scams

Traditionally, Canadians have been known for doing almost anything to avoid losing their homes to foreclosure. And for good reason: not only will it ruin your credit rating, but also losing your home to foreclosure is one of the scariest experiences a family can go through.

In the United States, scam artists have been preying on people who are in danger of losing their houses, offering them phony foreclosure-prevention schemes. In Canada, the scam artists take a different tack, using fraudulent titles to obtain large mortgages on homes they don't own.

Here's how these low-lifes operate: When they see a For Sale sign on the front lawn of a house, they search the title, find out the name of the owner and how much the person owes on the house. Then one of them assumes the identity of the owner, forges the owner's signature on a purchase and sale agreement, and uses a crooked lawyer to transfer ownership to the phony purchaser. The phony seller pays off the existing mortgage, while the new but phony owner takes out a much bigger one on the property. And that's the last that anyone ever hears of the fraudsters.

Meanwhile, the original owner of the property discovers the scam only when the new mortgage lender comes calling for their payment. In most cases, the owners have no choice other than to pay off the debt. Otherwise, the lender will evict them.

The onus is on the victims of title fraud to prove they've been swindled and that the bank or mortgage lender that extended the loan to the fraudsters did not do its due diligence. Only then can they make a claim to the provincial government's land-title assurance fund, which is financed by land-title fees.

Fortunately, according to First Canadian Title, which insures owners against title fraud, these scams affect fewer than 4% of their clients, which is reassuring unless you're one of the 4%. In the average case of title fraud, home owners have about $300,000 at stake. Few of us can afford to lose that much money.

Variations of this scam occur when people rent their houses to strangers. The tenants pose as the owners of the property and use a phony title to obtain a mortgage. Then, as with all scammers, they disappear with the money.

The Canadian Association of Accredited Mortgage Professionals (**www.caamp.org**) advises homebuyers and purchasers alike not to divulge personal information to strangers and to use a real estate professional and a reputable lawyer when buying or selling a house.

Payment Shortfalls

If you're having trouble making your mortgage payment, here's what you should do.

1. CALL YOUR LENDER IMMEDIATELY. The single biggest mistake borrowers make when they fall behind on their mortgage is not contacting their lender. As soon as you realize you have a problem, you've got to make that call. The foreclosure process for most lenders has a set schedule, so the longer you wait, the fewer options you'll have.
2. ASK TO SPEAK TO THE "LOSS MITIGATION" DEPARTMENT. See if your monthly statement contains the phone number to the lender's loss mitigation department. If not, call the customer service number and ask for that department. At most lenders, the loss mitigation department helps borrowers determine which workout option they qualify for. Keep in mind, though, that some lenders have their collections departments advise borrowers on workout options, so don't be alarmed if you're sent straight to collections.
3. BE PREPARED TO REVIEW YOUR SITUATION IN DETAIL WITH YOUR LENDER. Your lender will ask a series of questions to assess your financial situation. Some lenders have specialists with both the training and technology to pre-qualify a caller for a workout option right over the phone. If you have the right financial documents in front of you when you make the call, you might be able to get a resolution within minutes. So organize your bills, statements, and anything else that will help give an accurate picture of your current financial status. And resist the temptation to make your financial situation sound better than it really is. All that will accomplish is to get you a workout agreement that won't really help you. (By the same token, don't exaggerate how bad your situation is. That may lead your lender to think there's no way you can keep your house.)
4. KNOW THE WAYS YOUR LENDER CAN HELP YOU AVOID FORECLOSURE. According to Consolidated Credit Counseling Services of Canada Ltd. (**www.consolidatedcredit.ca**), most people take out a second mortgage when they get behind in their mortgage payments.

Depending on how serious your situation is, your lender can offer you other retention options (ways to keep your house) or liquidation options (ways to give up your house without going into foreclosure). Other retention options include forbearance (which generally lets you pay less than the full amount of your mortgage payment for a temporary period), a repayment plan (where you pay off your overdue mortgage payments in instalments), reinstatement (where you agree to pay your lender everything you owe in one lump sum by a specific date) and loan modification (where your interest rate and other loan conditions are changed). Liquidation options include a short sale (where your lender agrees to accept an offer to buy your house for less than the amount you owe—which then cancels the debt), deed in lieu of foreclosure (where you voluntarily transfer your property to your lender), and assumption (which allows a qualified buyer to take over your mortgage and make the payments). If you have a CMHC-insured loan, you may have additional options available to you. It's important to check with your lender for details.

5. KNOW WHERE TO TURN IF YOU AREN'T GETTING THE HELP YOU NEED FROM YOUR LENDER. There are a number of non-profit credit counselling organizations that will help you if you get into trouble paying your mortgage. Consolidated Credit Counseling Services of Canada is one. Another is Credit Counselling Canada (**www.creditcounsellingcanada.ca**).

What to Do if Things Go Wrong

If you feel a mortgage professional has taken advantage of you or otherwise treated you unfairly, the first step, as always, is to write a polite but firm letter to his or her immediate superior—or, if you're dealing with bank or other large financial institution, to the customer service department. In it, you should set out the nature of your complaint and what you expect them to do about it.

If this does not lead to a resolution of the problem, it's time to go higher up the chain, first to the banking ombudsman if you've borrowed a mortgage from a bank, or, if the problem lies with your broker, to your province's independent mortgage brokers association and to the Canadian Association of Accredited Mortgage Professionals, which offers a formal complaint-resolution process.

Getting Out of a Bad Mortgage

As I noted earlier, once you sign a mortgage contract, you're on the hook. There's no cooling-off period during which you're allowed to change your mind and pull out of the deal. You cannot cancel it even if you feel the lender has taken unfair advantage of you. But this doesn't mean you're screwed.

What you should do is immediately consult a lawyer with experience in residential mortgage issues. Particularly in cases where there is any basis for a claim that you were victimized by predatory practices, you might be able to renegotiate the contract to get better terms from the lender. If you can't afford a lawyer, you might qualify for free legal assistance from your provincial legal aid program. (You can find them through your provincial law society, which is listed on the web site of the Canadian Bar Association (**www.cba.org**).

Fight for Your Money Action Steps

- ☐ Understand that before you start shopping for a house, you need to shop for a mortgage.
- ☐ Figure out how much you can afford to spend.
- ☐ Go to **www.myfico.com** to order your credit score and credit report. Then get to work on fixing any errors and raising your score so you qualify for the best mortgage possible.
- ☐ Shop for a trustworthy lender.
- ☐ Protect yourself by asking your lender all of the specific questions outlined on page 174.
- ☐ Become an educated homebuyer. Read *The Automatic Millionaire Homeowner* and visit my web site at **www.finishrich.com** to find first-time-homebuyer workshops in your area.

Home Building and Remodelling

As a financial advisor helping clients plan for the cost of home-remodelling jobs, the number-one thing I learned was that construction projects always cost more than the estimate—and they ALWAYS take longer than expected. In fact, it's not uncommon for a remodel to cost as much as twice the estimate and take twice as long to complete as planned. The stress that results from this can be phenomenal. I have watched clients lose both their health and their marriages over the course of remodelling jobs.

We have all heard the nightmare stories of contractors who take six months to do a one-month job. Or, even worse, who promise to redo your kitchen for $15,000 and get you to pay them half in advance—only to demolish a wall and half the ceiling, and then disappear for good. Sadly, they are not urban legends.

According to the Better Business Bureau, home renovations consistently rank among the top 10 causes for consumer complaints in Canada. In Ontario alone, the Ministry of Small Business and Consumer Services receives more than 2,600 complaints a year against contractors.

There's no getting around it. If buying a home is the biggest single investment most of us will ever make (and it is), building or remodeling may be the second-biggest financial investment we make BUT the biggest potential headache. If done right, building or redoing a house to meet your own personal specifications can be enormously satisfying. But if you get stuck with a dishonest or incompetent contractor, the project can turn into a money pit that will take over your life, drain your savings, and possibly even ruin your marriage.

Despite the risks, about three out of four Canadian homeowners make renovations or repairs to their homes. How many of these people get ripped off by dishonest builders is anybody's guess. Given that we spend a total of more than $50 billion annually on home repair and remodelling projects, it's safe to say that building and remodelling rip-offs cost us millions of dollars a year. So proceed with caution.

How to Fight for Your Money

The number-one predictor of whether your project will go right is choosing a competent and honest contractor. But even if you do, you must still monitor the process closely. Home building is a great example of how fighting for your money can require you to sweat the details.

Whether you are building a new house from the ground up or remodelling an existing one, your ability to get the finished product you want at the price you want will depend on five main factors:

- hiring good people
- making—and sticking to—a budget
- drawing up a well-thought-out plan before construction—and then sticking to it
- understanding the construction contract you are signing
- staying on top of the project

It's really that simple. If you can do these five things, you will get your house built or remodelled without going broke (or crazy) in the process. Here are some guidelines to keep in mind.

Making the Plan

All successful construction projects begin with a good plan, and except for the simplest remodels that means the first thing you should do is find yourself an architect. It's one thing to sketch out a plan yourself; it's something else entirely to create workable blueprints that accomplish what you're looking for and comply with building codes. Get referrals from friends and colleagues who've been through projects similar to what you're planning. Particularly if you're building a custom home, make a note of houses you like in your area and find out who designed them. (Architects often place a sign outside their residential projects. In addition, records of all new construction, which include the name of the architect, are usually on file and available to the general public at your local city hall.) You can also locate an architect through the Royal Architectural Institute of Canada (RAIC), which operates an electronic directory on its web site (**www.raic.org**) or through the web site of *Canadian Architecture* magazine (**www.canadianarchitecture.com**).

As with hiring any professional, you should interview at least two or three candidates. You want to make sure both that their taste matches yours and that you get along. This is also the time to agree on a fee structure (some architects charge by the hour, others set a flat fee for the job, and some charge a percentage of the total construction cost), the proposed time frame for the project, and how cost overruns and delays will be handled. A web site called **ShowMeTheGreen.ca** contains a list of questions to ask about an architect you're considering (including: "Does the architect have experience in projects of this size?" and "How good is the architect at accepting criticism?").

Don't Try to Do It Yourself

As crucial as the architect is, the most important decision you will make when you're building or remodelling a home is your choice of contractor. About half of Canadians try to save money by acting as their own contractor, but unless you have some experience in the building trades and nothing else to do with your time, this is probably not a good idea.

Lining up materials and subcontractors and overseeing the progress of the job is only part of what a contractor does. Whether you're building a skyscraper or remodelling a kitchen, the success of any construction project depends in large part on your ability to get subcontractors arriving and departing in a smooth flow. The tight scheduling of workers in the correct sequence is essential, and if you don't have the kind of relationships that most established contractors have, you may have trouble getting the subcontractors you need when you need them. Subcontractors tend to show up more reliably when they're called by someone with whom they have worked in the past and for whom they hope to work again in the future. From a subcontractor's point of view, the do-it-yourself contractor represents nothing more than a one-time opportunity—meaning, if they have time, maybe they'll squeeze you in, but don't count on it.

To Find a Good Contractor, Dig, Ask—and Check

Despite what you may have heard, not all contractors are crooks. In fact, there are plenty of responsible, reliable contractors who take great pride in their work. The question is, how do you find one of them?

It's really not that complicated, although it does take a little effort. You begin by asking for recommendations from relatives, friends, and business associates. You should also make a note if you happen to see a custom home or remodelling project that you like. Contractors generally post signs on their job sites with their names and contact information. In the case of a remodel, you might even knock on the door and ask the homeowners if they'd recommend the professionals they are working with. Local building-supply outlets can often refer you to contractors who have purchased their materials from the outlet and have a consistent track record.

You can also get leads from the Canadian Home Builders' Association (www.chba.ca). And check the Yellow Pages.

Your aim should be to compile a list of at least three good candidates you can ask to bid on your job. Once you've got a few names, you should meet personally with all of them in their offices. If a candidate doesn't have an office, scratch him off your list. Not having an office is the definition of fly-by-night, and you want somebody who is established.

The three most important questions you should ask a prospective contractor are:

1. ARE YOU LICENSED AND BONDED? Bonding is a financial guarantee provided by most reputable contractors that they will honour their contracts.
2. DO YOU GUARANTEE YOUR WORK IN WRITING?
3. CAN YOU PROVIDE NAMES AND TELEPHONE NUMBERS OF AT LEAST THREE RECENT CLIENTS AS WELL AS SOME SUPPLIERS OR SUBCONTRACTORS? You want to talk to his subcontractors or suppliers to make sure he pays his bills—because if he doesn't, you will be responsible for them.

The only acceptable answers are yes, yes, and yes. And make sure to actually look at his license and call his references. Too much is at stake here to take anything on trust. Ideally, you should ask former clients if you can come to their homes and see the work your candidate did for them. In addition, contact your local Chamber of Commerce and Better Business Bureau (www.ccbbb.org) as well as your province's consumer complaints bureau. In Ontario, for example, you can check with the Consumer Beware web site of the Ministry of Small Business and Consumer Services (www.consumerbeware.mgs.gov.on.ca).

Figure Out What You Want and What It's Going to Cost

The key to a successful construction project is creating a detailed, specific budget. A good budget not only tells you how much you can expect to have to spend, but also can be used as the basis for a request for bids from contractors.

Start by writing out the scope of the work you want done—describing exactly what the job is, how long you expect it to take, and when you need to have it finished. On a simple project, you can do this yourself. On more complicated projects—and all custom home construction—you do this with your architect. The more detail the better. Next, list your specifications: how many square feet of floor will be covered? It's good if you can say that you'll use a medium-priced granite for your kitchen countertops. It's better if you can specify exactly which granite product, with the product number.

The key to a successful construction project is creating a detailed, specific budget.

To get a realistic idea of the prices and options available to you, you should comparison shop online or in person at hardware and specialty stores. Typically, a remodeller or builder will suggest that you establish an allowance for specific items—appliances or bathroom fixtures or flooring, for example. The trouble with this approach is that all too often the allowance doesn't come close to covering the cost of the products you want. You can avoid disappointment—as well as the temptation to spend more than you can afford—by pricing things out in advance.

For custom home-building projects, a U.S. web site called Building-Cost.Net (**www.building-cost.net**) has a really terrific cost estimator that takes into account the size and shape of your proposed house, the kind of finishes you want, and where you live. It may not give you a precise estimate for the cost of a project in Canada, but it will show you the many factors that contribute to the cost of a custom home, no matter where you build it.

You can also find out average construction costs per square foot for your region from local home builders' associations, available through the Canadian Home Builders' web site (**www.chba.ca**). The CMHC lists several books on its web site (**www.cmhc-schl.gc.ca**) that you can use to calculate costs of home building and renovating. (Look under Renovations, Frequently Asked Questions.)

For remodelling jobs, you can get a ballpark idea of costs for basic upgrades or replacements at web sites like Pillar to Post (**http://pillartopost.com**). You can also find out which renovation is likely to add more to your home's resale value at web sites like the Investor Education Fund (**www.investored.ca**).

Put Everything in Writing

Once you've selected a contractor and agreed on what he's going to do and how much it's going to cost, you need to put it all in writing. Drawing up a contract actually isn't all that difficult. ShowMeTheGreen.ca lists the ten essential components of a standard contract. You can also download a standard renovation contract from the CMHC's web site, **www.cmhc-schl.gc.ca**.

Whether or not you use a standard CMHC form, your contract should include:

- the contractor's name, company name, and address
- your design plans
- detailed specifications of all materials and appliances to be used, right down to the brand name, model, color, and features
- when the work will be started and when it will be finished
- the total price you will pay for the job, including permit fees and sales tax
- a payment schedule (also known as a "draw" schedule), under which specified partial payments are made as the contractor completes specified project milestones and the final payment is contingent on receiving proof that all subcontractors and suppliers have been paid
- how much of the final payment (usually at least 15%) you will withhold until the work is completed to your satisfaction
- a system for authorizing changes in your plans once work has started (known as change orders), a description of the final review and sign-off process, and the plan for cleaning up the work site
- a warranty that guarantees all work for at least one year, including specifics about what is and is not covered, instructions on how to proceed if you have problems, and the name of the individual whom you should contact

The point is that everything should be in writing. If it's not in your contract (or in the change orders that get added to the file over the course of the project), don't expect it to be in your house when the job is done.

Keep an Eye on Things—Inspect, Inspect, Inspect

Construction projects, both big and small, are the ultimate example of Murphy's Law—if something can go wrong, it will. There's also a related law of home construction that a friend of mine who recently built a house told me about: if someone can take advantage of you, they will.

So you need to keep a sharp eye peeled and take nothing for granted. Check credentials and licenses and ask to see a contractor's proof of insurance. Make sure the materials and appliances used in your job are the ones you contracted for.

For bigger jobs, which include all custom home construction, you should have a professional project manager who can ride herd on the contractor and verify that the required work has actually been completed before any payments are made. If you are building a house, your architect can take this role. If he's not willing to or if your project isn't quite that ambitious, it might be worth your while to spend a few more dollars and hire a building inspector. The point is, you need an objective third party who is knowledgeable about construction to make sure things are being done correctly and to sign off before any payments are made.

What to Watch Out For

Unlicensed Contractors

General contractors in Canada do not need to be licensed to do home renovations. That can make your life difficult if you hire a bad one. Unlicensed contractors generally do shoddy work, rarely have proper insurance, and can actually hold you responsible if they get hurt on the job.

Unlicensed contractors can actually hold you responsible if they get hurt on the job.

To be fair, most people don't deliberately hire a shoddy contractor. They get tricked into it. Here are some warning signs:

- He can't or won't show you his license or supply references.
- He doesn't have an office you can visit.
- He claims he can do the job for much less than anyone else.
- He insists on a large down payment—or even payment in full—before he will start work.
- He says you won't need any permits for jobs that involve electrical, plumbing, or structural work, or he asks you to get the permits yourself.

- He suggests you can make it easier for yourself by paying him off the books in cash, or he offers you a discount in return for letting him use your home as an example of his work.

You should be especially wary of contractors who try to pressure you into having home-improvement work done immediately. If they tell you your roof is about to collapse or your water heater to explode, before you sign a contract obligating you to thousands of dollars in repair work, spend a couple of hundred dollars to hire an inspector who can give you an informed, objective second opinion.

Contractors Who Show Up at Your Door

One of the oldest home-repair scams is for a guy to show up at your door claiming he's a licensed contractor who "just finished a job down the street" and noticed something wrong with your house. Don't hire anyone who shows up uninvited at your door, no matter how persuasive they may sound.

And if you do get talked into signing anything, keep in mind that, by law, you usually have a few days in most provinces to back out of any purchase made at your home. Even worse, if you get talked into writing a cheque, call your bank immediately and put in a "stop payment" order.

Storm Chasers and Disaster Vultures

Contractor scams are especially prevalent after disasters—when government and insurance money is pouring into a region, there's lots of work that needs to be done quickly, and homeowners are desperate for help. As tough as it may be, this is a time to be more careful than ever. In particular, you should beware of anyone claiming to be a government-certified contractor, electrician, roofer, or plumber. Neither the federal nor provincial governments certify building trades professionals. What's more, all government staff workers and inspectors carry photo identification; ask to see it if you're approached by a stranger claiming to work for a governmental organization.

"Cost-Plus" Contracts

Some contractors will try to talk you into what's called a cost-plus contract, claiming it will save you money. Don't believe it.

Under a cost-plus contract, instead of setting a fixed price for your project in advance, you agree to pay whatever the contractor's costs turn out to be plus a percentage (usually 8% to 25%) for overhead and profits. The problem, of course, is that with a cost-plus arrangement, the contractor has absolutely no incentive to try to keep expenses down.

What you want is a fixed-price contract. That way, it's in the contractor's interest to watch costs—since the more he spends, the less likely he is to turn a profit.

Losing Your House to a Lien

Contractors and subcontractors who haven't been paid in full can file what's called a mechanic's lien against your home. A mechanic's lien is a legal claim on a piece of real estate made by someone who is owed money for supplying either the labour or materials to improve that real estate. If one is placed on your house, you won't be able to transfer the title until it's cleared. And in the most extreme case, you could be forced into foreclosure.

To guard against this happening to you, you should insist on getting a lien release or waiver every time you pay a bill from a contractor, supplier, or subcontractor. If they won't give you the release, don't give them the cheque.

On bigger projects, of course, your contractor will be paying most of the bills. But you can still stay on top of the situation. One of the main protections homeowners have is that a subcontractor or supplier can't file a mechanic's lien unless he previously filed a notice of intent when he first started work. In fact, among the most disconcerting aspects of building a house or doing a major remodel is that early on in the project you start getting legal notices from all the suppliers and subcontractors warning that if they are not paid, they will put a lien on your house. The good thing about this is that it gives you a complete record of everyone your contractor is dealing with.

You shouldn't make your final payment to your contractor until you have verified that he's gotten lien releases from all his subcontractors and suppliers.

With this knowledge in hand, the most important advice I can share is you shouldn't make your final payment to your contractor until you have verified that he's gotten lien releases from all his subcontractors and suppliers.

What to Do if Things Go Wrong

You'll find a list of consumer protection agencies in each province at the web site of the Consumer Information Gateway (**http://consumerinformation.ca**). The Gateway's an invaluable tool in itself for preparing and filing a complaint. It shows you how to do it, who to contact, even what to say when you complain.

Canada's Office of Consumer Affairs also lists all the provincial consumer ministries, with email addresses, phone numbers and websites (www.ic.gc.ca), as well as contact information for the Financial Consumer Agency of Canada and the Canadian Competition Bureau.

In general, if you suspect fraud or cannot get a contractor to finish work you've paid or contracted for, complain to your province's consumer affairs office. You should also complain to your local consumer protection agency and the local chapter of the Better Business Bureau (www.ccbbb.ca).

Fight for Your Money Action Steps

- ☐ Hire a reliable, trustworthy team, including an architect and a contractor—and possibly a project manager. Get recommendations, check credentials, and get copies of licenses.
- ☐ Comparison-shop to make your budget detailed and realistic. Once your budget plan is written up—stick to it!
- ☐ Have a contract drawn up. Everything needs to be in writing. (See page 186.)
- ☐ Never make your final payment to your contractor until you have verified that he's gotten lien releases from all his subcontractors.

Home-based Business Opportunities

We've all seen the ads tacked onto telephone poles, peeking out of the classified section of the newspaper, and popping up on computer screens.

"Make big money without leaving home!"

"Earn $1,400 a week stuffing envelopes!"

"Receive $1,000 or more per day by simply returning phone calls!"

"No selling! No explaining! No meetings!"

"Immediate income! No experience necessary!"

Who wouldn't jump at deals like that? The problem, of course, is that virtually all of them are scams. Instead of enabling you to "make big money fast," as the ads typically promise, they often wind up costing you anywhere from several hundred to several thousand dollars—and in some cases, they can even get you mixed up in illegal schemes that could leave you subject to arrest and criminal prosecution.

How to Fight for Your Money

Thousands of Canadians are duped each year by would-be employers promising work-at-home paydays that never materialized. There are so many of them that work-at-home schemes are on the U.S. National Consumers League's list of Top 10 Frauds.

Typically, work-at-home rip-offs involve phony opportunities to make big bucks doing simple tasks like stuffing envelopes, assembling small products or crafts, or processing medical insurance claims. What the ads don't tell you is that before you can start raking in the dough, you've first got to take a training course (which costs you money) and order software or supplies (which cost you even more money). And then all a lot of them do is merely send you a list of potential clients—most of whom have absolutely no interest in hiring home workers to do anything.

Not All Home-based Businesses Are Scams

The good news is that there actually *are* legitimate home-based business opportunities, where you can make your own schedule, working when you like, as much or as little as you like. None of them will make you a fortune, but they won't swindle you out of any money either. While I don't personally endorse any companies, legitimate work-at-home jobs include:

DATA ENTRY. Companies like e-adjuster (www.e-djuster.com), which processes claims for insurance companies, occasionally use home-based workers to type information into computers for electronic processing and storage.

CUSTOMER-SERVICE REPRESENTATIVE. We've all heard how big companies have outsourced their call centres to India, but in fact many North Americans earn around $8 an hour handling customer-service calls in their own homes. U.S. companies hire most of the home-based workers for these jobs, and they will not employ Canadians. But you can occasionally find similar jobs on the web site of www.workopolis.com.

MYSTERY SHOPPING. This may sound like a scam, but market research firms really do pay people to visit stores posing as typical customers and then provide what are called "customer experience evaluations"—essentially, a review of how you liked the place. Rates can run from $5 to $100 for each evaluation. Among the more reputable mystery-shopping contractors are ICC Decisions Services (www.iccds.com), Corporate Research International Mystery Shops (www.mysteryshops.com), Mystery Guest (www.mysteryguestinc.com), and Service Intelligence Experience Exchange (www.experienceexchange.com).

SURVEY TAKING. Market research firms also pay consumers to participate in online surveys and focus groups. The pay isn't great. You might earn $10 to $15 for filling out a long questionnaire. But then the work is pretty easy. You can sign up online with firms like American Consumer Opinion (www.acop.com) and Survey Savvy (www.surveysavvy.com).

Be Skeptical—Appearances Can Be Deceiving

No matter how legitimate a home-based business opportunity may seem, investigate it thoroughly before you sign on. Don't be taken in by a slick-looking web site or fancy marketing materials. These days, anyone with a laptop and some halfway decent software can make themselves look like a Fortune 500 company.

As a rule, you should always check with your local Better Business Bureau and your provincial consumer affairs department to see if either the company or its owner has been the subject of complaints. Of course, not finding any complaints doesn't mean this company is clean. Unscrupulous operators generally change business names or move to avoid detection. You might also post a question about the company on a work-at-home forum like whydowork.com to see if other people have ever encountered the firm and to find out if it's legitimate.

> **Unscrupulous operators generally change business names or move to avoid detection.**

What this means is that once you've completed the initial checks, it's up to you to ask the promoter some hard questions. What tasks will you have to perform? Will you be paid a salary or commission? Who will pay you and when can you expect your first cheque? Will you have to pay for anything, including supplies, training, equipment, and membership fees?

If you don't get specific answers or the promoter tells you that you will have to fork over any money in advance, bail.

What to Watch Out For

Work-at-home scams are generally not that hard to spot. There are almost always at least two dead giveaways:

- They will claim you can make pots of money by doing work that requires very little effort or experience.
- They will ask you to send *them* some money upfront for instructions or supplies.

These scams come in numerous varieties, but here are five of the most common ones.

The Old Envelope-Stuffing Scam

Who wouldn't want to earn $350 a week just for stuffing envelopes in the comfort of your own home? Lots of ads say you can. In fact, in 2007, thousands of people around the country responded to a classified ad claiming you could earn at least $17.50 an envelope and be guaranteed a weekly income of as much as $1,400. All you had to do to get started was pay a $45 registration fee.

By the time authorities caught up with him, the Florida man who had placed the ad had swindled more than 25,000 people out of more than $1.2 million.

Envelope stuffing happens to be one of the oldest work-at-home scams, dating back to the 1930s. The fact is, there isn't any such business as home-based envelope stuffing. Companies that need envelopes stuffed either do it themselves or outsource it to firms that use sophisticated machinery that work much faster—and more cheaply—than any human being. So don't be taken in.

Phony Medical Claims Processing

I got an email recently from a 62-year-old woman named Anna, who told me about her experience with another classic work-at-home rip-off. Anna is disabled, and when she saw an ad from a health care services outfit offering the opportunity to make good money processing medical claims on her home computer, she jumped at it.

The first thing the company told her was that she had to pay $195 for training. So she borrowed money from a friend and signed up.

During her training, which consisted of three 20-minute phone calls, Anna drew constant praise for how quickly she was catching on. But when she finished her training and was ready to start earning the big bucks, the cheers turned to jeers. The company sent her a bunch of claims to process, but each time she turned them in, they said her work was unacceptable and refused to pay her a dime.

Eventually, Anna figured out that there never really was any work. The claims she had been sent to process were phonies. All the company wanted from her was that $195 training fee. As it turned out, she was hardly the only victim of that particular scam. The same health care services company also swindled at least 67 other people out of a total of $13,000.

If anything, Anna may have gotten off easy. Medical-billing scammers sometimes charge thousands of dollars for training, software, and what they describe as a list of potential clients. Usually, the client lists they provide are nothing more than out-of-date professional directories, not rosters of people who have asked for help. In fact, most doctors' offices process their own claims, and the ones that do contract out their billing use established firms.

Small-Products Assembly

Another popular scam involves work-at-home deals where you're hired at some exorbitant piece-work rate to assemble small products or crafts—usually things likes stuffed clowns, Christmas bells, artisan earrings, crosses, or baby burping pads. The technique here is similar to that of the claims-processing scam. Once you sign up—and pay a fee that's often several hundred dollars—the employer will send you supplies and instructions. But when you send back the assembled goods, the company typically refuses to pay—claiming that your work doesn't meet its standards.

Two Work-at-Home "Opportunities" That Can Get You Arrested

There's actually something worse than being swindled out of your money by a work-at-home scam. It's being swindled out of your money—*and then getting arrested for your trouble.* This really can happen if you fall for one of the two most terrible home-business rip-offs around today: work-at-home shipping and work-at-home payment processing.

In the shipping scam, you're promised big bucks simply to receive, repack, and then re-ship merchandise, usually to a foreign address. The catch is that the merchandise is stolen goods, usually the result of credit card fraud, and what you're doing by receiving and sending it on is participating in a fencing operation. When the police come knocking on your door—and they usually do before very long—you're going to have a hard time convincing them you didn't know what was going on.

Payment-processing scams are even worse. Scammers recruit unsuspecting people by offering them lucrative home-based opportunities to work as a sales representative or transfer manager processing payments and transferring funds. The way it works is that you give them your bank information so that money can be transferred into your account and then you use a wire-transfer service to send the proceeds to some other account, usually out of the country. For your trouble, you are promised a commission of as much as 10% of all the transfers you handle.

Sounds simple enough—but what you're really doing is helping criminals launder money.

An even crueler variation on this scam is one in which you are sent certified cheques or money orders, which you are instructed to take to your bank and cash. You are then supposed to bring the cash—sometimes tens of thousands of dollars—to the nearest Western Union office and wire it all to an offshore account. In fact, the cheques and money orders are actually forgeries, and when the bank discovers this—usually a day or two after you have wired the money to your employers—you are the one who will be held responsible for paying it back. In other words, you're now guilty of money laundering, forgery, and theft—*and* you owe the bank several thousand dollars that you may not have any way of repaying.

What to Do if Things Go Wrong

If you find you have been swindled by a phony work-at-home operation, your best chance to recover your money is to make a lot of noise.

Start by calling the company you believe is scamming you and ask for a refund. Let company representatives know that you'll be contacting the authorities—and possibly the media as well—about your experience.

Keep a record of all your conversations and correspondence as well as the time you spend trying to obtain the refund. Send all correspondence via certified mail, return receipt requested, to document what the company received from you.

If you get the cold shoulder, go to the authorities. This includes your province's consumer affairs department (which you can find at **http://consumerinformation.ca** under Related Sites, Provincial), PhoneBusters.com, local law enforcement, the Better Business Bureau, and the news media.

You should also contact Competition Bureau Canada (**www.competitionbureau.gc.ca**) at 1-800-348-5358.

Being a squeaky wheel really can work. After Anna, the disabled woman who signed up to process medical claims, took her complaint to the Better Business Bureau, the BBB contacted a local television station, which then called the owner of the company that had swindled her. Two days later, Anna got a cheque refunding her $195 training fee.

Fight for Your Money Action Steps

- ☐ If it sounds to good to be true, it usually is. Claims that a work-from-home opportunity will earn you tons of cash with little time, effort, and experience simply aren't true.
- ☐ If you're asked to send money upfront for supplies or instructions, walk away.
- ☐ Identify legitimate opportunities only after fully checking out the company and getting all your questions answered to your satisfaction.

RPPs and RRSPs

Nothing you will do in your lifetime other than buy a home will impact your wealth more than deciding to set up a Registered Retirement Savings Plan (RRSP) for yourself and to enroll in your employer's Registered Pension Plan, Group RRSP or Deferred Profit Sharing Plan (DPSP) at work. Depending on where you work and what kind of retirement benefits your employer provides, you can take one or all of these steps. We'll get to the details in a moment.

No matter how you do it, you have to make sure you pay yourself first. If you've read any of my previous books, you'll know that I believe in making this process as easy as possible. You can arrange to have your employer's pension plan take your regular contributions automatically. You should make the contributions to your own personal pension plan automatic, as well.

Now you'll have a portion of your paycheque deposited directly into your employer's pension plan and another, usually smaller, portion deposited directly into your RRSP. All of this forces you to pay yourself first—and if you start young enough, this alone will make you financially secure. In fact, if you do it right and save enough, paying yourself first this way will make you a millionaire.

Registered Retirement Savings Plans

There's no getting around it —contributing as much as you can to a Registered Retirement Savings Plan is almost always a true no-brainer.

Why? Well, for one thing, fewer employers offer traditional pensions anymore. For another, the Canada Pension Plan (CPP) and Old Age Security (OAS) system will probably not provide you with enough money in your retirement years to cover more than the basic necessities. The CPP was designed to provide about one-quarter of your income. As for OAS, the program pays a maximum of $516 a month, but you have to repay some or all of it as soon as your income from all sources exceeds about $65,000. You might think that $65,000 is a lot of money, but by the time you're ready to retire, you might not think so. In any case, the median income in Canada for an entire family is about $55,000 a year. If you take a quarter of that amount and add another $500 a month, you'll still end up with about $20,000 a year for you and your partner, wife or husband, and that's assuming that you're both eligible for CPP and OAS in the first place.

So don't be short sighted. Think long term. An RRSP is probably your best shot at being able to enjoy a decent—and potentially fantastic—retirement. This is not just theory. It is real. During my days as a financial planner at Morgan Stanley I worked closely with many clients who were able to retire as millionaires—in many cases, multimillionaires—simply because they had set up their RRSPs early in their careers.

Making the RRSP "No-Brainer" Decision Intelligently

Just because an RRSP is a no-brainer doesn't mean you can set it up and then stop thinking about it. The fact is that the people who administer managed RRSPs, which is the way most Canadians set them up, don't always have your best interests at heart.

Don't misunderstand me here—the basic idea and intention of the RRSP program is a great one, and most banks, fund companies, and, other financial institutions that offer them really want to do something good for the plan holder. But the big banks, brokerage firms, and insurance companies that administer these plans are in the business for one reason and one reason only—to make as much money as they can.

With a self-directed RRSP, you can choose the way you invest your contributions. That means you can invest in anything from equities to Canada Savings Bonds to mutual funds to exchange-traded funds. The decision is up to you.

With a managed RRSP, the financial institution that manages the fund usually decides where to put the money, and it's not surprising to find that your money usually ends up in a mutual fund or GIC sold by the financial institution itself.

For people who don't want to think about their investments from one year to the next, this might seem fine. But when you consider that some of these mutual funds charge a management fee of as much as 3% of the investment, it's worth paying attention. That fee means that you have to make a return of 3% just to break even and hang on to the full amount that you invested. With interest rates around 2% at the time of writing, you may not break even at all, let alone make enough on your investment to build your retirement nest egg. So you should think twice before you choose a managed RRSp, even if it seems to offer the easiest route to retirement saving.

Financial institutions may siphon as much as 3% of all the money we've got invested in their products through managed RRSPs.

How to Fight for Your Money

As of 2008, some 6.3 million Canadian workers had invested in RRSPs over the previous year. But the $34.1 billion that they invested in their plans amounted to only 6% of the total amount that eligible Canadians could have invested. In other words, Canadians could have invested a total of more than $500 billion in their RRSPs if everyone had taken full advantage of the program. They could have deducted their contributions from their taxable income, reducing the taxes they paid in 2008. And the money that they sheltered in their RRSPs would have grown tax-free. By the time you start withdrawing your contributions, you will have had the opportunity to make full use of the miracle of compound interest and you will likely be in a lower tax bracket than you are now.

You don't pay a cent in taxes on the earnings you put into the plan or on any of the returns your money generates over the years.

What an opportunity!

What makes it even more baffling is that fewer and fewer Canadian workers—only about 38%—are covered by their employers' pension plans. Even though RRSPs are not perfect, if you are eligible for an one, you should definitely take advantage of the opportunity. One big reason is that they entitle you to FREE MONEY. This is too good a deal to miss out on.

A key feature of these plans is that you get to decide how much money you put in and how it will be invested. Having this kind of control can be great, but it also means there are no guarantees. How much money you will have at retirement will depend mainly on what kind of investment decisions you make along the way. So you've got to pay attention.

You don't pay a cent in taxes on the earnings you put into the plan or on any of the returns your money generates over the years.

The impact all this can have on your ability to build wealth is phenomenal. If you're like most people, the government normally grabs about 30 cents from every dollar you earn before you ever even see the money. That leaves you with only about 70 cents. But when you make a contribution to an RRSP, you get to do so with the entire dollar. It's now the government that gets bypassed. This is what gives tax-deferred investments such a terrific advantage over regular investments. The following table shows just how terrific they are.

	RRSP (Pretax)	Regular Investment (Taxable)
Gross income	$1.00	$1.00
Taxes deducted	−0	−30%
Amount available to invest	$1.00	$0.70
Annual return	+ 10%	+ 10%
Balance after one year	$1.10	$0.77
Are gains taxable?	No	Yes

How much would you rather have after a year—$1.10 or 77 cents? This is a no-brainer. But wait—it might get better. If your company is one of those that offer to match a percentage of employee retirement contributions in a Group RRSP, you could come out really far ahead.

	Group RRSP (with Employer Match)	Regular Investment (Taxable)
Gross income	$1.00	$1.00
Taxes deducted	−0	−30%
Amount available to invest	$1.00	$0.70
Typical employer match	+ 25%	0
Amount invested	$1.25	$0.70
Annual return	+ 10%	+ 10%
Balance after one year	$1.38	$0.77
Are gains taxable?	No	Yes

Think about it—$1.38 vs. 77 cents. You get almost a 100% increase in your net savings simply by using a Group RRSP! That's huge—and it's only year one.

The catch, to the extent that there is one, is that if you take out any money before you're 71, you have to pay a withholding tax of as much as 30% of the amount you withdraw. That means that, if you take $18,000 out of your RRSP before you're eligible to start making withdrawals, your financial institution or bank that administers your RRSP will withhold $5,400.

Here are some key tips to making the most of your RRSP opportunity.

Aim to "Max Out" the Plan

The first decision you have to make when you open an RRSP is how much of your income you're going to contribute every pay period. You can figure out the total amount that you're eligible to contribute by checking the back of your previous year's tax assessment from the Canada Revenue Agency (CRA). On the back of the assessment, you'll find a line that says "Your RRSP deduction limit." This tells you how much pre-tax money you can invest, tax-free, within your own personal RRSP. If you can't find your assessment, you can call the CRA hotline in your area, listed in the Blue Pages of your phone book. (Have your Social Insurance Number handy.)

Based on this amount, you can then figure out how much you want to contribute from every paycheque. I recommend that you contribute the maximum amount, if you can. I also recommend that you make your contributions automatic. You can do this in several ways: through payroll deductions, where money is automatically taken out of your paycheque and transferred directly to your RRSP; through automatic withdrawals after your employer deposits your paycheck electronically into your chequing account, or through an online bill payment service that you've set up to withdraw a specified amount to deposit into your RRSP every week or month.

No matter how you do it, your goal should be to max out the plan. This means making the maximum contribution every year. As of 2008, the CRA allowed you put 18% of your earned income, up to a maximum of $20,000 a year, into an RRSP. In 2009, the maximum rises to $21,000, and it goes up to $22,000 in 2010. Beyond that, the ceilings will be adjusted annually to keep up with inflation.

Your goal should be to "max out" the plan.

Putting aside $1,000 OR $2,000 OR $3,000 a year may not sound like much, but don't forget the power of compound interest. If at age 25 you started putting $250 a month (or $3,000 a year) into an RRSP that earned an annual return of 10%, by the time you were 65, you'd have a nest egg worth nearly $1.6 million. Even if you waited until you were 40 to get started, you'd still wind up with a hefty sum—roughly $335,000.

Obviously, the earlier you start, the easier it is to accumulate major wealth. Still, it's really never too late to begin. Some money is better than no money.

Begin by Saving One Hour a Day of Your Income

Even though I just said that your goal you should be to "max out" your RRSP contribution, I am a realist. I know you may read this and say to yourself, "There's no way I can save the maximum that my plan allows." Saving $20,000 or 18% of your salary may seem impossible. But you can do it.

The trick is not to think about percentages. Instead, when it comes to funding your retirement plan, think in terms of how many hours you work each week. If you work a 40-hour work week, I believe you DESERVE to at least keep one hour a day of your income. That's five hours of income a week—or 12½% of your gross income. If you are starting late on your road to retirement savings, your goal should be to save the absolute maximum–1.4 hours a day—or 18% of your income.

Right now, only one-quarter of the Canadians who contribute to an RRSP put in the maximum amount. The rest don't come anywhere close to the maximum. When you consider that we are trading our time for a paycheque, the idea that you deserve to keep 1.4 hours a day of what you are working for seems to me like the ultimate no-brainer.

Right now, only one-quarter of Canadians who contribute to an RRSP save the maximum amount.

If you have to start small and feel the most you can save is, say, 4% of your income (which amounts to just under 20 minutes a day), then make it a goal to increase that percentage periodically—every month, if your plan allows it. Remember, if you started out putting just 1% of your salary into your RRSP and then raised your contribution rate by 1% each month, within a year you would be at the one-hour-a-day goal I suggested—and you would be saving a lot more than the average Canadian saves.

With Pensions, Everyone Gets the Same Tax Break!

No matter what type of plan—Registered Pension Plan set up by your employer or a Registered Retirement Savings Plan set up by you—or even if your employer has no pension plan at all, the combined contributions of the employer and employee to a registered pension plan or RRSP are tax-deductible up to a specified amount.

The government wants to make sure that all Canadians get the same tax breaks when they save for their retirement, and this means getting the same tax advantages. An employee who belongs to his private employer's RPP should not be able to make a larger tax-free contribution to his or her pension than a person who belongs to a public-sector RPP or a self-employed individual administering his or her own RRSP. They all get the same tax break on their retirement savings.

If You Have the Choice, Put Your Money Where it Will Grow

As a rule, you don't get much help when it comes to figuring out how to invest your money in an employer-sponsored pension plan, whether it's a Group RRSP or a defined-contribution plan. The folks from HR may give you a few pamphlets and the URL of a web site you can check out, but that's pretty much it. So it's no wonder that many people just stash their contributions in a savings account or Canada Savings Bond and leave it at that. That's too bad, because what they are doing is shortchanging them selves. These investments are safe, but they don't generate anywhere near the kind of returns you will need to build up a decent nest egg.

A savings account or Canada Savings Bond doesn't generate anywhere near the kind of returns you will need to build up a decent nest egg.

You need to put your money where it will grow. So take some time to learn about your investment options and, if you need it, get some professional advice on putting together an investment plan. Your goal should be to diversify your investments with a variety of mutual funds that give you wide exposure to the stock and bond markets, both in Canada and internationally. If all this seems confusing (and it should), ask your benefits office if your investment choices include a target date or life cycle fund. This is a fund specifically designed for retirement savings. These funds are just becoming popular in Canada, although they've been around in the United States for several years. Basically, with a target date fund, you pick a target date close to when you plan to retire, and the fund automatically ensures that you will have the appropriate mix of investments for someone your age—more aggressive when you're younger, gradually becoming more conservative as you approach retirement.

In the United States, money invested in these funds by workers saving for retirement increased by 100% between 2006 and 2008. Target-date funds are growing so fast in the United States that some experts believe that by 2013 they will account for 75% of all assets in certain types of pension plans.

This concerns some critics, who worry that target-date funds can be riskier than they seem. The basic idea is that as you approach retirement age your investments should be geared less toward growth and more toward capital preservation—meaning that over time you should be moving away from stocks and towards fixed-income securities. The problem is that not everyone agrees on how quickly this shift should occur. In fact, while some funds aim to have just 10% of their assets invested in stocks by the target date, the stock total for others is as high as 65%.

Still, most experts agree that a good target-date fund can do a much better job investing for your future than you can do for yourself. Indeed, a 2008 John Hancock study showed that over the previous 10 years 84% of those who selected their own pension plan investments in the United States earned an average annual return two full percentage points lower than they would have gotten by investing their money in a Hancock target-date fund.

Most experts agree that a good target-date fund can do a much better job investing for your future than you can do for yourself.

As of the summer of 2008, there were 36 target date funds in Canada offered by BMO, Fidelity, Clarington, London Life, Scotia, RBC, and a few other fund companies. How do you select the right one for you? It's tricky. Because the concept is so new, there is no accepted standard for comparing the performance of different target-date funds. Of course, when it comes to picking one for your RRSP, you may not have a choice if you have a managed RRSP with one of the companies or banks that sells this type of product. Most companies that offer target-date funds to their RRSP clients offer only one family of funds.

Since target-date funds have been around for only a short time in Canada, their rankings don't mean much, especially since many of them were set up just as the global markets became as volatile as they've been in decades.

When Your RRSP Ends

At the age of 71, you're required by law to take the money you've sheltered in your RRSP and either use it to buy an annuity or deposit it within another tax-sheltered vehicle called a Registered Retirement Income Fund (RRIF). In both cases, you'll receive a monthly income from the money that you've set aside in your RRSP. With an annuity,the monthly income depends on the kind of annuity you buy (which we'll talk about a bit later). With a RRIF, you calculate the minimum monthly payment using a formula developed by the government, based on your age. (Your RRIF administrator will make this calculation on your behalf.) You can take more than the minimum monthly payment from your RRIF, but you have to pay tax on the payment, so the more you take out, the more tax you pay.

You can hold the same investments in a RRIF as you do in your RRSP, and they accumulate tax-free. Once you've rolled your RRSP savings into a RRIF, you can't make more deposits to the fund. Otherwise, the only big difference between a RRIF and an RRSP is that you must withdraw a certain amount every month from your RRIF.

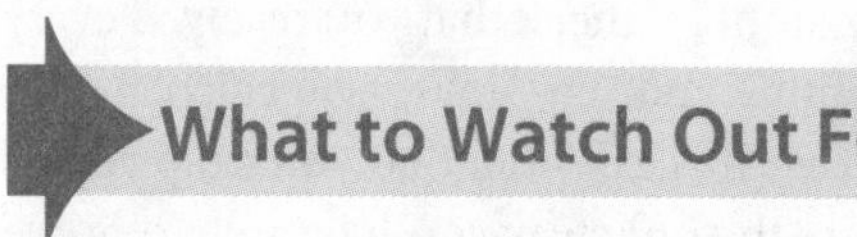

What to Watch Out For

Putting Your Nest Egg in One Basket

If you belong to a group RRSP or a defined-contribution plan, a form of employer-sponsored Registered Pension Plan, you can choose where to invest your retirement savings. Depending on your employer, your choices may include the stock of the company where you work.

In recent years, too many overly loyal employees have lost their entire nest eggs because they invested all their retirement money in the their own company's stock. Keep in mind names like Laidlaw, AIG, and Royal Trust. Until the roof fell in, everyone thought these companies were sure things—no one more than the people who worked for them.

Think about it. What happens if most of your RRSP or RPP money is invested in your own company's stock and the company goes out of business? Not only do you lose your job, but also your retirement savings at the same time. Talk about a double whammy!

In my view, you should never invest more than 10% of your retirement money in your own company's stock. In fact, I have said for years that you simply cannot afford to have more than 5% to 10% of your net worth in one stock. In the aftermath of the 2008 meltdown, I now feel this more strongly than ever.

And you should regard your company's stock as a relatively high-risk investment, even if it's a conservative company. This is because owning a single stock reduces your diversification—and therefore increases your risk.

An Overly Long Vesting Schedule

While your own pension contributions always belong to you, the money your employer puts in your account may not really be yours until you have worked for the company for a certain number of years. If you leave the company before then, you get a refund of your contributions, but you may not be entitled to any benefits based on your employer's contributions.

The entitlement process is called vesting. Typically, it takes only two or three years for you to be fully vested—that is, to enjoy full ownership of your employer's contributions. In Ontario, for example, you become vested after two years of continuous membership in a plan. Make sure you understand your company's vesting schedule. And don't count on that money until it's really yours.

And when you leave your company, double-check that you received every penny of your vested funds. Don't assume your employer will calculate the amount correctly. This is one reason that it is essential that you keep copies of all your pension statements. They are the only way you'll be able to prove anything if your employer did make a mistake.

What to Do if Things Go Wrong

Be alert for mistakes on your retirement account. Check your pension statements regularly to make sure your account is being properly credited. Notify your employer at the first sign of a problem, and always do it in writing. If you can't get the issue resolved, or if you suspect that your employer is stealing money from the plan, complain to the plan administrator, if applicable. The administrator will likely be a financial institution or insurance company.

You can also contact the Financial Services OmbudsNetwork (**www.fson.org**) and the Canadian Consumer Information Gateway (**http://consumerinformation.ca**) about irregularities in your employer's pension plan.

Fight for Your Money Action Steps

- ☐ Make the decision to pay yourself first!
- ☐ Make sure you're signed up for your retirement plan at work.
- ☐ Start contributing at least one hour a day of your income, with the ultimate aim of maxing out your plan.
- ☐ Investigate your investment options and allocate your savings in order to build your nest egg.
- ☐ Avoid borrowing money from your account—and don't cash it out when you leave an employer!

Pension Plans

The traditional pension plan is generally a great deal. You don't have to contribute anything yourself and, as long as you put in a certain number of years on the job, once you retire you're guaranteed a set monthly benefit for the rest of your life.

Unfortunately, like most great deals, traditional pension plans are no longer as common as they used to be. As I mentioned earlier, about 38% of employees in Canada belong to an employer-sponsored registered pension plan (RPP). The vast majority—about 80% of them, almost 4.6 million workers—belong to what's called a defined-benefit plan.

If you do have a pension coming to you, you definitely have a leg up on retirement. But don't assume your golden years are all set. As millions of workers have discovered in recent years, just because you're entitled to a pension doesn't mean you're actually going to get it. Faced with tough economic conditions, as we are at the time of writing in 2008, an increasing number of companies are cutting back their pension plans or getting rid of them entirely. Although a company can't take away benefits you've already earned, it can eliminate those you were expecting to earn in the future. This is particularly a risk when companies merge.

In the United States, companies like Boeing, Coca-Cola, Dupont, and IBM either stopped offering pensions to new employees or terminated their plans entirely between 2005 and 2008. The same trend hasn't occurred in Canada, although pension experts wonder if it will, especially in the volatile markets of 2008.

Under the economic conditions prevailing over 2007 and 2008, your plan may be seriously underfunded, which means it may not have enough money to pay out all the benefits that it's supposed to. The Office of the Superintendent of Financial Institutions Canada (OSFI), which regulates about 1,200 federal pension plans for large corporations such as banks, airlines, and telecommunication companies, reported recently that about half of them were fully funded, up from only one-quarter in 2006. That means that, under federal regulation, the plans have enough money to meet their obligations to plan members. But as the economy went topsy-turvy in 2008, though, the Bank of Canada said that more than six in 10 Canadian chief financial officers had reported their defined benefit plans face severe problems. Pension plans, like all investments, go through ups and downs, and the regulations that govern them are based on very conservative estimates. So you shouldn't panic, even if your employer's fund is among the ones that are underfunded.

In any case, the good news is that you don't have to be a victim. There are steps you can take to protect yourself. It's simply a matter of educating yourself and asking the right questions.

How to Fight for Your Money

Make Sure You Know the Rules—Get the Summary Plan Description

Every pension plan is different, so it's important to know the rules governing yours. When you go to work for a company or government agency that offers workers a pension plan, you're supposed to be given, by law, an information package that describes your rights and obligations regarding the plan. The package also describes how your pension plan works—what your benefits are, how they're calculated, what you need to do to earn them, and so on. Make sure to read this document and then put it in a safe place. And make sure you keep a record of the plan's registration number and whether it's registered with the province where you work or with OSFI, which regulates pensions federally. (If your employer never gave you one, or if you can't find it, ask your plan administrator for a copy.) You should also read and save any notices you get from your employer about changes to the plan. The old rules will still apply to the benefits you've already accrued, but the new rules will govern all future benefits. If you want to know more about how your plan works—especially if you have concerns about how it's being managed— ask your plan administrator for a copy of the full plan document.

Keep a Record of Your Work History

Since your pension benefits depend largely on how long you worked for your employer and how much you earned, it's vital that you keep as complete a record of your work history as possible. Don't assume that the HR department will have an accurate record.

You need to keep your own records in case you wind up in a dispute with your employer. Keeping each year's final pay stub is generally the easiest way to do this. If you started or stopped employment during the year, note that on the stub.

Know the Vesting Rules

By law, you're entitled to pension benefits after you've belonged to a pension plan for a certain continuous period. In most plans regulated provincially and federally, that period is usually two years. This requirement is known as vesting. Every employer has its own vesting policy, and it's essential that you understand yours if you want to be able to make an intelligent decision about when to leave your job.

Many pension plans also have other service thresholds that confer additional benefits. For example, if you stay at least 20 years, you may be entitled to start collecting full benefits at age 59, rather than 65. After 30 years, you might be entitled to retire with full benefits whenever you like, regardless of how old you are.

Sometimes staying in a job just a few months longer than you planned can be worth tens of thousands of dollars.

So if you're considering leaving a job that comes with a pension plan, make sure you figure your employer's vesting rules into your calculations. Sometimes staying in a job just a few months longer than you planned can be worth thousands of dollars in pension benefits.

Use the Pension Formula to Your Advantage

Most pension benefits are calculated using your most recent earnings, such as the average of the highest three out of the last five years or the highest five out of the last fifteen. With this in mind, you may be able to increase your pension by ramping up overtime work that increases your total compensation during those crucial years. Similarly, you may want to avoid doing anything that will decrease compensation during those years—such as switching to part-time status. Check your plan documents and consult with your plan administrator to see what makes sense for you.

Review Your Payout Options *Very* Carefully

Deciding how you want your pension benefits paid out to you is one of the most important decisions you will make for the rest of your life. Consider getting professional advice from an unbiased source before doing anything other than taking a joint benefit that will include survivors' benefits for your spouse.

If you are offered the option of taking a lump-sum payout (as opposed to monthly payments for the rest of your life), ask an accountant or financial planner to compare its value to the value of regular payments. A lump sum can be a smart choice if you manage the money well, but this requires a detailed review of whether or not your money-management efforts generate a better return than the fixed payment offered by the pension plan. It can also be smart if your pension fund is underfunded and you have doubts about whether you'll actually receive all the benefits to which you're entitled. Then again, if you opt for a lump sum with the idea of investing it and living off the proceeds, you have to be prepared for the risk of losses as well as gains. And you may be giving up such valuable benefits as cost-of-living adjustments and extended health insurance.

You will also have to decide between a "single life" benefit, which you get as long as you live but ends when you die, or a "joint and survivor" payout, which your spouse would continue to receive even if you were to die before him or her. The single life benefit generally gives you a bigger monthly cheque, which makes it a reasonable choice if you expect to outlive your spouse. But if you expect to leave your spouse behind, the lower joint payment makes more sense. Given that women tend to live longer than men, it's not surprising that 69% of married women go for the single life payment, while 72% of married men choose the joint payment option.

Insurance agents often suggest that if you expect your spouse to outlive you, there is a way you can take the more lucrative single payout and still protect your surviving spouse. What they propose is that you protect your spouse by using the extra income from the single life benefit to buy a life insurance policy that will provide your spouse with a lump-sum payout that, if managed correctly, could be worth a lot more than the continuing joint pension benefit. It's a clever idea, but be wary. Would your spouse really be able to manage a lump-sum insurance payout to produce the same income as the survivor benefit? What's more, under this scheme, your surviving spouse would miss out on the extended health insurance and other advantages that often go along with a survivor's benefit.

Don't Give Up Your Spousal Benefits Without a Fight

A spouse must agree to give up his or her survivor benefits. If your spouse is the one with the pension and he or she wants to take the single life option, don't sign away your rights without getting the opinion of an unbiased advisor. There are times it makes sense and times that it doesn't. One time it definitely doesn't is if you are getting divorced, in which case you should make sure your spouse's pension is part of the negotiations.

What to Watch Out For

Employer Mistakes

Employers can and do make mistakes when figuring pension benefits, especially when there have been changes in plan rules over the course of your employment. So when you receive your pension plan statements, double-check the pension calculations.

Often, a company that has reduced the size of its annual pension contribution (say from 1.5% of a participant's salary to just 1%) will mistakenly calculate retirees' pension benefits as if the lower percentage applied to all their years of service even if they worked some of them when the higher rate was still in effect. Other common errors include inaccurate or incomplete records, such as an incorrect date of birth or failing to include bonuses in the participant's total compensation. Since even a small error can cost you tens of thousands of dollars in benefits, go over your statements carefully.

Shaky Finances

Given the growing concern about pension plan underfunding, it's a good idea to learn as much as you can about the state of your plan's finances. As I noted earlier, if they are shaky and you're approaching retirement, you might want to consider taking your benefits in the form of a lump-sum payout.

You can generally get information about your pension plans directly from your agency's plan administrator. You'll likely receive an annual report from your pension plan administrator that lists your plan's assets and liabilities, funded status over the past three years, and how the assets are invested. You may also get more information from the government commission that regulates pension plans in the province. In Ontario, for example, where plans covering almost half the pension-plan participants in Canada are registered, you can get detailed information about your pension plan at the web site of the Financial Services Commission of Ontario (FSCO) at **www.fsco.gov.on.ca**. To do this, you'll need your plan's registration number.

If you find anything in these reports that troubles or confuses you, ask your plan administrator for a full explanation.

Losing Touch with an Old Employer's Plan

You don't have to work for someone until you're 65 to be entitled to a pension. As long as you worked long enough to be vested, you may be eligible for a pension benefit from an employer you left many years before you reached retirement age. Most people transfer their accumulated pension savings to their new employer when they leave their old one or take the savings in the form of a tax-sheltered locked-in RRSP. But if you chose instead to leave your accumulated pension savings with your old employer's plan, you should make sure you always keep your employer informed of your current address, regardless of whether or not you still work for the company.

You may be eligible for a pension benefit from an employer you left many years before.

If you've neglected to do this, write to the company's pension plan administrator today. If the company is no longer around—or if it claims to have no record that you ever worked for it—you should contact your province's pension commission.

If Your Employer Goes Out of Business

Your pension investments are protected in a number of different ways, depending on your location and the type of plan. Group RRSPs, for example, may be protected by the Canada Deposit Insurance Corporation (CDIC), which I discussed earlier in the chapter about banks. CDIC guarantees deposits and other types of savings on deposit with financial institutions.

With defined-contribution plans and group RRSPs, you control the money that's deposited on your behalf for your pension. Even if your employer goes out of business, the insurance company or trust company that holds the money for you and your company's other employees will continue to administer your pension savings as long as you want them to continue.

With defined-benefit plans, provincial or federal regulators try to ensure that plans have enough money or funding to meet their obligations in the future. When they become underfunded, employers are required by law to deposit more money in their plans. In Ontario, most employers of defined benefit plans belong to the Pensions Benefits Guarantee Fund. Even if the plan can't meet its obligations, the PBGF guarantees certain benefits. Pension plans registered in Ontario cover about half the employees in Canada with employer-sponsored pension plans. In the rest of the provinces, though, there's no similar program, so you should check with your employer to see if they've made some other arrangement to guarantee your pension.

What to Do if Things Go Wrong

If you have a problem with a company pension that your plan administrator is not willing or able to resolve, you should check with your federal or provincial pension regulator.

In Ontario, where most pension plans are registered, you can write to:

Pension Plans Branch
Financial Services Commission of Ontario
5160 Yonge Street, Box 85
Toronto, Ontario
M2N 6L9

In other provinces, you should contact your province's pension commission or regulatory body, listed under Links on the website of the Office of the Superintendent of Financial Institutions Canada (**www.osfi-bsif.gc.ca**). If you work for a bank, airline, railway, or other federally regulated organization, OSFI itself handles pension-related matters.

Fight for Your Money Action Steps

- ☐ Find your pension plan document. If you don't have it, get a copy from your plan administrator.
- ☐ Create a work history file for your records.
- ☐ Educate yourself on the state of your plan's finances.
- ☐ Consult an accountant or financial planner to understand your payout options when you are considering retirement or leaving your employer.
- ☐ If you're eligible for a pension with a former employer, be sure to be in touch with the plan administrator.

Canada Pension Plan and Old Age Security

Some people, including several actuaries who work in the field of pension-plan design, suggest that people can live comfortably on their income from the Canada Pension Plan and Old Age Security when they retire. They say that your expenses are much lower by the time you retire, because you've sent the kids off to work, paid for your house, and don't go on expensive vacations anymore.

In my opinion, CPP and OAS will just keep your head above water. That's because the most anyone can possibly hope to get from Old Age Security and Guaranteed Income Supplement is about $15,000 a year. If you manage to receive more than that, the government starts to take back some of your OAS benefits.

In fact, Old Age Security was never intended to be a retirement plan. At most, it was designed to provide an income supplement.

To be fair, the people who say you can live comfortably on your CPP and OAS income are trying to put things into perspective for working people who think they should save most of their income for retirement. What's the point of living like a pauper till you turn 65, only to find that you're almost too old to enjoy all the money you've saved?

The key is to take a balanced view of retirement, including CPP and OAS, just as you do with all your other financial planning.

Canada Pension Plan

The Canada Pension Plan (CPP), which was set up in 1966, will provide you with the equivalent to 25% of your average monthly pensionable earnings.

The maximum amount you can get from your CPP, as of writing in 2008, is $884.58.

The good news is that you qualify for the CPP even if you've made only one payment to the plan over the course of your working life.

You can start collecting CPP at the age of 60, but you don't get the full monthly payment unless you wait till you're 65 to start. Before that, your payments are reduced by a certain percentage. You can also collect CPP while you're still working, if you're over 60, as long as your total income doesn't exceed the maximum monthly CPP payment of $884.58.

You can also wait until you're as old as 70 to start collecting CPP payments. The longer you wait, the more you get. For example, as the government explains at the Service Canada web site (**www.hrsdc.gc.ca**), "if you start your pension at 60, your monthly payment is 30 percent lower than if you wait until you're 65. However, by starting it sooner, you will likely receive it for a longer time. If you start your pension at 70, your monthly payment is 30 percent higher than if you had taken it at 65. There is no financial benefit in delaying receiving your pension after the age of 70."

Old Age Security

You're eligible to receive OAS payments when you turn 65, as long as you've lived in Canada for at least 10 years after you turned 18. You get the full pension if you've lived in Canada for 40 years or more.

Remember, though, that OAS is supposed to supplement your income—not provide you with all the money you'll need for your retirement. That doesn't mean that a lot of people don't depend on OAS. For the poorest families in Canada, OAS makes up more than 80% of their income.

The most anyone can possibly hope to get from Old Age Security and Guaranteed Income Supplement is about $12,600 a year. That may be okay for walking-around money, but you sure wouldn't want to have to live on it.

Guaranteed Income Supplement

If you have little or no other income than the OAS, you may be eligible for the Guaranteed Income Supplement. If you're married to someone who receives OAS payments but you're not 65 yourself, you may also be eligible for an allowance of as much as $1,000 a month.

How to Fight for Your Money

Your CPP retirement pension and OAS payments do *not* start automatically. *You must apply for them* unless you're receiving a CPP disability benefit. (If you are, your disability benefit automatically becomes a retirement pension when you turn 65.).

Your CPP retirement pension and OAS payments do not start automatically. You must apply for them.

The rules that I'm talking about now, in 2008, might change and probably will, however. So you should try to keep yourself informed about OAS and CPP, especially as you get closer to retirement age.

That's because, when it comes to complicated regulations and massive bureaucracy, these programs are right up there with the Canada Revenue Agency and the people who administer your health care program.

OAS rules in particular have been changed many times—when Spouse's Allowance was extended to all low-income widows and widowers aged 60 to 64, for example, and when same-sex common-law partners became eligible for certain benefits—and they will likely change again, so keep on top of them by reading the information packages and brochures you get from the government, your employer, and the bank. Check from time to time with the government at Service Canada (**www.hrsdc.gc.ca**) to see if any changes are in the pipeline. Don't forget, nobody is giving you any benefits—you earned them. So don't be reluctant to stand up for your rights.

Here are some other important tips to keep in mind.

Make Sure Your Earnings Record is Accurate

The size of your CPP retirement benefit is largely based on how much you paid over the years in taxes and deductions. (That's the dreaded CPP deduction on your payroll cheque.) So it's vitally important that your earnings record is accurate. Every year, the government is supposed to send you a statement listing your CPP eligibility over the course of your working life. You should contact Service Canada if you have any concerns or questions:

By telephone (toll-free)
1-800-277-9914 (for service in English)
1-800-277-9915 (for service in French)
1-800-255-4786 (TTY)
On the Web at: **www.servicecanada.gc.ca**

The CPP keeps a record for each person who pays into it, with information supplied through Canada Revenue Agency and Revenu Québec. When you receive your statement of earnings every year from your employer (called a T4 slip), you should check it to make sure your name and Social Insurance Number (SIN) are the same as they are on your SIN card. If they are not, your CPP contributions may not be credited to your CPP record. This could mean not getting benefits to which you are entitled.

Figure Out When You Want to Start Collecting

The longer you continue working, the higher your CPP retirement benefit will be until you reach the age of 70. So to get the maximum benefit, you should delay retiring as long as you can. Here's how it works.

Your retirement benefit is based on the 85% of your working years when your income was the highest. It's calculated according to your income, from a minimum of $3,500 a year to a maximum of $44,500 a year (in 2008). In making its calculation, the government drops the 15% of your working years when you made the lowest yearly income.

As I mentioned, the longer you wait to start receiving benefits (up to age 70), the bigger your benefit will be. For every year you wait to collect CPP after you turn 65, the government adds another 0.5% to your monthly payment. (Don't get too excited. On the average Canadian's CPP payment, that adds up to about $2.50.)

Based on this, you might think that waiting until 70 to start collecting benefits is a no-brainer. But that's not necessarily the case. It's true that most people who make it to retirement age will probably live into at least their early eighties. Nonetheless, I have always advised most of my clients to start collecting their CPP benefits as early as possible.

Why? Because even though most people will live long enough to take it later, many won't. Or if they do, they will struggle financially in the meantime. So I believe that even if you can live without your CPP and OAS benefits when you're 65, you should take it anyway. Use the money to help your grandchildren save for university. Take your family on a vacation. Enjoy your life with the extra money! And if you do need the money, you'll be glad to get it.

I believe that even if you can live without your CPP and OAS benefit when you're 65, you should take it anyway.

Many experts disagree with this approach. But the bottom line is that the question of when to start taking CPP and OAS is a very personal one. You need to look at your life and what impact taking the money early vs. taking it later will have. Then weigh whether waiting makes sense.

If You Change Your Mind

If you change your mind and decide to wait a bit longer before collecting your CPP, you have up to six months to do it after you start receiving payments. You have to do it in writing, and you have to pay back *all* the benefits you received and pay more CPP contributions on any earnings you made while you were receiving the pension.

Take Advantage of the Quirks

Although the OAS and CPP systems are complicated and quirky, sometimes those quirks can work for you. In particular, there is one that every married couple should take advantage of.

Under CPP rules, spouses or common-law partners who are together, who are both at least 60 years old, and who receive CPP retirement pensions can share their pension benefits. This may result in tax savings. If only one of you is a CPP contributor, you can still share the single pension.

You can get more information about this at the Service Canada web site (**www.hrsdc.gc.ca**).

What to Do if Things Go Wrong

If you have problems with CPP or OAS, your best bet is to contact Service Canada. If you use the toll-free number, remember that the lines are busiest at the beginning and end of the month, so it's best to call at other times. You should have your Social Insurance Number ready, as well. The toll-free numbers are:

1-800-277-9914 for service in English
1-800-277-9915 for service in French
1-800-255-4786 (TTY)

If you can, you're better off going in person to your local Service Canada office. Click on the Service Canada web site to find the location near you (**www.servicecanada.gc.ca**).

Write down the claim number you're assigned and the name of every person you speak with. Dealing with a bureaucracy can be extremely frustrating, but if you keep good records and stay focused, you can generally get your issue resolved.

Fight for Your Money Action Steps

- ☐ Check your CPP statement and T4 slips diligently. Errors in your earnings history should be addressed as soon as possible with your employer or Service Canada.
- ☐ Know the exact year that you'll be eligible for full CPP and OAS benefits.
- ☐ Weigh your options when it comes to deciding whether to collect your CPP payments sooner vs. later.

Annuities

With more and more baby boomers heading into their sixties—and stock market returns no longer looking like a sure thing—annuities are becoming an increasingly popular investment vehicle for retirees. Sales in Canada of individual annuities totalled $15.1 billion in 2007. Annuities are more popular in the United States, for various reasons, but Canadians are buying them in greater numbers, as well, primarily for their retirement income.

Basically, an annuity is a contract between you and an insurance company. You give them a bunch of money to invest and, depending on what kind of annuity you are buying, they promise you a regular stream of monthly payments that could last anywhere from a few years to the rest of your life and beyond. What's supposed to make annuities a good deal is that the investments the insurance company makes for you are tax-deferred (meaning you don't pay any tax on the earnings until they are distributed to you). Even better, annuities usually come with some sort of guarantee. In some cases, it may be a particular rate of return or a pledge that no matter how badly the stock market does, your investment will never decrease in value; in others, it's a promise that the company will pay out at least as much as you put in (if not to you, then to your heirs).

There's no getting around it—annuities are complicated. There are literally hundreds of different kinds and making comparisons is very difficult. One thing all annuities have in common is they are all either *immediate* (meaning they start paying out right away) or *deferred* (meaning you have to wait a set period of time before the payments start). They are also either *fixed* (meaning they offer a guaranteed interest rate for a set number of years, much like a Guaranteed Investment Certificate) or *variable* (meaning your money is invested in stocks and bonds, as a result of which your rate of return will rise and fall with the market).

What makes annuities different from other kinds of investments is the insurance component—the fact that different kinds of protections can be built in for the investor. Some annuities will guarantee you a monthly payment for the rest of your life—no matter how long you live. Others will guarantee you a minimum rate of return or that your principle will never decline in value or that your survivors will receive certain benefits. In general, the more protection you try to build into your annuity plan, the more it will cost you. Not surprisingly, salespeople love to push the more complicated plans that include all sorts of bells and whistles—and hence are much more expensive.

Insurance companies pay hefty commissions (sometimes as high as 15%) to agents who can convince people to pull hundreds of thousands of dollars in retirement savings out of other investments and put them into annuities. Some unscrupulous agents prey on the elderly, calling themselves "elder advisors" or "senior specialists"—though as one securities industry official points out, "the training they receive is often nothing more than marketing and selling techniques targeting the elderly."

This doesn't mean you should avoid annuities, but it does mean you need to be careful.

RRIFs and Annuities

Most people in Canada don't think much about annuities until they're about to retire. That's because annuities are an important part of retirement planning, especially for people who have accumulated substantial investments within their Registered Retirement Savings Plans (RRSPs).

By law, you cannot hold an RRSP after you reach the age of 71. On or before your 72nd birthday, you just take the accumulated savings in your RRSP and either put them into a similarly tax-sheltered vehicle called a Registered Retirement Income Fund or use them to purchase an annuity.

In both cases, the government wants to make sure that you receive an income as you grow older from the money you've saved during your working life. The difference between a RRIF and an annuity is that you have more choices about how to invest your money with a RRIF, although most people choose to let their financial institution or the administrator of their RRIF make those choices for them, just as they do with managed RRSPs, which I talked about earlier.

With an annuity, you also get a monthly income, but it can take several forms, as we'll see in a moment. It can be guaranteed, so that you receive the same amount, month in, month out, no matter what happens in the financial markets to affect your original lump-sum payment. Or your monthly payments can vary depending on the performance of your investment in the market.

How to Fight for Your Money

The simplest annuity is what's called a fixed lifetime immediate annuity—a life annuity, for short. This is the plain vanilla of annuities and it's meant for retirees who don't have a pension and are afraid of outliving their savings. It's also good for people who do have pensions but aren't sure they can count on them and so choose to collect their benefit in one lump-sum payment. You invest a chunk of your savings, the proceeds from the sale of your house, or your lump-sum payout, and, starting right away, the insurance company sends you a cheque every month for the rest of your life. The insurance company, of course, is betting that you will die before they start losing money on the deal. If you don't—well, the law of averages says that enough other customers will probably die prematurely to keep the company ahead of the game.

A life annuity can be an effective substitute for a traditional pension, but it does have drawbacks. One catch—and it's an important one—is that, like any immediate annuity, it locks you in. Once you sign off on the payment schedule and the cheques start arriving, that's it—you can't get your money out any faster. If you've purchased the annuity with your RRSP investments, you're probably more concerned about the steady income than you are about using the lump sum. But don't go this route if there's any chance you're going to need the cash sooner than the schedule calls for.

Another problem with fixed annuities is that you are trusting the insurance company or bank that sold it to you to do a good job managing your money. While it's true that a fixed annuity comes with a guaranteed rate of return, that guarantee is only as good as the company that stands behind it—and as we saw in 2008, even the biggest and most reputable insurance companies can stumble badly and even collapse.

One way to maintain some control over how your annuity is invested is to get what's called a variable annuity. In Canada, variable annuities are more commonly called segregated funds or seg funds. There are now more than 2,700 seg funds in Canada to choose from.

A seg fund is basically an annuity where your money is invested in a portfolio of investments that you choose yourself. Unlike a life annuity, you must hold your seg funds within a Registered Retirement Income Fund (RRIF). This isn't a major obstacle, and the insurance company that sells you the fund will set up the RRIF for you.

A seg fund offers a guaranteed payment like a fixed annuity, but also the chance to earn more if your investments perform well. The key word here is "choice." There are variable annuities that allow you to choose from as many as 30 of the best mutual funds around. So you can pretty much custom tailor your portfolio to what suits you best.

Because this sort of investing can be risky, the insurance company will be more than happy to sell you all sorts of protections that limit (or even eliminate) your downside. And because you may not live long enough to actually see any of the proceeds, they will be happy to write insurance guaranteeing that your heirs will receive at least as much money as you paid in.

The downside for variable annuities is that they can be expensive. That's because you have to pay both an insurance fee and a money-management fee for each investment you select. According to Morningstar, total fees for variable deferred annuities average nearly 2½% of assets. This is more than *twice* what most mutual funds charge! And sometimes they exceed 4%!

Total fees for variable deferred annuities average nearly 2½% of assets. This is more than twice what most mutual funds charge!

Seg funds have become enormously popular in Canada. In 2007, sales reached $2.7 billion, increasing by more than 33% over the previous year. More than $75 billion is now under management in seg funds in Canada. Sales are being driven primarily by Canadians worried about outliving their savings as they enter their retirement years.

The good news is that insurance companies such as Standard Life (www.standardlife.ca) and Canada Life (www.canadalife.com) now offer no-load seg funds that come with lower management fees and other bells and whistles.

Here are some other tips to keep in mind when considering annuities.

Don't Be Bamboozled by the Bells and Whistles

Surveys show that nearly one-third of us are guilty of making an investment we shouldn't have because we really didn't understand what we were buying. This is particularly true when it comes to annuities. The fact is that unscrupulous salespeople love to push complicated products like equity index annuities simply because they are so difficult to figure out.

Don't let yourself be bamboozled. Don't buy an annuity unless you really understand exactly what you are getting. With all the talk of bonus interest rates and no downside risk, it's easy to miss the fact that you're getting stuck with outsized fees or ridiculous surrender penalties that can cost you all of your gains if you need to make an early withdrawal. Read the contract carefully and make sure you understand it all. And even if you do, take it to an accountant or financial advisor for a second opinion before you write anyone a cheque.

Never Put All Your Savings in an Annuity

Annuities are best used in combination with other investments. Putting all your eggs in one basket is never a good idea, and putting it in one with extended surrender penalties is particularly risky because you might need access to the money.

Trust, but Verify

Back in the 1980s, Ronald Reagan used a famous phrase to describe his attitude toward negotiating arms agreements with the Soviets: "Trust, but verify." That's good advice for dealing with annuity providers. Before you do business with an agent who wants to sell you an annuity, check with your province's financial services commission or similar body to verify that he or she is properly licensed. (You'll find a list of provincial organizations at the web site of the Office of the Superintendent of Financial Institutions Canada at **www.osfi-bsif.gc.ca**.) And ask them whether the agent has ever been disciplined for improper behaviour. You should also verify the financial strength and stability of the company that's providing the annuity. You can do this through a credit-rating company like Dominion Bond Rating Service (**www.dbrs.com**).

What to Watch Out For

Salespeople Who Call Themselves "Financial Advisors"

The folks who hawk annuities often call themselves "financial advisors" or retirement consultants, but they are generally just insurance agents who are not licensed to sell anything but insurance products. That's why no matter what your financial situation and goals may happen to be, their solution is always the same—buy an annuity! Given the high commissions they generally earn from selling annuities, you should take their advice with a huge grain of salt.

Salespeople Who Won't Tell You How Much Commission They Earn from Selling You an Annuity

Insurance agents often tell customers they shouldn't worry about how much commission they make from selling annuities since the customer isn't the one who has to pay it. But like so many other things they say, that's not really true. Yes, insurance companies do pay agents upfront commissions as high as 15% of the amount of every annuity they sell (meaning they can pocket as much as $37,500 cash for selling you a $250,000 annuity). But the cost of that commission is passed right back to you in the form of smaller payouts and higher fees—particularly surrender charges. As a rule, if the agent's commission is higher than 4%, the terms of your annuity will probably be lousy. So it's important to know how much your agent stands to earn. And if he or she won't tell you, it means you're probably getting a bad deal.

As a rule, if the agent's commission is higher than 4%, the terms of your annuity will probably be lousy.

You can usually figure out how much the commission was by looking at your annuity's surrender charge. As a rule, the surrender charge for the first year is almost always just a bit higher than the commission that your broker or financial advisor got when he sold you the annuity.

Promises of Huge Gains

Variable annuities—segregated funds in Canada—are like any other investment: they can go up and they can go down. While it's true that for an extra charge (usually a substantial one), you can buy an annuity that is guaranteed to maintain some minimum value, there is no way an insurance company or anyone else can guarantee you huge returns. Of course, that doesn't stop unscrupulous salespeople from claiming they can.

Colleen and Rich Powell, a retired couple I know, had never invested in anything but GICs, until a friend recommended her "financial advisor" to them. The advisor, who was really an insurance agent, immediately began pushing the idea of a seg fund. "We stressed we could not afford to lose any principal," Mrs. Powell says. "We also told him we were completely naïve about investing and the stock market. He said his own parents had the variable annuities he was recommending for us. He was so convincing but still we hesitated. And then he told us we'd never make less than 11% a year, and could make as much as 25%. It sounded like an answer to our prayers. We foolishly trusted him."

Needless to say, the Powells never made anywhere near the gains the salesman promised. In fact, the value of their account began falling almost immediately. They filed an arbitration complaint against their broker and eventually won a $50,000 award, but there was no happy ending for them. The broker filed for bankruptcy and, as Mrs. Powell notes sadly, "We've yet to collect a penny."

Getting Trapped in a Low-Yielding Annuity

If you're considering a fixed annuity that guarantees you a relatively good interest rate for the first several years, make sure that the interest-rate guarantee lasts at least as long as the surrender charge period. With many fixed annuities, the interest they pay falls sharply as soon as the guarantee expires, and if you've still got a surrender charge hanging over your head at that point, you could find yourself stuck in a low-yielding investment with no easy exit.

The Switch-and-Roll

Some advisors will push you to roll over your assets to a new annuity as soon as your surrender period is up. They will give you all sorts of reasons that this makes sense—for example, that you may be able to lock in a higher death benefit or get some new special feature—but the real reason they want you to "switch and roll" is that if you buy a new annuity, they will earn a new commission. So before you agree—and in the process subject yourself to a new six or eight years of surrender fees—make sure the "new" bells and whistles you're getting aren't already provided by your current policy. You should find this out by calling your current annuity company and asking them directly; don't just take an agent's word for it.

What to Do if Things Go Wrong

There aren't many businesses more heavily regulated than insurance—except maybe the securities industry. Since annuities involve both insurance and securities, there are an awful lot of places you can go for help if you think you've been scammed, swindled, or otherwise mistreated in the course of buying one.

You should probably start by contacting the brokerage that employs the person who sold you the annuity. Talk to the salesperson's supervisor. If the supervisor agrees the sale was inappropriate, he or she may be able to cancel the transaction. Your next call should be to the insurance company or financial institution that issued the annuity. Start with customer service and work your way up the chain to someone with the authority to unwind your annuity. Explain politely but firmly just how you were misled and make it clear that although you have no desire to sue anybody for fraud, you will have no choice but to do just that if the situation can't be resolved amicably.

If this doesn't produce results, it may be time to call in the big guns. Complaints about fixed annuities and insurance agents should go to your province's financial services commission. (As I've mentioned, you'll find a list of provincial organizations at the web site of the Office of the Superintendent of Financial Institutions Canada at www.osfi-bsif.gc.ca.)

Fight for Your Money Action Steps

- ☐ Get the advice of an accountant or financial advisor before investing in an annuity—and remember, the agent who sells annuities is not a financial advisor!
- ☐ Check your agent's credentials with your province's financial services commission and check out if they've ever been disciplined for improper behaviour.
- ☐ Bottom line—don't buy an annuity unless you really understand what you're getting.

Online Shopping and Auctions

Who doesn't buy stuff on the Internet these days? In 2007, Statistics Canada estimated more than 8.4 million Canadians bought $12.8 billion worth of goods over the Internet. Online shopping has exploded because it's quick, easy, and convenient. But all that convenience comes at a price. Internet sales scams—particularly those involving online auctions—are among the fastest growing category of consumer complaints, and many of them originate in Canada, according to the Internet Crime Complaint Center (IC3), a joint operation between the FBI and the U.S. Justice Department's National White Collar Crime Center. The Edmonton Police department says more than half the population of the country have lost money to online fraud in Canada. Phonebusters, Canada's online crime fighting agency, reported that Canadians lost $4.6 million to just one type of fraud in the month of January 2008 alone. And that's just the people who filed complaints. The actual total is probably several times that.

How to Fight for Your Money

About half of all the complaints about online shopping involve problems related to Internet auctions, and there's no question that sites like eBay and

Ubid are a world unto themselves. But whether you're bidding for something at an online auction or buying a fixed-price item from an Internet merchant, the ways scam artists try to rip you off are similar. Here's how to protect yourself.

Know Your Seller

Where possible, buy from sites you know. If you're buying from a site that's unfamiliar, research them before you place an order. Virtually anyone can set up a shop online and start doing business. Try calling the seller's phone number to make sure you can reach them. Type the site's name in a search engine to see if you can find any reviews. For auction sites like eBay, check the seller's feedback rating. Steer clear of those with less than positive ratings—or no ratings at all. Be aware, however, that feedback ratings can be manipulated. To protect yourself, always check the seller's history to make sure he or she has previously sold items similar to what you're thinking of buying. As one expert says: "If it's all been for very low-priced items and suddenly the person is selling laptops, for example, you should be very suspicious." You should also look for the "Buy Safe" seal. Buy Safe (www.buysafe.com) is an independent company that certifies online merchants as being trustworthy and reliable. (Shoppers in Canada are protected through a corporate guarantee, according to BuySafe's web site, and enjoy the same level of protection as U.S. shoppers.)

It's easy to tell whether a site is encrypted. Your browser will display a small icon of a closed padlock or unbroken key.

Make Sure Your Internet Connection Is Secure

Before you buy anything from an e-commerce site, make sure it uses encryption technology, which scrambles sensitive information such as your credit card number to keep computer hackers from stealing it. It's easy to tell whether or not a site is encrypted. Just look at the web address in your browser display. If it begins with "https," instead of "http," the site is encrypted. In addition, your browser will display a small icon of a closed padlock or unbroken key. (You can usually find this icon in either the lower right-hand corner of the browser or in its address bar).

Most reputable e-commerce sites also display the words "Secure Sockets Layer (SSL)" or a pop-up box that says you are entering a secure area. The most secure sites will display something called Extended Validation (EV)

SSL Certificates. A site with one of these has had its authenticity verified by a reputable authority such as VeriSign. If a website doesn't have a security certificate, it's probably too risky to shop there.

Make Online Purchases with a Credit Card—Not with a Debit Card or Cheque

If something goes wrong with an online transaction—like, say, you get cheated—you'll be glad you paid with a credit card. When you charge something to a credit card, you can have the charge reversed if the item turns out to be defective or simply never arrives. You can also stop payment if you are dissatisfied with the quality of any goods and services you've purchased with a credit card. (For more details, see the section CREDIT CARDS on page 81.) When you pay with a debit card, you have no such protections.

And never pay with a personal cheque. That's an open invitation to identity theft, since it contains your bank account number and home address.

If you're buying something from an individual who is unable to accept a credit card charge, insist on paying through an online payment service like Escrow.com or PayPal.com, which protect buyers against fraud. (But if the seller suggests a service other than Escrow.com or PayPal, check them out carefully. There have been cases where scammers have set up phony escrow services to con both buyers and sellers out of their money.)

Guard Your Privacy

Be wary if an online merchant asks for information that's not pertinent to your purchase, such as your date of birth, social insurance number, or annual income. When you're filling out an order form, provide only the basic information that is required (usually it's marked with an asterisk) and don't volunteer anything beyond that. (Some outfits sell this information to marketers; others may be fronts for identity theft.) And never share your passwords with anyone. In fact, if you ever set up accounts with online merchants, make a point of using different passwords for different web sites.

Be Careful When You're Bidding

Before you place a bid for anything at an online auction, read the description of the item carefully. Ask questions if you're uncertain about any aspect of the transaction—especially the item's condition. Find out who pays for shipping and delivery. Generally, sellers specify shipping cost and give buyers the option to pay for faster delivery. Check the seller's return policy. Can you return the item for a full refund if you're not satisfied? If you do return it, will you be required to pay shipping costs or a restocking fee?

Don't place a bid until all your questions have been answered to your satisfaction. And before you start bidding, figure out the maximum price you're willing to pay for the item and don't go beyond it. This approach will protect you from being fooled into paying an inflated price by shill bidding—a scam in which confederates of the seller try to bid up an item way beyond what it's really worth. In any case, never bid on anything unless it's an item you really want, since if you turn out to be the highest bidder, you will be obligated to buy it.

Keep Your Receipts

Receipts are always important, regardless of where or how you bought something. But they are especially crucial when you're shopping in the virtual world, where it's often difficult to know who you're dealing with. So whenever you complete an online purchase, always print and save the confirmation page. In fact, until you actually receive the merchandise you ordered, keep all the associated documents, including the product description and price as well as copies of any emails you may have exchanged with the seller or merchant.

Know Your Rights

Consumer affairs guidelines require online merchants to honour their promises to ship goods by a certain date—or, if they didn't specify how long it would take, then within a reasonable period after you place the order. If the goods aren't shipped by then, the seller should notify you and give you a chance to cancel your order and receive a refund. What's more, you can reject merchandise if it turns out to be defective or not what was promised.

Wire-Transfer Requests

Be suspicious if a seller insists that you pay by wire transfer. Even if he is an individual (as opposed to a business) and so has no way of processing a credit card charge, there is absolutely no reason that he can't accept payment through an online payment service like **Escrow.com** or **PayPal.com**. Except, of course, if he is trying to scam you.

Foreign-Based Sellers

Be extra cautious when dealing with sellers or buyers located outside Canada and the United States. Our consumer protection laws and regulations do not apply to them, and you will have little if any recourse if they rip you off.

Discount Prices for Designer Labels

In June 2008, a French court ordered eBay to pay a $63 million judgment for allowing counterfeit Louis Vuitton bags, Christian Dior clothing, and Guerlain, Kenzo, and Givenchy perfume to be sold on its site. Luxury brands like Hermès and Rolex won similar cases against eBay in previous years. Counterfeit designer goods are a problem everywhere, but especially online. So be extremely skeptical of any seller who is offering designer products at bargain-basement prices. Chances are, they're fakes.

Sellers Who Want Direct Contact

Online auction sites generally provide bidders with the seller's direct contact information *after* they make a bid. So be wary of a seller who puts his address or phone number in the description of the item he's trying to sell. Chances are, he's trying to get around the site's antifraud protections.

Suspicious Photos

The kind of photos used in an online auction listing can often tell you more than the seller may intend. Look at them carefully. You want them to be of the actual item the seller is offering—NOT stock photos of the product from the manufacturer's web site—unless perhaps the item is being sold as overstock. The use of stock photos generally means that the item is in lousy condition, is a fake—or doesn't even exist.

Being Phished to a Phony Site to Be Swindled

If you receive an unsolicited email from an Internet merchant and you're interested in what he has to sell, don't click on any links that may be embedded in the message. Instead, find your own way to the merchant's web site by using a good search engine like Google or Yahoo. Online scammers often pose as reputable merchants and send out email solicitations containing what are called "spoofed links"—links that look like they'll take you to a good vendor but in fact direct you to a phony site where they can "phish" your personal data.

What to Do if Things Go Wrong

If you have problems during a transaction, you should first try to work them out directly with the seller or site operator. If that doesn't work and you paid with a credit card, contact the credit card company to dispute the charge. (For details on how to do this, see page 89 in CREDIT CARDS.) You should also complain to your province's consumer affairs department (see the list on the federal government's Consumer Information Gateway at **http://consumerinformation.ca**) and your local chapter of the Better Business Bureau (**www.ccbbb.ca**).

If you've been victimized by any kind of Internet scam, file a complaint online with the Internet Crime Complaint Center at **www.ic3.gov/complaint**. Include your name, mailing address, and telephone number as well as the name, mailing address, and web address of the person or business that defrauded you. You should also include specific details of how you were defrauded and any other relevant supporting information. After you file the complaint, you'll be assigned a complaint ID and password so you can update your complaint as you get new information. After reviewing your complaint, analysts with the IC3 may refer it to appropriate government authorities.

Fight for Your Money Action Steps

- ☐ Make sure your online purchase is from a legitimate merchant.
- ☐ Buy only from secure sites.
- ☐ Use a major credit card.
- ☐ Check the seller's rating before placing a bid on an auction item. Has he sold similarly priced items before?
- ☐ Keep your receipts and correspondence.

Appliance Protection Plans/Extended Warranties

Every time I buy a new computer, iPod, cell phone, DVD player, or even a microwave, I go through the same drama. I've finally figured out which model I want to get and I tell the salesperson to write it up, and then he stops me cold by saying: "And you're going to want the extended warranty, right? I mean, you never know with these things. It's worth it just for the peace of mind."

But is it really worth spending 10% to 20% of the purchase price for a plan you may never use, for coverage you may already have?

In the three months before Christmas, Canadians spend upward of $1 billion on cameras, photographic equipment, and small appliances. That means they could spend another $1 million or more on protection plans and extended warranties to get extra protection for everything from $20 toasters to $9,000 PCs. The irony is that in the vast majority of cases we are shelling out good money for protection we already have or don't really need.

This is why, except for computer purchases for my company, I almost never purchase an extended warranty. Experience has taught me that when you do buy an extended warranty, the hassle of actually using it (returning the defective product, paying the shipping and restocking fees, pulling together all the paperwork) simply isn't worth the time and trouble it takes. In fact, it's often cheaper to buy a brand new product than to pay the deductible on an extended warranty for an old product that they may or may not be able to fix to my satisfaction. So when the salesperson asks me if I want the extended warranty, my answer is: "No thank you!"

A Good Deal for the Retailer—but What About You?

Extended warranties are definitely a great deal for the folks who sell us the products we're paying to cover. A retailer typically keeps at least half—and often more—of the purchase price of every extended warranty he or she sells. On a $500 service contract for a $3,000 flat-screen TV, that can mean at least $250 in pure profit for the dealer—which is why you'll rarely get out of a store without being subjected to a strong sales pitch for the extra coverage.

But the fact is that, with a few exceptions, most consumer products are so reliable these days that they rarely break down during the period covered by most extended warranties. As a result, the cost of the warranty is almost always far higher than any repair bills you are likely to incur. Indeed, according to a 2007 *Consumer Reports* survey, two out of three new-car buyers who bought extended warranties said they had spent a lot more on the warranty than they saved in repair costs. Fewer than one in 20 said they actually came out ahead.

Two out of three new-car buyers who bought extended warranties said they had spent a lot more on the warranty than they saved in repair costs. Fewer than one in 20 said they actually came out ahead.

When it comes to electronics and appliances, the situation is even worse. Experts estimate that for every 100 warranties sold on electronics and appliances, only 15 people ever file a claim. And most of those problems are not the result of defective workmanship but rather of consumers not reading the directions properly.

How to Fight for Your Money

As a rule, if a product is so unreliable that you need to supplement the manufacturer's warranty with additional protection, you probably shouldn't be buying it in the first place. That said, there are some items—like laptop computers and rear-projection TVs—for which extended warranties may make sense. Here's what you should keep in mind.

You May Already Be Protected

Virtually every consumer product comes with a manufacturer's warranty that offers protection for anywhere from 30 days to three years. On top of this, many credit card companies will give you as much as a year's additional coverage if you buy the product with their card, while some big retailers automatically tack an extra year or two of warranty coverage onto products they sell. And most homeowner's insurance policies cover accidental damage, loss, or theft of household items, including electronics. So before you fork over any additional dollars for an extended warranty or protection plan, make sure you really need it.

Make Sure You Know What's Covered

Most warranties are loaded with fine print, and it's important to understand in advance what's covered and what's not. According to one report, **Amazon.com**'s extended warranty lists 35 cases in which protection doesn't apply,

I Fought for My Money!

A few years ago, I bought a top-of-the-line computer at a top-tier store with a renowned reputation for service. Because things often do go wrong with laptops, I forked over $500 for a three-year extended warranty. Sure enough, in the third year, my screen died. I immediately dug out the paperwork and sent the computer back to the retailer. Three weeks later, they sent the computer back to me with a note saying that the computer had water damage that was not covered by the warranty and that it would cost me $850 to get it fixed. I knew there was no water damage, so I fought back—hard. I insisted the problem was covered by the warranty; they insisted it wasn't. Finally, after eight phone calls, half a dozen emails, and a letter to the manager sent via both certified mail and fax, they relented and agreed to fix the computer.

It would have been very easy for me to give up on my computer. This is exactly what the stores that sell these warranties count on. They know you are busy, and so they will attempt to stonewall you. This did not work with me—and it shouldn't work with you. If you ever buy an extended warranty and get the runaround like I did—FIGHT BACK! Don't ever give up, speak to management, and put your complaint in writing.

including "plasma TVs used in altitude levels above 6,000 feet above sea level." When it comes to major appliances or large items like flat-screen TVs, it's crucial to know what kind of service the warranty provides. Will they come to you to fix it or will you have to bring it to them? And when it's fixed, will they hook it back up? Also keep in mind that while the salesperson may insist that *everything* is covered, including your three-year-old flushing your cell phone down the toilet, his verbal assurances are worthless. If it's not in the warranty contract, you're out of luck.

And find out about the deductible. Many warranties make you pay the first $25, $50, or $100 of each repair. When you add in shipping fees, service fees, and the like, a deductible can render an extended warranty pretty much worthless.

Consider Who's Protecting You

Some extended warranties are administered by the manufacturer, some by the retailer, and some by third-party warranty companies. When you buy this kind of protection, it's important to know who stands behind it—especially in tough economic times. That's because if the company goes out of business, your warranty may disappear along with it. In 2007, a company called Ultimate Warranty went bankrupt, leaving nearly 140,000 customers who had paid upward of $45 million for extended warranties holding contracts not worth the paper they were printed on. So find out who is actually guaranteeing your warranty and make sure you're comfortable that they'll be around to honour it.

Take Your Time

Because their profit margins are so huge, most retailers will do everything they can to keep you from leaving their store without buying an extended warranty. But the fact is that there's no reason you have to decide right then and there. Typically, you have 30 days from the date of purchase to buy an extended warranty. So if you think you may need one, take your time. At the very least, take the contract home and read it carefully BEFORE you hand over any money.

Pay Attention to the Calendar

Most extended warranties go into effect the day you purchase the product, so at the beginning at least they will merely duplicate the manufacturer's warranty coverage that comes with the product. What this means is that if your product has a one-year warranty, a three-year extended warranty will give you only two years of extra coverage.

Don't Pay Too Much

As a rule, a warranty costing more than 15% of the price for three years of coverage is not worth it.

Most three-year extended warranties go for somewhere between 10% and 20% of the product's price. Given the likelihood that you'll never use the protection, you want to pay as little as possible for it. As a rule, anything more than 15% of the price for three years of coverage is not worth it.

Consider the Extras

Extended warranties not only provide for repairs if a product turns out to be defective, but also sometimes include valuable extras such as tech support. This can make a protection plan worthwhile for items like computers. For example, Apple offers first-rate tech support for its Macs, but it's free for only the first 90 days. After that, the company charges $49 for every phone call—unless you buy its three-year AppleCare warranty, in which case you can make as many tech-support calls as you want for no extra charge. Given that AppleCare costs only $169 for an iMac, you'll be ahead of the game if you make just three or four tech-support calls.

What to Do if Things Go Wrong

If you have an issue with your extended warranty or appliance protection program, you should first try to resolve the problem with the retailer who sold you the defective product. If that doesn't work, contact the manufacturer. It's usually best to do this in writing, with a letter sent by certified mail, with return receipt, in which you detail the nature of your problem and how you would like to see it rectified. Include copies (not originals) of your sales receipt and other relevant documents.

If the manufacturer doesn't help, file a complaint with your province's consumer affairs department. (The federal government's Consumer Information Gateway at **http://consumerinformation.ca** has a list of them.) Also contact your local chapter of the Better Business Bureau (**www.ccbbb.ca**).

Finally, you should consider taking legal action. Disputes involving less than $750 can usually be handled without lawyers in small claims court.

Fight for Your Money Action Steps

- ☐ Find out what kind of manufacturer's warranty is already included with the product.
- ☐ Find out if the retailer offers an additional warranty free of charge.
- ☐ Call your credit card company in advance to determine what kind of coverage you'll have through them if you purchase the product on your card.
- ☐ Know what's covered through your homeowner's insurance.
- ☐ Check reliability statistics of the product through *Consumer Reports* or J.D. Power and Associates.
- ☐ If you're leaning toward buying the extended warranty after all, find out what the deductible is and who the warranty is actually through—the manufacturer, the retailer, or a third party.

Gift Cards

Gift cards may be the perfect solution for that hard-to-please teenager or guy-who-has-everything uncle on your Christmas or birthday lists, but in general they are a much better deal for the retailers who issue them than they are for you. For one thing, when you buy a gift card, you're basically lending money interest-free to the merchant who sold it to you. For another, gift cards are often so difficult or inconvenient to redeem that millions of recipients wind up throwing them away—in effect, turning your interest-free loan into an outright gift *to the merchant*!

Canadians spend about $6 billion a year on gift cards. But one in four cards is never used, according to the Consumers' Association of Canada—meaning that gift card issuers wound up pocketing about $450 million. Canadians are more likely to use their cards on inexpensive items like groceries than on expensive things like fur coats, so the value of unused gift cards may be even higher. In 2006, Best Buy earned $16 million from unredeemed gift cards. That's a big gift—to Best Buy.

How to Fight for Your Money

For all the convenience they offer, gift cards are often incredibly frustrating to use. Indeed, in an effort to protect consumers, some provinces such as Ontario, B.C., and Manitoba have passed laws imposing restrictions on gift cards, eliminating expiry dates, for example, and transaction fees charged to administer the cards. Still, the rules governing them remain hard to follow.

So if you're thinking of buying a gift card—or if someone has given you one—here are some tips to keep in mind.

Read the Fine Print

If you think that a gift card is as good as cash, think again. Some of them not only have expiration dates, but also charge a laundry list of fees for all sorts of routine services—and in some cases for doing nothing—that can reduce a card's value sharply. To make matters worse, many merchants restrict how and where their cards can be used. For example, Starbucks gift cards are not good at many Starbucks outlets in airports, supermarkets, and bookstores. And some bank-issued gift cards aren't accepted at gas stations, car-rental companies, and cruise lines.

The worst offenders in terms of fees and expiration dates are the bank-issued Visa and MasterCard gift cards.

The worst offenders in terms of fees and expiration dates are the bank-issued Visa and MasterCard gift cards. For example, if you buy a Visa-branded Citizens Bank gift card online, you'll be charged a $2.00 load fee. You'll get to check your balance by phone once for free, but after that it's 50 cents a call or 75 cents if you want to talk to a live agent. At restaurants and some other places, you need 15% more on your gift card than the amount of your bill or else you can't use the card at all.

After six months, many cards begin to lose their value, some by as much as $2.50 a month.

The point is that when you receive a gift card, you should read the fine print to make sure you fully understand expiration dates, fee schedules, and other rules that could affect your ability to redeem the card. If the person who gave you the card didn't include this information with it, check the retailer's web site or call them for a copy of all the applicable terms and conditions.

Use Them or Lose Them

The worst thing you can do with a gift card is to throw it in a drawer somewhere and forget about it. I've been guilty of this myself and now I always make an effort to use the card immediately. Gift cards may be made out of plastic, but they do not last forever. Even if yours doesn't have an expiration date, the merchant that issued it might. When Sharper Image declared bankruptcy in 2008, it stopped accepting its gift cards—leaving consumers stuck with an estimated $40 million of suddenly worthless plastic.

So if you're given a gift card, use it as soon as you can.

Don't Expect Change

If you use a $50 gift card to buy a $40 item, don't expect to get back any change. The $10 will stay on the gift card. And don't assume that you can put it toward another purchase of something that costs more than $10. If you're using a retailer's card, split tender transactions—where you pay for part of a purchase with a gift card and the rest in cash—are usually not a problem. But some merchants will not let you do that with a bank-issued gift card. So if you're the recipient of one of these, keep in mind that you probably won't be able to use it to buy anything that costs more than the card's face value, and you may even need more than the card's face value to make a purchase, so do your best to buy something as close to the value of the card as possible.

Don't Throw Away the Paperwork

Pretty much the worst thing that can happen to a gift card is that it gets lost or stolen. If yours goes missing, you can usually get a replacement card from the issuer—for a fee of $15 or so—if you know the card number and can provide some proof (such as a receipt) that you actually owned it. So when you are given a gift card, don't throw away the paperwork. Keep the receipt that came with it, make a copy of both sides of the card or write down the card's ID number, and make a note of the customer service telephone number on the card's back. (Keep in mind that you must report a loss right away. As far as the issuers are concerned, you are responsible for any transactions on the card before it was reported missing.)

Get the Most Out of Your Card by Registering It

A growing number of issuers will let you register your gift card. Indeed, some—such as Starbucks—won't replace a lost or stolen card unless it's been registered. But you can also register your gift cards at a number of consumer web sites designed to help you manage and protect them. Probably the best of these is **GiftCardTracker.com,** a totally free service that's been around since 2004. Its founder, a Virginia native named Ken Hawkins, got the idea after he walked into his local Office Max with a $50 gift card he had been given two years earlier—only to learn that it was no longer worth anything. In addition to keeping track of your gift card account numbers, customer service contact information, and other key data, **GiftCardTracker.com** will also send you e-mail reminders when your card is nearing its expiration date and keep you up to date on the latest offers involving thousands of gift cards.

If You Don't Want It, Swap It

If you've gotten a gift card from a store you don't like, there's a better alternative to throwing it away. You can swap it online for a gift card from a store you do like. Sites such as **CertificateSwap.com** provide a marketplace where you can trade cards with other dissatisfied recipients, put your card up for sale, or purchase one at a discount.

What to Do if Things Go Wrong

If a gift card issuer doesn't seem to be following his own rules or otherwise drops the ball, you should first try to resolve the problem directly with that company. If that doesn't work, you should go to the authorities.

If the card was issued by a retailer, file a complaint with the retailer first. If that doesn't achieve what you want, contact your province's consumer affairs department. You'll find a list of them at the federal government's Consumer Information Gateway at **http://consumerinformation.ca**. And contact your local chapter of the Better Business Bureau (**www.ccbbb.ca**).

Fight for Your Money Action Steps

- ☐ When you receive a gift card, read the fine print!
- ☐ Make a photocopy of the front and back of the card and file it in a safe place along with the receipt. (And when you give a gift card, always include the receipt.)
- ☐ Go the extra step and register your card.
- ☐ This weekend, you're going shopping! Pull out all those cards that are stashed away—and use them before they expire.
- ☐ Never give a bank card. Write a cheque instead.

Rebate Offers

How many times have you been talked into buying some expensive new product—say, a new microwave oven or a digital camera—mainly because the manufacturer is offering a rebate that will knock forty or fifty or maybe even a hundred bucks off the price? But when you get home, the forms you're supposed to complete and the instructions on what part of the box you're supposed to cut out and send in are so confusing that you can't be sure you've done any of it right. So you wind up doing one of two things. Either you stuff the forms in a drawer, telling yourself you'll get to it some other time (which, of course, you never do). Or you send in all the paperwork, fingers crossed—and nothing happens.

Then, to add insult to injury, when you contact the manufacturer to find out what happened to your rebate cheque, they tell you they have no record of your ever applying for one, and anyway the program expired months ago.

Rebates are the deal that consumers love to hate—and for good reason. As University of Toronto Marketing Professor Sridhar Moorthy told the CBC, "From the manufacturer's point of view, they're having their cake and eating it too. They've gotten you to buy the product because you thought you would redeem the rebate. Then once you went home, you forgot about the rebate."

REBATES ARE RIGGED TO FAIL YOU

Value of products sold with a rebate offer:	$800 million
Percentage that is ever redeemed:	2%–50%

That's no exaggeration. According to experts, an attractive-sounding rebate can goose the sales of a product by as much as 500%. So every year companies offer millions of rebates on products ranging from cars to cell phones to computer software to food. In the United States, four out of five rebates never get redeemed. In Canada, it's even lower, depending on the amount of money involved. And that's not because consumers are lazy. As Professor Moorthy says, it's because a $50 rebate "is not just a $50 deal. It's a $50 deal plus a lot of work."

How to Fight for Your Money

Why do manufacturers make it so hard to redeem rebates? The answer is simple: greed. The fewer customers who qualify for rebates, the more money the companies get to keep. As one industry expert told *The Wall Street Journal*, "Rebates are a good business plan only when consumers fail to claim them."

So how do you protect yourself when the game is rigged against you? Here are some basic tips.

Don't Forget to Apply for It

That sounds simple enough, but once you get your new purchase home, open the box, and misplace the receipt, it's easy to zone out on the whole rebate process. If you are counting on a rebate to make the price you paid affordable, take care of it as soon as possible. Dallas entrepreneur Daniel Pentecost, who successfully cashes in on six to eight rebates a year, told *U.S. News & World Report* that he tracks his rebates in a spreadsheet. "As soon as I have the product in my hands," he said, "the very first thing I do before I use it is I cut off the UPC code, then put it in the envelope. I know that if I don't, it will slip my mind."

Read the Fine Print

Then read it again. And then once more for good measure. Manufacturers all have different rules, which makes the rebate game hard to master. Most rebates require some proof of purchase and a receipt, but what exactly you need to send in varies from one company to another. Some require the original receipt, while others will be fine with a copy. Some might ask for the UPC Code, which can be confusing when merchants put their own bar codes on packaging. So don't throw out the box until your rebate cheque arrives, just in case you mailed in the wrong proof of purchase.

He Fought for His Money!

Chris, a photographer, makes a practice of using certified mail with return receipt whenever he files for a rebate worth more than $20. "That way I have proof of when they received it and who signed for it," he says, which makes it tougher for companies to claim they never got anything.

Chris' vigilance paid off when a rebate he filed for a Netgear computer router apparently fell into a black hole. After waiting six months, he went to Fry's Electronics, the retailer that sold him the router. "Since I had copies of everything I'd submitted," he says, "including a return receipt showing that the fulfillment house had received my paperwork before the cutoff date, Fry's agreed to refund me the amount of the rebate."

Also, pay attention to the dates. Deferred rebates don't start until weeks after you purchase the item. It's possible too that the promotion is over but the store hasn't removed the materials yet.

Document Everything

The key to rebate success is good record keeping.

The key to rebate success is good record keeping. Keep notes on exactly when you mailed in which rebate applications, make copies of everything you send, and be sure to keep the initial rebate offer containing contact information. All this will come in very handy if you get into a dispute over an unpaid rebate.

Don't Be Too Patient—and Don't Give Up

Too many consumers are too patient. If your rebate is overdue, don't just sit there. Under Canadian consumer regulations, companies are required to send rebates within the time frame promised, or if no time is specified, within a reasonable time. And if they tell you your application has been turned down because you missed a deadline that you know you made or failed to send them documentation that you know you sent, fight back. Rebate rejections can be reversed if you are persistent. As Chris the photographer notes: "Rebates are a game and you have to play it in order to get paid. But if you play it, you will get your money."

What to Do if Things Go Wrong

If more than a month has gone by and you haven't received your cheque, make a fuss. The way to start is with a call to the manufacturer or the fulfillment house the manufacturer uses to handle its rebate programs. Contact information is usually included in the original rebate offer, which is why you should make sure to keep it. If you haven't, check with the retailer who sold you the product or go online and do a search for rebate contact information along with the name of the company that offered the rebate you want to inquire about.

When you reach a customer service representative, explain that you followed all the instructions but haven't yet received your rebate and would like to know why. Be prepared to have him or her ask you to resend all the documentation you originally sent. (This is why it's essential to keep copies.) If they tell you there's nothing they can do or are otherwise unhelpful, ask to speak with a manager.

If the phone call does not get you any results, you should write a polite letter to the manufacturer, setting out the details of what you bought, where you bought it and when, and noting that your decision to purchase the product was based on their offer of a rebate. Add that your purchase of the product constituted an acceptance of their offer, and that if you don't get your rebate cheque within 30 days, you will complain to the authorities and begin legal action for breach of contract. (You'll find a sample letter you can use as a model on page 328 of the FFYM Toolkit.)

Send copies of the letter to regulators such as your province's consumer affairs department as well as the Consumers' Association of Canada (**www.consumer.ca**) and the Better Business Bureau (**www.ccbbb.ca**).

Fight for Your Money Action Steps

- ☐ Apply for the rebate as soon as possible.
- ☐ Read the fine print.
- ☐ Keep all packaging, proofs of purchase, and receipts.
- ☐ Know the dates of the promotion.
- ☐ Keep good records. Keep notes on exactly when you mailed in which rebate applications, make copies of everything you send, and be sure to keep the initial rebate offer containing contact information.

- ☐ Use certified mail with return receipt for rebates over $20.
- ☐ Follow up if you don't receive your rebate within a month. Be diligent!
- ☐ Organize and keep track of your rebate submissions at **www.rebatetracker.com.**

Tax Preparation

Tax preparation is a huge business. In all, Canadians spend as much as $4 billion on it each year. Many taxpayers hire someone to help them fill out the forms and calculate what they owe. Among the many tax-preparation services in Canada, H&R Block alone operates more than 1,000 outlets. Many more rely on computer programs like QuickTax. Unfortunately, taxpayers don't always get their money's worth.

It's not hard to understand why. The tax code is so complicated and hard to understand that even if your finances are relatively simple, filing your income taxes can still be a nightmare. Critics say that many taxpayers submit far more in a year than they should have because they didn't understand their tax forms. And 32% of taxpayers themselves say they probably skip exemptions and writeoffs that they could have taken because they just can't figure out how to do their tax returns properly.

How to Fight for Your Money

I'm a huge believer in having your taxes done professionally—especially if your income exceeds $50,000 a year. In my experience, the savings you realize from a professionally done return will more than cover the cost. In fact, the savings are usually somewhere between five and ten times your investment. So if you spend $500 having your tax return done, you will more than likely shave $2,500 to $5,000 off your tax bill.

That said, deciding whether to prepare your taxes yourself or to hire a pro pretty much depends on how much time and patience you have and how complicated your finances are. If you're self-employed or have just inherited money, purchased rental property, exercised stock options, or gone through a major life change (like getting married or divorced or becoming a parent), it's almost always worth your while to pay a professional to do your taxes.

If you spend $500 having your tax return done, you will more than likely shave $2,500 to $5,000 off your tax bill.

The catch is that pretty much anyone can hang up a shingle and call themselves a tax preparer. As a senator in the United States, Chuck Grassley, once said: "It's incredible that we have legal requirements for a barber to cut your hair, but there are no requirements for someone to prepare your taxes. The worst that can happen when you get a lousy barber is a bad hair day. But if you get bad tax advice, you may be audited, owe thousands of dollars, and even face jail time." He could have made the same observation about Canada.

Tax preparers range from the guy who tacks a card to the grocery store bulletin board every winter, to the big storefront chains like H&R Block, to professional accountants and enrolled agents. Here's how to pick a good one.

Bigger Doesn't Always Mean Better

Those international chains such as H&R Block (**www.hrblock.com**) and Liberty Tax Service (**www.libertytax.com**) may seem like a good bet. After all, they process millions of returns annually, they have thousands of retail locations where you can meet with someone face to face, they have fancy websites, and everybody's heard of them. But the fact that these companies are well known doesn't guarantee success. That's because at the end of the day, how well your return is prepared depends on who actually does the work. Local newspapers throughout Canada compare tax preparation services almost every year. And every year, they conclude, as the Government Accountability Office did in the United States, that "nearly all of the returns prepared for us were incorrect to some degree."

Many firms just use a software questionnaire similar to the kind of program you can buy for yourself for $50.

That's not really surprising, because many firms use high school graduates (as opposed to more expensive university graduates) to process your return. They just use a software questionnaire similar to the kind of program you can buy for yourself for $50. If you don't like the idea of a part-time employee with only a high school diploma doing your taxes (and you shouldn't), make sure you ask up front about who will be doing your return and what kind of experience he or she has.

Look for Real Professionals

Your best bet for quality tax preparation help is to use a certified professional. Professional tax preparers are certainly more expensive than the chains—an accountant will typically charge $100 to $300 an hour vs. a total fee of $200 or so for an itemized return at H&R Block—but spotting just one missed deduction or credit (say, the deduction for interest on a student loan or the credit for a home office if you work from home) can easily save you the difference.

There are two professional designations that you should consider: chartered accountants (CAs) and certified general accountants (CGAs).

CHARTERED ACCOUNTANTS (CAS) have been certified by the Canadian Institute of Chartered Accountants (**www.cica.ca**) to work in public practice, industry, government, and education as business professionals with expertise in tax- and finance-related activities. Their training covers a much wider range of topics than just tax matters, including accounting, auditing, and personal financial planning. You should probably use a CA to handle business tax matters or more complicated individual returns.

CERTIFIED GENERAL ACCOUNTANTS (CGAS) work in sectors such as manufacturing, commerce, and finance, as well as the public sector, private accounting firms, and other sectors that require accounting or financial management services. Among their wide range of training and expertise, they have been trained to prepare income tax returns in the course of obtaining their CGA designation from the Certified General Accountants Association of Canada (**www.cga-canada.org**).

Other people who prepare income tax returns in Canada include bookkeepers, financial planners, and lawyers. They may do a perfectly good job of preparing your tax return, but it's more difficult to assess the level of their expertise from their credentials alone

Ask for Referrals

The best credential any tax preparer can have is a steady stream of satisfied, repeat customers. So regardless of the professional designation (or lack of one), ask for recommendations from relatives, friends, and coworkers who are in roughly the same financial circumstances as you are. If someone you know and trust swears by their tax preparer, make an appointment and check him or her out.

Reputable professionals never promise you a big refund before they have reviewed your situation and run your numbers. They also never ask you to sign a blank tax form or other tax document.

Basically, you want to make sure they have experience in the kind of issues your taxes typically involve. You also want to know that they're up to speed on the latest tax changes. Ask what publications they read, whether they attend continuing education courses, and how many of their clients are audited. And in this age of identity theft, find out how they safeguard your personal information.

Look for Protection

A problem with a tax preparer often means a problem with the Canada Revenue Agency (CRA). So before you hire a tax preparer, find out what (if any) protection you will have in the event they make a mistake. The big chains typically promise to cover any fines, penalties, and interest you might get hit with as a result of their work. Many CAs and CGAs will do the same. But this is not something you can just assume. So make a point of asking about it in advance. And if they tell you that nothing is guaranteed, take your business elsewhere.

Don't Wait Until the Last Minute

If you start looking for a tax professional after the beginning of February, chances are, you're not going to have much luck. All the good ones are usually fully booked up by then. The time to start shopping is in the fall, when a top preparer will have the time to consider your situation and discuss what he or she might be able to do for you.

You May Be Eligible for Free Tax Assistance

If you earn a low income and have a simple tax situation, the CRA offers free help with your tax return through its Community Volunteer Income Tax Program. If you can't prepare your own tax returns, look for one of these Volunteer Tax Preparation Clinics using CRA's web site (www.cra-arc.gc.ca).

If Your Situation Is Relatively Simple, Do It Yourself with Software

If you're a wage earner with run-of-the-mill deductions like child-care or educational expenses, there's no reason you can't do your taxes yourself with one of the many brands of tax-preparation software you can buy today, either over the Internet or in stores. There are dozens of programs and online tax prep services to pick from, but your best bet is to stick with one of the best-sellers: QuickTax (**http://quicktax.intuit.ca**), eTaxCanada (**www.etaxcanada.com**), and TaxTron (**www.taxtron.ca**).

You can find dozens of different packages listed under Canadian Tax Preparation Software for personal use on Wikipedia. Some of these packages cost as much as $60. Others are much less, even free, and all work pretty much the same. They lead you through a long list of questions about your income, personal finances, spending, and family situation. On the basis of your answers, the software then fills out the appropriate forms, prints them out, and, in some cases, even helps you file it all electronically with the federal government's NetFile service (which speeds up any refunds you may be entitled to).

Regardless of which brand you choose, don't pay full price. Tax software is often discounted or bundled with other finance-related software at an affordable price from New Year's Day right through the middle of tax season. Surf the web and check ads in the Sunday paper for the best deals.

What to Watch Out For

Unannounced Outsourcing

Some accounting firms outsource their tax-prep work to chains. Others send returns to overseas subcontractors in places like India, where they can be processed overnight for as little as $50. Either way, you're being ripped off—*and* subjected to the danger of identity theft. As Beth Givens, director of the Privacy Rights Clearinghouse, told *Smart Money* magazine, tax returns contain so much data "in one bright, shiny package"—everything from your Social Insurance Number to your date of birth to your bank and brokerage account numbers—that sending them anywhere, no less halfway around the world, is "a great gift to the identity thief." So make sure your return will be prepared in-house. If

Some accounting firms outsource their tax-prep work to chains.

your preparer won't guarantee that, find another one—or at a minimum, find out how they protect your Social Insurance Number and other sensitive information.

"Related" Products You Don't Really Need

Many preparers make their real money not by filling out tax returns but by selling you related products such as insurance and loans. Many tax preparers will give you your refund today, with a discount for their service, and then collect your full rebate themselves when CRA sends it out. This is perfectly legal, but you may want to think twice about whether you really want less money now or more money when Ottawa sends out your cheque.

Software "Up-Selling"

Just about every brand of tax-prep software has a web site where they allow you to start filling out your tax return free of charge using a bare-bones version of their program. But along the way, they will try to get you to buy a more sophisticated version. This is called upselling—and the added bells and whistles are not always worth the price. A friend of mine who was doing her taxes on one of these sites was persuaded to upgrade from the $49.95 Deluxe version to its $74.95 Premier version because she had sold some stock during the year. The difference? Premier asked her two questions about her stock sale that Deluxe didn't, and it made absolutely no difference in the amount of tax she wound up owing. In other words, she paid $25 more than she needed to for no reduction of her tax bill. Companies will try to up-sell you at every turn. Think hard before you take the bait.

Tax Rebate Discounting

Some tax preparation firms used to offer their clients immediate cash if they qualified for a tax refund. The cash payment would amount to far less than the refund itself, though. In return, the client would sign over the refund to the tax preparer, who would receive the cheque directly from the CRA for the full amount. Since a lot of people needed money immediately, they had little choice but to sign away a substantial refund in return for cash, even if they got only 75% or even 50% of their full refund.

Quebec outlawed this practice altogether. Manitoba passed legislation that required tax rebate discounters to register with the province, pay a $500 fee, and limit the discount to a small percentage of the total refund. Last year, the federal government passed the *Tax Rebate Discounting Act*, which requires rebate discounters in every other province to provide rebates of no less than 85% of the estimated refund up to $300 and 95% of the refund over that amount. The discount includes the fee for preparing the return. The government fines anyone who violates the act and asks taxpayers to report anyone who provides a rebate at a discount larger than the law allows.

What to Do if Things Go Wrong

When you get lousy service from a tax preparer, the problem is compounded by the fact that you still have to deal with CRA. Remember, even if someone else prepared your return, you are still responsible for what's in it. So if you think it was done inaccurately or incorrectly, don't just send it in. Instead, redo it. If there isn't enough time to do it correctly before May 1, then submit it later. You'll have to pay a penalty of 5% or more of your balance owing, but you can then apply for a refund. You have to do this by mail, using a form that you download from the CRA's web site (www.cra-arc.gc.ca) or pick up at your local government office. And CRA will take its time to repay you, probably a year or more, if it approves the repayment at all. But usually that's still better than submitting an improperly prepared return.

If you believe your tax preparer has acted unprofessionally—whether by treating you badly or abusing the law—you should report them to the professional organization that licensed them. You should do it by mail and detail just what your preparer did (or didn't do). The letter should also include any documents that support your claim, along with the practitioner's address and telephone number. Send your letter to:

The Canadian Institute of Chartered Accountants
277 Wellington Street West
Toronto, Ontario M5V 3H2
Tel.: 416-977-3222
Fax: 416-977-8585

or

Certified General Accountants
Suite 100, 4200 North Fraser Way
Burnaby, British Columbia V5J 5K7
Toll-free: 1-800-663-1529

If your preparer is not a certified professional but rather an uncertified preparer (say, some university student working at a storefront chain), you have little recourse with CRA. Unlike the U.S. Internal Revenue Service, CRA doesn't handle complaints from taxpayers. (It treats most of us as if we're suspect to begin with.) As an alternative, you may contact the Better Business Bureau (**www.ccbbb.ca**).

Fight for Your Money Action Steps

- ☐ If you're going to outsource your tax preparation, hire a CA or a CGA.
- ☐ Start your search early.
- ☐ Get a recommendation for a professional from someone you know and trust, but make your final decision after you've interviewed the tax preparer.
- ☐ Find out what their guarantee is if mistakes are made on your return—and how your privacy will be protected, too.
- ☐ If your finances aren't complicated consider filing your taxes yourself with a software package like QuickTax.

Charitable Giving

Practically every morning when I walk from my apartment to my office in downtown Manhattan, I'm stopped by at least half a dozen people asking for contributions to some worthy cause. Some claim they're raising money to protect the environment. Others say they're collecting for victims of domestic violence. Still others mention hurricane relief or Darfur.

For all I know, they're all telling the truth. But I still don't give them any money.

It's not that I'm cheap. I actually believe deeply in the importance of giving. In fact, in most of my books I tell readers that tithing—giving at least 10% of your income to charity—should be part of everyone's financial plan. It's certainly been part of mine for years. But I want the money I donate to really do some good. I don't want it to be wasted.

The fact is that not all charities are legitimate—and even among the legitimate ones some are more efficient and effective than others. Of the 78,000 charities registered in Canada, at least a few of them don't deliver what they promise. It's just not always easy to know which ones don't, unless you do some homework.

Some charities, for example, spend as much as 30% or more of the donations they receive to pay the fundraisers who solicit the donations in the first place. Combined with administrative costs of even 15%, that means that as much as half of every dollar you donate to the charity goes to something other than the cause that the charity represents.

Unless you're careful and do your homework, the hard-earned dollars you contribute to charity could be wasted—or, worse, wind up lining some scam artist's pocket.

How to Fight for Your Money

Canadians give more than $8.5 billion a year in pledges and donations to charities that raise money by tugging at our heartstrings with moving stories about the important work they do and the desperate needs they fill. And it's hard to resist tales of woe and photos of needy children. But if you really want to do good with your money, you need to give smart. Here's how.

Develop a Plan

Be a thoughtful, informed giver. Ask yourself what causes are most important to you and what charities fit best with your interests and sympathies. Then figure out how much you can afford to donate and make that an item in your budget. This will not only make it more likely that you will actually follow through on your good intentions, but also some telemarketer phones you at dinnertime asking for a contribution to some charity you never heard of, you can politely and truthfully end the conversation by explaining that you have a charity budget and they are not on it.

When some telemarketer phones you at dinnertime, explain that you have a charity budget and they are not on it.

Do Some Research

Before you start writing any cheques to a specific charity (no matter how worthy it may seem), you should do some research about how it handles its finances. Experts recommend looking for charitable organizations that pass through at least 75% of what they raise—meaning that at least 75% of every donation should go to support the cause itself (whether it's feeding hungry kids in Africa or buying books for inner-city libraries). They recommend that you stay away from ones that pass through less than 50% due to high administration, management, and fundraising costs.

Charities that subscribe to Imagine Canada's Ethical Fundraising and Financial Accountability Code will provide, upon request, their records on gross revenue, net proceeds, and costs of any fundraising activity (including the fundraising costs categorized as education and/or public awareness) that they undertake. (Check out Imagine Canada's web site at **www.imaginecanada.ca.**)

The Internet makes it easy to find this kind of information. There are numerous rating organizations with web sites that provide extensive information about how virtually every major charity and countless minor ones raise and spend money.

Three of the best information sources are:

Charity Intelligence Canada
Box 124
King City, Ontario
L7B 1A4
Tel: 905-833-0075
www.charityintelligence.ca

Better Business Bureau's Charity Review
2 St. Clair Avenue East, Suite 800
Toronto, Ontario
M4T 2T5
Tel: 416-644-4936
www.ccbbb.ca

Imagine Canada
2 Carlton Street, Suite 600
Toronto, Ontario
M5B 1J3
Toll-free: 1-800-263-1178
www.imaginecanada.ca

If none of these organizations can provide data about the charity of your choice (or if the information they do have is incomplete), check with Canada Revenue Agency's Charities Listing (**www.cra-arc.gc.ca**). It identifies charities whose tax status has been revoked, suspended, or annulled as well as all the other 78,000 organizations that have registered with CRA.

You should also ask the charity itself for a copy of its financial statement. Of course, financial statements can be hard to interpret and figures can be manipulated. So rather than relying solely on the annual report of a group you're thinking of supporting, call them up directly and ask to speak to someone in the development office. Explain that you are considering making a donation and then pepper them with a lot of questions. Which of their programs need money the most? How do they monitor the effectiveness of their programs? Who is on their board? Do any board members make money by providing services to the organization?

If a charity doesn't want to talk about its mission statement, its spending habits, or its financial health, think twice about making a donation. Your willingness to give money gives you the right to ask questions and receive straightforward answers about a charity's health.

Be Wary of Telephone Solicitations

You should be particularly skeptical of telephone solicitations. Don't be afraid to question the person on the phone about his or her relationship with the charity they are touting. It's not uncommon for telemarketers calling on behalf of charities to pocket as much as two-thirds of all the donations they manage to bring in. So if it turns out that the solicitor works for a telemarketing firm, ask what percentage of your contribution will actually go to the charity itself. If you don't like the answer—or if they refuse to tell you—hang up. (If the cause they're touting happens to be one you want to support, you can always contact the charity directly for information about how to make your contribution without going through a middleman.)

It's not uncommon for telemarketers calling on behalf of charities to pocket as much as two-thirds of all the donations they manage to bring in.

Take Advantage of the Tax Breaks—But Not Everything Is Deductible

People will tell you that the great thing about charitable contributions is that they allow you to do good *and* reduce your income-tax bill at the same time. But don't be fooled—not all charitable donations are tax-deductible.

Maybe you gave money to a sick friend at a benefit or to one of those police organizations that calls you up at dinnertime to solicit for funds. Or maybe you donated to a political campaign or spent $50 on raffle tickets for your child's after-school program. These are all worthy causes, but that alone doesn't cut any ice with CRA. Unless the recipient is a registered charity, your contribution is not tax-deductible. (And don't be misled by organizations that describe themselves as tax-exempt. All that means is that *they* don't have to pay taxes; it doesn't necessarily mean that contributions to them are tax-deductible.)

So if your goal in charitable giving is at least partly a tax deduction, make sure the recipient of your donation is a registered charity. (You can find them listed on CRA's web site, **www.cra-arc.gc.ca**.) And if you don't want to get in trouble with CRA, make sure you subtract from your deduction the value of any goods or services you received in return for your contribution.

For instance, say you got a copy of your favourite band's latest CD as a premium for contributing to your local public-radio station's pledge drive. If so, you can't deduct the entire amount of your contribution. You've got to subtract the cost of the CD. Or say you spent $100 on tickets to a charitable gala; if the food and entertainment were worth $30, you can claim only a $70 deduction on your taxes.

How do you know how much to subtract? The charitable group should provide you with a tax receipt telling you the value of any goods or services you may have received in connection with your contribution. If they don't, ask them for it.

Be Careful About Donating Noncash Gifts

Of course, money isn't the only thing you can give to a charity. You can also donate cars and boats, household goods and clothing, stocks and bonds, mutual funds, you name it—if it has value, some charity will probably be happy to take it.

Deducting the value of noncash contributions can be tricky. If you're one of those people who thinks that donating your old junk is a great way to clean out your attic and cut your tax bill at the same time, think again. In recent years, CRA has tightened up the regulations regarding deductions for noncash charitable gifts.

To begin with, donated goods must be assessed not at what you think they're worth but at fair market value, which is the price that a seller could actually get a buyer to pay.

For stocks, mutual funds, and other securities, that's relatively straightforward (although in late 2008, as I write, with stock and bond prices going up and down like a yo-yo, it's not as easy as it once was.) You are entitled to deduct 100% of whatever amount the security happens to be trading at on the day you make the donation. This can be a terrific deal tax-wise if you are donating a long-term investment that is worth a lot more than you originally paid for it. By transferring the security directly to the charity (as opposed to selling it and donating the proceeds), you avoid having to pay any capital gains tax, yet you get to deduct the investment's full market value on your tax return.

The benefits are slightly less generous when you donate stuff you own—like appliances or books or clothing. In most cases, you have to have these items professionally appraised, and you can't claim your old TV or tennis racket is worth what it would cost you to buy a new one, or even what you originally paid for it. eBay is another acceptable source of prices for used goods.

If you are unsure of the rules, go to CRA's web site (**www.cra-arc.gc.ca**) and check Line 349—Donations and gifts. And whatever else you do, be sure to keep good records. CRA requires a receipt or cancelled check for any donation, no matter how small the amount. So when you're giving money, try to pay by cheque or with a credit card. Actual cash is not only hard to track, but also can too easily wind up in the wrong person's pocket.

What to Do if Things Go Wrong

When it comes to supporting charities, you can't afford to let your guard down. It's sad, but there are scammers out there eager to take advantage of those of us who want to make a difference and support a cause. So be skeptical if you receive an unsolicited phone call or email from an organization asking for money or from an individual claiming to be a victim—particularly around the holidays or in the aftermath of a major disaster. At the very least, never provide any credit card or bank information unless you are absolutely sure that the solicitor is legitimate.

If you have any suspicions that a solicitor is falsely posing as a representative of a well-known charity like the Salvation Army, United Way, or Canadian Red Cross, you should contact the real charity directly. They will either verify the solicitor's affiliation with them and deal with any complaints you may have about his or her behaviour—or they will take steps to deal with the scam.

If you suspect a solicitor of shilling for a nonexistent charity, you should contact a law-enforcement agency such as your local police or Phonebusters (**www.phonebusters.com**).

Complaints about the behaviour or management practices of existing charitable organizations should go to CRA. You should also notify the Better Business Bureau (**www.ccbbb.ca**).

Fight for Your Money Action Steps

- ☐ Be proactive. Figure out what issues are most important to you and how much you can afford to donate, then go on a charity-rating web site and find out which organizations that work on these issues are the most financially sound.
- ☐ If getting a tax deduction is important to you, make sure you are donating to a charity registered and in good standing with CRA.
- ☐ Follow the rules for valuing noncash donations when you deduct them from your taxes.
- ☐ If you suspect charity fraud, report it.

TV AND PHONE

Cable and Satellite TV

Cable TV service is truly a joke. On any given night, you may have 150 channels to choose from and for the most part there is nothing on any of them that's worth watching. (Is it just me—or do you feel this way too?). One of the first things I always do when I present a money makeover on some TV show is look at how much the family is spending on cable. In my experience, it is often more than $100 a month. One hundred dollars a month is $1,200 a year. Do you know what that means? Figuring the taxes you have to pay, you have to earn nearly $2,500 a year to pay the cost of receiving 150 stations you don't watch! There are families right now in Canada that literally work a full month every year just to pay their cable bill.

There are families right now in Canada that literally work a full month every year just to pay their cable bill.

The good news, I guess, is that if you really love television, you now have a lot to choose from and many more ways to get it.

What Do You Really Watch—and Do You Really Need It?

For a nation of TV watchers, the explosion of channels available to us over cable and satellite TV in recent years might seem like a great thing. And for some people, it is. But for most of us, it's a huge rip-off.

I'm not talking about bad programs. That's a matter of taste. If you don't like what's on, you don't have to watch—and you certainly don't have to shell out $75 a month for cable or satellite service. But if there are programs you do like, then, chances are, you are going to be ripped off. That's because in order to get the channels that carry them, you'll also have to subscribe to other channels that you may have no interest in watching.

As most cable and satellite TV subscribers know, you can't really pick and choose the channels you get. You have to order them in packages (or "tiers," as some of the companies call them), starting with a basic lineup of 25 to 50 or more channels. So if all you're interested in is CBC Newsworld and the Weather Channel, that's too bad—you're still going to get CTV, YTV, The Shopping Channel, and CPAC as well, depending on your location and the company that services your area.

With the explosion in the number of channels available by cable and satellite, the average Canadian home receives more than 75 television channels. But if U.S. viewing habits are similar to Canada's, the average home watches only about 15 of them with any regularity. What's so terrible about getting channels that you don't watch? Well, nothing really—*except that you're paying for them*. In all, some experts estimate that we consumers fork out as much as $600 million a year more than we should for channels we don't want and wouldn't subscribe to if we could choose on an à la carte basis.

This doesn't mean you should throw your cable or satellite box out the window. But don't be fooled into thinking that you're getting a great bargain from any of the cable or satellite companies.

How to Fight for Your Money

For all that the lack of à la carte pricing is a rip off, there's no question that consumers have benefited from the bitter competition between the two systems. While prices are still relatively high, they are no longer increasing the way they used to. And the variety and quality of services you can get—from high-definition programming to video on demand to built-in digital recorders—is nothing short of amazing.

It may seem as if everyone with a TV has either cable or satellite service, but the fact is that some 1.5 million Canadian households still get their TV the old-fashioned way—with an over-the-air antenna. But they are a dying breed. Roughly 8 million of the nation's 12.5 million TV households are wired for cable, while around 3.5 million homes subscribe to one of the nation's two DTH (for direct to home) services, Bell TV and Star Choice.

If you're fortunate enough to live in one of the areas where fibre-optic service is already available, you should probably give it serious consideration, since its huge bandwidth gives it the ability to offer superior picture quality, better interactive services (like video on demand), and more HD channels than either cable or satellite. The catch is that it will be years before it will be available everywhere—or even in most places. So for the time being at least the real choice for most of us is between cable and satellite.

Here are their pros and cons.

Cable

PROS: Simplicity, economy, versatility. You don't need to buy any equipment (except for a TV) and if you're willing to forego all premium and HD channels, you can get a bare-bones basic package for as little as $30 a month. With a digital box, (which will cost you an extra $10 or so a month) you can sign up for all sorts of more costly premium programming, such as National Geographic and Showcase, as well as for video on demand and elaborate HD packages.

CONS: Lack of competition. Most communities wired for cable are served by only one provider. So if you want cable but don't like the company that has the franchise for your area, you're out of luck. This may be why customer service problems (like waiting for days for the cable guy to show up) are legendary. Cable is also not available in some rural areas.

Satellite

PROS: High customer-satisfaction ratings—perhaps because no matter where you are, you have a choice between Bell TV and Star Choice. Satellite offers phenomenal sports offerings (NHL Centre Ice, for example, and NFL Sunday Ticket for $25 a month on Star Choice), and dozens of HD channels (Star Choice has 33; Bell TV has more than 60).

CONS: Substantial upfront costs to buy or lease equipment and pay for installation, including around $150 for an HD dish and as much as $250 for a high-def PVR setup (though rebates can reduce or eliminate many of these charges). Local broadcast channels are not always available and there is no true video on demand (because satellite systems are not interactive like digital cable). You also need to be able to mount an 18-inch dish on your house with an unobstructed view of the southern horizon, and even then your signal can be distorted in bad weather. (The start-up costs are not charged if you live in an apartment complex or condominium building already wired with a dish. But even then, most companies still charge you an activation fee.)

Don't Panic—You Really Have Only Three Companies to Choose From

Given all the sports, movie, and HD packages the cable and satellite companies offer—not to mention the countless rebates, credits, and different kinds of contract commitments—picking a provider can seem to be a hugely complicated deal. The thing to remember is that, in most Canadian locations, you really have only three choices: whatever company has your local cable franchise or Bell TV or Star Choice. And if you've decided you'd prefer cable to satellite, you have only one.

This doesn't mean you're at their mercy. In fact, the opposite is true. The competition between the satellite and cable providers is so intense—and they're all so worried about the challenge posed by the new fibre-optic networks—that they are often willing to wheel and deal. This is particularly true when it comes to keeping existing customers from defecting. So if you currently have cable service, don't be afraid to call the company and tell them you're thinking of switching to satellite TV. They may offer to reduce your rates in order to keep your business.

Negotiate, Negotiate, Negotiate

In my experience, there is almost nothing easier than lowering your cable or satellite bill. Usually, you can do it with one phone call. That's because what you are paying now is almost certainly more than what a new customer would pay for the same service if they signed up today and took advantage of

He Fought for His Money!

I worked with one couple on a money-makeover TV show who were paying nearly $80 a month for cable—more than $1,000 a year. The husband insisted he needed TSN. I convinced him he didn't need it—that he could save $500 a year by living without it. Then we called the cable company and asked for a better package. Just dropping the sports-channel tier cut his bill in half. Later, I had him call back a second time and tell the cable company that he had just gotten a coupon from a satellite TV company offering introductory service at $19.95 a month for six months. Guess what happened? His cable company matched the offer—and threw in TSN for free, for a total savings of nearly $400!

one of the many new-customer specials that cable and satellite companies constantly offer.

There is almost nothing easier than lowering your cable or satellite bill.

So open your junk mail this week and see what is being offered in your area. Check your newspaper, too, and go online. The competition between cable and satellite TV providers is brutal—and their willingness to make deals is especially great in areas where the new fibre-optic service is available. Take advantage of the situation. Call your cable company and negotiate your bill down. If they won't work with you, threaten to cancel. And if that doesn't work, then SWITCH SERVICES to get yourself a better deal.

What to Do if Things Go Wrong

The first place to go if you have a service or billing problem with your cable TV provider is the company itself. Call the customer service number listed on your bill and see if you can work it out with them.

One thing to keep in mind when dealing with cable-company call centre employees is that they are often expected to handle all complaint calls they receive within a certain period of time or they get into trouble. As a result, they've been known to make promises that just aren't true, or even hang up on a customer who won't take no for an answer. In fact, these front-line customer-service representatives often don't have the authority to fix your problem; their instructions are to make excuses or even lie. So when you call, don't waste your time with the person who picks up the phone; instead, ask to speak to a supervisor.

If you can't resolve your problem with the company, you should file a complaint with the Canadian Radio-Television and Telecommunications Commission (CRTC). You can sometimes find a standard complaint form and instructions on the web site of your local municipality. That's because cable companies generally operate under franchises granted by local municipalities, and each municipality with a cable franchise designates one of its officials to handle complaints from residents.

You can contact the CRTC by telephoning toll-free at 1-877-249-2782 or writing to:

CRTC
Les Terrasses de la Chaudière, Central Building
1 Promenade du Portage
Gatineau, Quebec
J8X 4B1
Toll-free: 1-877-249-2782

Fight for Your Money Action Steps

- ☐ Ask yourself—can you make do with fewer channels?
- ☐ Gather together any promotions you can find from competing services in your area—check your mail and newspaper, and search online. Then get out your current bill and call your current provider.
- ☐ Review your current service with your provider, ask about other packages that might make more sense for you, then compare offers from their competitors.
- ☐ Negotiate! Let your current provider know that you're switching to the competition if they're not willing to offer a better deal.

Cell-Phone Plans

I remember my friend David's first cell phone. David had one in 1985, and when we took it into a restaurant, every single person in the place stared at us. Never mind that the phone was as big as a brick. It was portable, and no one had them yet.

Fast forward to today, and there are now 3.3 billion cell phones in use around the world. That's enough for every other person on the planet. Never in history has a technological device become such an essential part of our lives so completely. As I write this in 2008, there are more than 21 million wireless subscribers in Canada—roughly 65% of the population—yakking away on their cell phones an average of 15 minutes a day, and that's expected to increase to more than 75% of the population by 2010.

In all, Canadians spend about $15 billion a year on wireless phone services, far more, by comparison, than wireless customers in most other countries. The average bill runs $60 a month. This may not sound like very much, but it's a lot bigger than it needs to be. Why? Because most of us have the wrong cell-phone plan—as a result of which we wind up buying a lot more minutes than we really need. Indeed, while reliable figures are hard to come by, some experts estimate that the average cell phone user lets 40% of his plan minutes go to waste.

Why do we do this? Well, even though we all depend on cell phones to keep our lives on track, the fact is that most of us hate having to pick a cell phone provider and figure out the billing plan that makes the most sense for us. And for good reason. The three national cell phone carriers—Rogers, Telus, and Bell—offer such a confusing array of features, services, and pricing plans that it's often difficult to figure out who has the best deal.

The good news is that after years of phenomenal growth—the cell phone population exploded by nearly 700% between 1995 and 2007—we're reaching the point where just about everybody who wants a cell phone already has one. As a result, the number of new customers signing up for cell-phone service finally seems to be levelling out.

Why is this good news? Because with the market for new cell-phone users pretty much tapped out, the only way a cell-phone company can continue to grow is by stealing business from its competitors. And as one marketing expert told *USA Today*, "When operators have no choice but to try to take customers away from each other, they have a natural inclination to sharpen the pencils and make the best offer they can."

In other words, if you know what to look for, this may be the best time ever to be in the market for a good cell-phone plan. Just saving $10 a month on a plan could help you pocket more than $120 this year! And if you are a family and aim to save $30 a month, that's $360 a year in savings. Chances are, you can do this in an hour with just a little research and a little negotiating with your current provider.

How to Fight for Your Money

The key to getting a good cell-phone plan is knowing what you really need it for. Ask yourself the following:

- Do you live on your cell or do you keep one just for emergencies?
- Do you call all sorts of different people or mainly the same ones over and over again?
- Are most of your calls local or do you have friends and relatives in a different part of the country who you call a lot?
- Are you a single twentysomething who texts as much as you talk or do you have a family (and, hence, a need for several phones)?
- Do you often travel outside the country or do you stick close to home?

Your answers to these and other similar questions about the way you use your cell phone should determine which of the countless service plans out there is right for you. A good plan meets your needs. A bad one forces you to change your behaviour in order to achieve savings or keep from being penalized. Here's how to determine which is which.

Don't Buy a Bigger Plan Than You Need

There are three kinds of cell-phone users. Low-volume users generally use their cell phones only for emergencies or to give to their kids so they can call if they get stuck somewhere. Typically, they are on their cell phones less than 300 minutes a month. Medium-volume users, who use their phones to keep in touch with friends and family but don't spend half their lives on them, are in the 300- to 1,000-minutes-a-month range. And then there are high-volume users, who log north of 1,000 minutes a month—and whose phones are basically attached to their heads.

The key to getting a good deal on a cell-phone plan is never to buy a bigger plan than you need. Most people worry too much about the excess fees they will have to pay if they go over their plan's limit. It's certainly true that most carriers will charge you as much as 45 cents a minute for any time in excess of what your plan includes. But this is less of a problem than being locked into a plan that's bigger than you need. If you find yourself using more minutes than your plan allows, most carriers will be happy to let you upgrade. But they won't let you downsize if the reverse turns out to be the case. So be conservative. When in doubt, go for the smaller plan.

When in doubt, go for the smaller plan.

If You Are a Low-Volume Caller, Go with a Basic Plan for as Little as $10 a Month

If you're a low-volume user, you should probably get one of the basic plans offered by the major providers. For $30 to $40 a month, most big carriers will give you at least 300 minutes with no long-distance or roaming charges plus a free phone. If that's too much, you can get really inexpensive service from a specialty provider like Koodo. For as little as $15 a month, Koodo's super-simple Combo 15 plan comes with 50 minutes of calling time and no activation fee if you do it online.

You might also consider a prepaid plan, where you pay in advance and are charged only for the time you actually use the phone (often as little as 10 cents a minute). Prepaid plans also make sense if your credit is bad or you have teenage children whose phone usage you want to limit. All the major carriers offer them. Maybe you don't need a phone at all—maybe a phone card would do!

For medium-volume callers, there are plenty of good plans offering up to 1,000 minutes for between $40 and $80 a month, while high-volume users can get absolutely unlimited domestic calling (that is, as many calls as you want for as long as you want anywhere in Canada and sometimes the United

States too) for $100 a month. Keep in mind that these figures cover only regular phone calls. Extra services—such as text, photo, and video messaging—will cost you extra.

Think About Who You'll Be Calling

Most people tend to make most of their calls to the same small group of numbers—their home, their office, their spouse or sweetheart, their best buddies, and so on. If this is true of you, you should probably consider a plan that allows you unlimited calling to several specific numbers that you pick in advance. (Rogers, Telus, and Bell have plans that let you choose up to 20 numbers.) In many cases, this feature can make it possible for a high-volume caller to use a less expensive medium-volume plan without going over the monthly usage limit.

Think About Where You'll Be Calling

All the major carriers put most of their marketing efforts into pushing national calling plans that let you phone anywhere in Canada without incurring any long-distance or roaming charges. These are generally terrific deals if you make a fair number of long-distance calls. But if you don't, you might want to consider getting a local or regional plan, where in return for agreeing to pay extra for long-distance, you get extra-cheap rates for calls within your home city or region. (Local plans generally cover a single metropolitan area, while regional plans may include several provinces.)

Basically, the smaller your coverage area, the less your plan will cost—but the more you will have to pay for out-of-area calls. For example, while a basic national plan gives you 1,000 minutes for $49.95 a month, a regional plan gives you 3,000 minutes for the same price—though calls made from outside the region or to a number outside the region will cost you 49 cents a minute. Similarly, for $39.99 you can get a national plan that includes 500 minutes or a regional one that gives you 700 minutes.

At the opposite end of the spectrum, if you travel outside the country a lot—or make a lot of overseas calls—you'll want to pick a carrier with good international calling capabilities. Ideally, you want one that uses Global System for Mobile (GSM) technology, so its phones can also be used outside Canada.

Don't Forget About the Cost of Nonvoice Features

The thing about cell phones is that telephone conversations are the least of their uses these days. If we're not texting or sending photos to friends, we're using our phones to access our favourite web site, play games, or listen to music. Unfortunately, it's easy to forget that none of this is free. So if you think you might be using any of these nonvoice features—and, chances are, you will be—make sure you get a plan that includes them. Texting can cost as much as 15 cents a message if your plan doesn't include it—and as little as a penny per message when it does.

Before You Pick a Carrier, Check Out Their Coverage

Location, location, location!

Just like in real estate, location is critically important when it comes to cell-phone service. Though all of the major carriers provide what's described as nationwide service, the coverage they offer varies considerably from region to region. And in some places, it's nonexistent. So before you pick a provider, you should find out what kind of on-the-ground coverage they have in areas that matter to you—like your house or apartment, your neighbourhood, your workplace, and places you often visit.

All the major providers offer coverage maps on their web sites, but take them with a grain of salt, if you can get them to work at all. (Try Rogers's wireless maps, for example. Good luck.) The carriers' maps tend to be fairly general and they don't always show the random dead spots that drive most cell-phone users crazy. So always check with friends and neighbours about their experiences and visit such independent web sites as **www.deadcellzones.com**, where you can punch in your address and see reports on what kind of coverage you're really going to get.

If You Have a Family, Get a Family Plan

All the major carriers offer family plans, where Mom, Dad, and the kids all have separate phones with separate numbers but share the same pool of monthly minutes. The advantage is that under the family plan, the separate lines cost you far less than if everyone had his or her own individual account. If you have a family—or for any other reason need more than one cell phone—signing up for a family plan is as close to a no-brainer as anything you'll find in the cellular universe.

CHEAPER BY THE DOZEN	
Two separate cell numbers:	$79.98 a month
Two numbers on a family plan:	$69.99 a month
You save:	**$9.99 a month**
Three separate cell numbers:	$119.97 a month
Three numbers on a family plan:	$79.98 a month
You save:	**$39.99 a month**

Choose Your Carrier Before You Choose Your Phone

Each carrier has a specific set of cell phones that work with its network. So do you pick a phone and then see which carriers support it? Or do you pick a carrier and then see which phones it allows? If you think about it for a minute, you'll realize that the best phone in the world isn't worth very much if your carrier has spotty coverage and lousy customer service. In other words, the chicken in this chicken-and-egg problem is the carrier. So make sure you've found yourself a good carrier before you worry about whether your phone will come preloaded with a sufficient number of cool ringtones.

Before you select your carrier, you should compare services on a web site like Mobilook (**www.mobilook.com/CarriersCanada.asp**) to see how Bell compares with Koodo, for example, or Telus compares with Rogers. You should also use the incredibly useful checklist at the Canada's Office of Consumer Affairs (**www.ic.gc.ca/epic/site/oca-bc.nsf/en/ca02270e.html**) to make sure you ask for what you need rather than what the wireless company wants to sell you.

Always Ask for a Trial Period

Given that it's so hard to get out of cell-phone contracts—and that there are so many variables involved in cell-phone service—it's always a good idea to ask for a trial period to test the service. There is really no substitute for real-world experience when it comes to knowing how well you'll be able to talk to the kids at school, your spouse at home or work, and friends and colleagues wherever they may be. Trial periods usually last for 15 days or more, after which, if you're not satisfied with the service, you can return your phone and get out of your contract without having to pay an early termination fee. If the carrier you're leaning toward doesn't offer any sort of test drive, see if you can sign up for service on a month-to-month basis—that is, without having to commit yourself for one or two years of service.

You May Not Have to Sign a Contract

To read the carriers' ads and visit their web sites, you'd think the only way you can get a decent cell phone and decent cell-phone plan is to sign a contract that commits you to at least two years' of service. In fact, most carriers will give you a monthly service plan without a long-term commitment as long as you're willing to forego some of the more attractive come-ons—like free phones and special data services. If you don't like the idea of paying full price for a phone (which, depending on the model, can easily run to several hundred dollars), ask if you can sign a contract for one year, rather than two. You'll have to pay part of the cost of the phone (typically between $50 and $100), but the flexibility you get is worth it.

Early-Termination Fees

Aside from dropped calls, nothing bugs cell phone customers more than the early-termination fees carriers force you to pay if you want to get out of your contract before it expires. With penalties running as high as $200 per phone line, it's hardly surprising that in a survey conducted by *Consumer Reports*, one in seven cell-phone subscribers said that if it wasn't for the early termination fee, they would have left their current carrier long ago.

It used to be that you would be charged the full termination fee regardless of whether you quit at the beginning of your contract or the day before its expiration date. But since May 2008, wireless carriers have begun prorating their fees—meaning that the further along you are in your contract, the lower the fee.

Of course, this doesn't help much if you want to drop your service near the beginning of your contract. But there are ways to get out of a cell-phone contract without paying a termination fee.

For one thing, the contracts of nearly all carriers include what's called a "material adverse change" clause. In plain English, this means that any time your carrier adds a new charge to your plan—which happens all the time—you have the right to cancel your contract without penalty within 14 days. The carriers obviously know this, and they interpret the clause as strictly as possible. So if you try to go this route, make sure you follow the contract

Anytime your carrier adds a new charge to your plan, you have the right to cancel your contract without penalty within 14 days.

provisions closely. You'll probably get an argument from the company, but it's one you have a good chance of winning.

Another way to avoid a termination fee is to transfer your cell-phone contract to someone else. All the major carriers allow customers to do this, though their rules for how it must be done differ slightly. Finding someone to take over your contract is simpler than you might think. For a fee of around $20 to $25, web sites like Cell Swapper Canada (**http://ca.cellswapper.com**) will hook you up with consumers who are eager to get a cell-phone account without having to pay an activation fee. You can also do this on craigslist (**www.craigslist.ca**).

Mandatory Contract Extensions

Once your initial contract ends, you are free to continue service on a month-to-month basis. The companies, however, will do everything they can to get you to sign a new contract. Their main tactic is to try to hook you by offering you a free new phone or sexy new data service. Buried in the fine print that accompanies these offers are provisions that say your contract will automatically be extended if you take the deal. So be skeptical of promotional come-ons. If you like your carrier and don't mind having your contract extended, then by all means take advantage of the offers. But make sure you know what you're agreeing to when you sign up for one of these free deals.

Unnecessary Phone Insurance

Cell phones may be free, but they are not cheap. As a result many consumers are tempted to buy the cell-phone insurance that all the major carriers offer. It's a temptation you should resist. That's because unless you wind up putting in a claim within the first few months, these policies are far more likely to cost you money than save you money. The problem is that the premiums generally total around $60 a year, while the deductibles run as high as $100. So if you lose or break your phone after having the policy for a year, you'll be out around $160—which is pretty much what you would have had to spend on a new phone if you didn't have any insurance.

What They Mean by "Unlimited Nationwide Calling"

One of the most attractive developments in cell-phone pricing in recent years is the wide availability of national calling plans that allow you to call nationwide without incurring any roaming charges. But not all nationwide calling plans are alike.

The problem is that not everyone defines the word "nationwide" the same way. While you may think that nationwide means anywhere in the country, some providers define nationwide as meaning anywhere within their network. So before you start travelling with your phone, check with your carrier to make sure your definition of "nationwide" agrees with theirs. Otherwise, even if you never leave Canada, you could find some hefty roaming charges on your next bill if you happen to make a call from somewhere outside your carrier's coverage area.

Roaming Charges for Overseas Calls

Roaming charges can be a huge issue if you travel outside the country with your cell phones. Calls placed from foreign countries can easily cost you upward of $1 per minute. So before you travel abroad you must call your carrier and find out the costs and see if they have an overseas plan you can sign up for. In many cases, you can add this service just for the time you'll be travelling.

What to Do if Things Go Wrong

There are basically two kinds of problems with cell-phone service providers—contract issues and service issues. Your first stop in the event of either kind of problem should be with the carrier itself. Either call their customer service number or visit one of their stores.

If you can't resolve the problem with them, you should file a complaint with the industry's Commissioner for Complaints for Telecommunications Services (CCTS). Telecom companies formed this nonprofit organization to handle complaints from consumers and small businesses about their telecommunications services. You can reach the CCTS at:

Commissioner for Complaints for Telecommunications Services
P.O. Box 81088
Ottawa, Ontario
K1P 1B1
Toll-free: 1-888-221-1687
Toll-free TTY: 1-877-782-2384
Fax: 1-877-782-2924

You can get more information on the Internet at **www.ccts-cprst.ca**.

Issues involving your cell-phone contract—say, early termination fees or mandatory extensions—can also be dealt with by your province's consumer affairs department. (A complete list is available through the Canadian Consumer Information Gateway (**http://consumerinformation.ca**)).

Finally, if you think your wireless service provider has misled you, you can file a complaint with Industry Canada's Competition Bureau:

Competition Bureau
Industry Canada
50 Victoria Street
Gatineau, Quebec
K1A 0C9
Toll-free: 1-800-348-5358
Toll-free TTY: 1-800-642-3844

If Your Cell Phone Is Lost or Stolen, 10 Steps to Protect Yourself

I recently saw a TV report that prompted me to write an entire article about what to do when your cell phone is lost or stolen. If this happens to you, you could get stuck with a *huge* bill for unauthorized charges—unless you know how to fight back! Consider what happened to Wendy N., who was hit with a bill for $26,000 after her cell phone was unknowingly stolen before she left for an overseas vacation. Her cell-phone company held her responsible for charges incurred after the phone was taken, up until the time Wendy discovered the theft and called the carrier.

Wendy was able to prove via airline and passport documents that she was out of the country and couldn't possibly have made the unauthorized calls during that time, but the company still held Wendy accountable for all charges.

Not only that, they advised Wendy that if she couldn't pay the bill she should consider filing for bankruptcy!

CAN THIS BE LEGAL?

If you dig through all the fine print in your cell-phone contract, you'll most likely discover a statement that reads something like this: "Should your cell phone be lost or stolen you are responsible for any costs incurred for unauthorized calls made prior to reporting the cell phone missing."

Unlike a credit card, cellular contracts are not required to limit liability for fraudulent charges. But it's important to realize that the extent of your liability as stated in your contract is your provider's policy—it's not a law.

AVOIDING AND RESPONDING TO A THEFT

Are we at the mercy of an unregulated industry that's free of consequences and penalties? Not if we learn how to defend ourselves.

Thousands of cell phones are reported lost or stolen every year. Here are the 10 things you need to know to protect yourself from cell-phone theft and fraudulent charges:

1. GUARD YOUR CELL PHONE AS YOU WOULD YOUR WALLET.
   Yes, this is obvious advice, but frankly the best way to not get stuck with fraudulent charges is to do what you can to prevent unauthorized calls in the first place.

   On a related note, think twice about what information you store on your device. A stolen cell phone can lead to not only a huge bill, but also identity theft as well.

2. PASSWORD-PROTECT YOUR DEVICE.
   Check the user guide that came with your phone and start using the "lock" or "password" feature to potentially prevent a thief from making unauthorized calls. There are ways to override passwords, but at the very least you might be buying yourself some time until you discover the loss and call your provider.

3. DON'T BE FOOLED BY CELL-PHONE INSURANCE.
   Purchasing cell-phone insurance will provide coverage for the device itself, but it won't protect you against charges for unauthorized calls.

4. CALL YOUR CELL-PHONE PROVIDER AS SOON AS YOU DISCOVER THE LOSS.
   Report your missing device, and be sure to keep meticulous records, including the date and time you called your carrier, the name and ID number of the representative to whom you spoke, and what you were told.

   Also note the province or region of their call centre, plus their telephone extension number. Finally, ask for confirmation in writing that your device has been disabled. Some companies can even email this to you.

5. FILE A POLICE REPORT.
   This may not help your chances of getting the stolen phone back, but it still provides an official record of the crime. Your carrier may even require the police report number when you phone in the loss.

6. OPEN AN INVESTIGATION WITH YOUR CARRIER IF NECESSARY.
   If you find that you're not getting an immediate resolution, don't

waste another minute. Call your carrier and request an investigation, then follow up in writing. Generally, requesting an investigation gives you a better chance of preventing any formal collections action from being taken and should also delay reporting to any of the credit bureaus.

When you request an investigation, advise your carrier that you'll be filing a complaint with the Commissioner for Complaints for Telecommunications Services (CCTS) and your province's consumer affairs office. Your carrier is more likely to pay closer attention to you when they know you're an informed consumer.

7. CONTACT THE CCTS.

The CCTS will forward your complaint to your service provider, requiring an RESPonse from them within 30 days.

8. CONTACT YOUR PROVINCE'S CONSUMER AFFAIRS DEPARTMENT.

You can find the contact information for your province's consumer affairs office at **consumerinformation.ca**.

9. CONTACT YOUR LOCAL BETTER BUSINESS BUREAU.

You can reach the Better Business Bureau at: **http://www.ccbbb.ca/**.

10. WHEN ALL ELSE FAILS, CONTACT THE MEDIA.

The wireless companies are particularly adverse to negative media attention, so until effective laws are put into place you may have to resort to contacting your local TV station.

In Wendy's case, that's just what she did, and her story has a happy ending. After many months of persistent determination and follow-up, all fraudulent charges were dropped. It seems the wireless industry wants to do the right thing after all—as long as they're forced to by the media.

Ultimately, her local consumer news reporter played a huge role in getting the situation resolved. But don't be tempted to skip steps 7 through 9. These industry and government authorities all need to see how serious a problem this is, so formal complaints serve an important purpose.

Fight for Your Money Action Steps

- ☐ Figure out the size of the plan that's right for you (and your family), then comparison-shop among the major providers. Be conservative. When in doubt, go for the smaller plan.
- ☐ Consider a prepaid plan if you're a low-volume user, have bad credit, or have children who need a phone for emergency purposes.
- ☐ If you don't make a lot of long-distance calls, opt for a regional or local plan, which can get you more minutes for less money.
- ☐ Check out the coverage area before you decide on a carrier.
- ☐ Choose your carrier, then choose your phone.
- ☐ Ask for a trial period. This is a great way to make sure the plan and the phone work for you before signing on the dotted line.
- ☐ If you change your service in any way, be sure your contract isn't being extended without your knowledge.
- ☐ If your phone is lost or stolen, contact your carrier immediately.

Residential Phone Service

If you go strictly by the numbers, dumping your landline can seem like a no-brainer. After all, most of us already have a cell phone, so why pay for a landline too? Cancelling it can save you $50 a month, which adds up to a quick $600 a year back in your pocket.

Unfortunately, it's not that simple. Landlines are convenient, and many people live in places where cell-phone reception isn't good. I live in New York City, which has to be one of the best-served cell-phone areas in the world, but my cell phone does not work in my building. So I have to have a landline.

The fact is, in this wireless world of ours, only 3.1 million households used landlines exclusively at the end of 2007, while more than 9 million had at least one cell-phone. But 3.1 million is still a lot of houses, all hooked up with old-fashioned landline service—where signals travel from a central exchange along copper wires that snake into our bedrooms and kitchens and plug directly into our telephones. That's probably because of Canada's geography as much as our preferences for wires. It's hard to use a cell phone if you live in parts of Canada that aren't served by a wireless network, which describes a vast part of the country and explains why Canada has lagged behind the United States in adopting the technology. And of the households with cell phones in Canada, only 6.4% of them used them exclusively in 2007. So there are still a lot of Canadians talking on the phone in the old-fashioned way.

Nevertheless, the number of landline phone subscribers in Canada has been declining ever since. Early in 2004, the number of cell-phone subscribers zoomed past the number of people with landline phones. These days, cell phones probably outnumber landlines by 3-to-1 or more.

Still, even if it's no longer the mainstay it used to be, landline service is a part of our lives, and for many of us it's not going away. For one thing, it's often cheaper than wireless service. For another, regular phones are generally more comfortable to use than cellular handsets, especially on longer calls. And because they have their own power supply (which comes in over the phone lines), landline phones are not as vulnerable to power outages as computer-based systems or cell towers.

One thing landline phones have in common with their wireless counterparts is the confusing maze of choices you have to sort through when you're picking a service provider. Once upon a time, the phone company was a monopoly. This definitely had its disadvantages but it did make the selection process very simple. Today, after decades of deregulation, there are dozens of telephone companies angling for both your local and long-distance business. The trick is to figure out which one is right for you.

How to Fight for Your Money

You can use the same company for local and long-distance service or two different ones.

To get residential phone service these days, you need to pick a local carrier for local phone service and a long-distance carrier for long-distance service. You can use the same company for both or you can use different companies for each.

In one sense, picking your local and long-distance phone companies is not very different from picking a cell-phone carrier. Your decision should be based on what kind of telephone consumer you are. In Canada, residential phone customers pay a flat monthly rate and have unlimited local calling. For long distance, they usually pay by the minute. Figure out how many minutes you're likely to need (dig out a few old bills, if you're not sure) and look for a plan that provides them at a rock-bottom rate. An easy way to do this is to call your current carrier and have them analyze your current usage. Tell them: "I'm looking to save money. Based on my usage, am I on the best plan? What else can you offer me?"

Even if you're not in the market for new service, I strongly recommend that right now (as soon as you finish this chapter) you give your current plans a fresh look—especially if you've had them for a while. Do you really know how much you're paying for phone calls? Review some recent bills

Do the math on your phone bills and see if you might want to think about switching.

and do the math. And then see if you can get cheaper service from a new provider.

I can't emphasize enough that the best way to save money NOW is to call your current carrier and simply ask for a better deal. Have them sell you on your current plan and push them to look at what special offers they have and how they can save you money by providing you the best plan based on your current usage. They know exactly how much you use, and they know that they can save you money. Trust me on this—they will not be calling you with ideas about how you can save money. You have to call them. (It's called FIGHTING FOR YOUR MONEY.)

For Local Service, It Pays to Stay Local

When it comes to local service, most residential phone customers stick with the established local company—which in most places these days is one of the telecommunication giants. That's not surprising, since in addition to reliable service, they all offer a variety of plans, some bundled with long-distance packages, some separate, some including special features like call waiting, voice mail, and caller ID. Typically, you should be able to get basic unlimited local calling from your local provider for $20 to $30 a month.

But that doesn't mean you shouldn't check out the competition. One way to find potential alternatives is to log onto your favourite Internet search engine and type in the words "local phone service" along with the name of your city or town.

What you'll discover is that some of these companies are simply repackaging and reselling the local telephone company's service, while others offer broadband phone service, otherwise known as VoIP, for Voice Over Internet Protocol. (More about this later.) In general, their prices tend to be lower than the big boys, but they don't always offer all the special features the big companies do. And most worrisome, many lack repair and maintenance capabilities.

For Long Distance, It Pays to Play the Field

The long-distance situation is slightly different. There are real bargains to be had from a wide variety of companies with names you've probably never heard of, like Eurotel, Gold Leaf, and Megatron. These outfits buy phone time from the big boys at wholesale rates and then resell it to you and me at what amount to discount prices. They can do this because they aren't spending tons of money on giant marketing campaigns (which is why you've never heard of most of them), nor do they have huge corporate infrastructures to support. But their calls go over the same fibre-optic networks as those of Bell and Telus, so the level of quality they provide is just as good as the giants'.

You can find which of these outfits offers service in your area—and how much (or little) they charge—by typing "long distance service" and the name of your city or town into your favourite search engine.

Focus on the Services You Actually Use

Many long-distance carriers make a point of emphasizing their rates from Canada to a particular country such as England, India, or China. But what if you make a lot of long-distance calls *within* your province—say, from Burlington to Sudbury, in Ontario, or from Montreal to Quebec City? Just because a particular plan has a low international rate that doesn't mean its intraprovincial rate will also be low. The point is that you should know the rates for the services you actually use—not just the services the company wants to brag about.

Always Review Your Bill—and Make Sure You Understand It

The more complicated and confusing your phone bill gets, the more tempting it is just to pay the darn thing without trying to figure out whether or not it's really accurate. This is a huge mistake. Precisely because phone bills have gotten so complicated—because they include so many different charges, fees, and rates—the odds are very good that the service provider has gotten something wrong. There is also a chance that someone may be deliberately trying to scam you.

Especially if you are a new customer or just switched some aspect of your service, you should make sure that you are being charged the rates you agreed to for the services you signed up for. Among the questions to ask yourself are the following:

- Are there any companies listed on my bill whose names I don't recognize?
- Are there any charges for calls I didn't place or services I didn't authorize?
- Are the rates and the line items not what the company told me they'd be?

If your answer to any of these questions is yes, you should contact your phone company immediately and demand a full explanation.

The VoIP Alternative

One way to save big time on residential phone service is not to use the phone lines at all. Instead, you can make your calls over the Internet, using what's called Voice Over Internet Protocol, or VoIP. From the user's point of view, VoIP is pretty much indistinguishable from regular phone service. The phones are the same, the voice quality is the same, and you can get all the same special services such as caller ID, voice mail, and call waiting. The big difference is the cost—particularly on international calls. Companies like vBuzzer, comWave, Lingo, and Vonage offer unlimited local and long-distance calling for around $25 a month. And most offer incredibly cheap—in some cases, free—international calling as well.

Of course, there's a catch. To be able to use VoIP, you need a high-speed Internet connection and all the equipment that goes along with it. This is likely to cost you around $40 a month, which wipes out at least part of the savings (particularly if you don't make a lot of calls). Moreover, not all VoIP providers offer full 911 emergency service. And if your power ever goes out or you lose your Internet connection, your phone service will be gone too—which is why it's probably a good idea to keep at least one basic landline, even if you don't use it much.

And Then There's Skype

An even cheaper—and increasingly popular—alternative to standard VoIP is Skype, an Internet phone service that lets you make and receive calls through your computer. (Most people use either their computer's built-in microphone and speakers or a Skype-friendly headset, but you can also buy regular phones that work with Skype.) Once you've downloaded the free software from Skype's website (**www.skype.com**), you can make unlimited calls to anywhere in the United States and Canada for just $2.95 a month. What's more, for $9.95 a month, you can make unlimited calls to 34 other countries, including most of Europe, Australia, New Zealand, Chile, China, Japan, and Korea. Even better, calls to any other Skype subscriber anywhere in the world are free.

With Skype, you can make unlimited calls to anywhere in the United States and Canada for just $2.95 a month.

Skype is not the only service of its type. Vonage and Packet8 also offer similar service, but they charge as much as $25 a month for it. The drawbacks are the same as with VoIP—plus your computer needs to be turned on and connected to the Internet for you to make or receive calls. Still, given how cheap it is, if you already have a computer and a broadband connection, Skype is a much better deal than even the cheapest landline long-distance service.

What to Watch Out For

Slamming

Given the intense competition between phone companies, it's probably not surprising that some unscrupulous operators try to take advantage of the fact that most consumers don't bother to review their bills. What these rip-off artists do is switch you, without your permission, from the local or long-distance provider you selected to some other company—usually, their own. They count on the fact that most consumers won't realize they're now paying a different company—and that their rates may have gone up a bit—and so will never complain.

This practice is called slamming, and it is most definitely illegal. The best way to protect yourself from it is to check your phone bill every month. If the name of your telephone company seems to have changed, call the number on the bill and ask them what's going on.

Another way to protect yourself is to be very careful when dealing with telemarketers who are selling phone services, telephone survey takers who ask you about your phone service, or sweepstakes forms you may receive in the mail. Quite often, slammers will try to trick you into authorizing a service change without your realizing it. So be careful about what you say over the phone and read the fine print before you sign up for any sweepstakes or drawings. To be extra safe, you can ask your selected carriers to "freeze" your account—meaning that they shouldn't allow your service to be transferred to any other company without direct written or verbal authorization from you.

And if you get a postcard in the mail asking you to "verify" a switch that you didn't authorize, don't ignore it. Instead, call your phone company immediately to let them know you haven't authorized any changes in your service. You should also contact the sender of the postcard and let them know the same thing.

If you discover you've already been slammed, call the slammer and tell them you want your original service restored. Also call your preferred company and tell them you want to be reinstated to the same calling plan you had before the slam. And insist that your bill be wiped clean of any "change of carrier charges" (which are generally imposed when a customer switches companies).

Keep in mind that you DO NOT have to pay anyone—neither the slammer nor your selected company—for service for up to 30 days after being slammed. If you unknowingly paid a slammer, you will be entitled to a full refund. After the initial 30 days, you must pay your authorized company for any service you've received, but at its rates, not the slammer's rates.

Cramming

An even more widespread scam than slamming is what's known as cramming—in which rip-off artists try to slip all sorts of unauthorized charges onto your phone bill. Like slammers, they count on the fact that bills today are so complicated and confusing that you won't notice another small item amid all the other legitimate fees and charges.

A tip-off that you may have been victimized by cramming is the appearance on your bill of small charges (often just $2 or $3) with vague descriptions such as "service fee," "service charge," "monthly fee," "other fees," "mail server," "calling plan," "psychic," and "membership." If you see any charge on your bill that you don't recognize, immediately call the company that billed it, ask for an explanation, and demand that your bill be adjusted. Also call your own phone company and find out the procedure for having an incorrect charge removed from your bill. Keep in mind that even if you did authorize a service, it's considered cramming if the provider misled you about its actual cost. A typical cramming technique is to get victims to authorize a service that they are led to believe is free.

What to Do if Things Go Wrong

The first place to go if you have a problem with any aspect of your home phone service is to the company that provided it. There are customer service numbers on every bill you receive from your various service providers as well as contact information on the companies' web sites.

If you can't sort out your issues with the company directly, your province's consumer affairs department may handle the complaint. The Canadian Radio-television and Telecommunications Commission, the federal regulatory body, also handles complaints, especially about slamming and especially if your telephone service provider doesn't address your complaint to your satisfaction.

The CRTC has a toll-free number, 1-877-249-2782, or you can submit a complaint by email using the CRTC web site: www.crtc.gc.ca.

Fight for Your Money Action Steps

- ☐ Call your carrier to have your current usage analyzed and ask them for a better deal.
- ☐ Compare deals online for both local phone service and long-distance phone service.
- ☐ Review your bill every month, not only for errors but also to avoid slamming and cramming.
- ☐ Consider VoIP services or Skype, which will usually save you a bundle—especially if you make a lot of long-distance calls.

Bundled-Service Plans

If your mailbox is anything like mine, it's been filled lately with pitches from your cable TV company, your telephone company, and your Internet provider—all of them trying to steal each other's business. They're all pushing the same idea: that we should get all our telecom services—TV, phone, and Internet—from the same place.

It's called bundling, and the theory is that getting all three services together (a "triple-play," in the industry's jargon) should be a better deal for you than buying them separately. It's certainly a big deal for the companies, especially in Canada, which leads the United States. in the rate of adoption of high-speed Internet, wireless, and other services. According to IDC Canada, 62% of consumers prefer to subscribe to bundled communications services.

But aside from getting one monthly bill instead of three, are there real advantages to bundling? As usual, the answer is that it depends. If you're a big telecom consumer—someone who regularly phones all over the country, is used to watching a lot more than basic cable, and needs the speed of a broadband Internet connection—bundling can deliver real value. But if you're not, it probably won't.

How to Fight for Your Money

When I was a financial planner, I used to urge my clients to diversify their investments. "Remember what your mother told you," I would say. "Don't put all your eggs in one basket." Bundling is putting all your eggs in one basket—big time. It's bad enough when your cable goes out, but how would you feel if every time it did, you also lost your Internet and phone service too?

Then again, most providers offer digital TV, cable telephone, and cable Internet for $59 a month to $79 a month (at least for the first few months). Purchased separately, this kind of phone, cable, and Internet service could easily run twice that. For example, my friend Allan spends about $150 a month on telephone service from Telus, $175 a month on cable TV service from Rogers, and $50 a month on high-speed Internet service from Bell—for a total of $375 a month. If he got all those services from Rogers, which offers a variety of bundled packages, it would cost him just $250 a month. So in his case, bundling could save him $1,500 a year. And even if you aren't as big a telecom consumer as Allan, bundling could still save you hundreds of dollars a year.

Here's what to keep in mind if you're considering it.

Price Is Everything

If you're not going to save money as a result of bundling, there is no point in doing it. So evaluate your current phone, TV, and Internet usage realistically. Unless you're really going to use all the services you're going to get, why bother? For instance, if you live in an apartment or condo, your building may offer wireless service at a much cheaper rate than you would pay if you were to purchase your own plan.

You should also make sure you know exactly what the bundled services are going to cost you. Not just the list price, but the *total* price—including taxes, surcharges, and those mysterious system access fees. All these charges can easily add as much as $15 or $20 a month to your bill. Are there extra fees for cable boxes, DVRs, modems, and remote controls? (Most cable companies basically rent you all the required hardware.) Will there be installation or activation fees? Will your first bill include a charge for an additional month of service (because most companies bill in advance)? Are these charges negotiable? Will the company waive them entirely? Will you have to agree to conditions—say, automatic bill paying? Are you comfortable with that? Since the telecom market is so competitive right now, you actually do have strong negotiating power. If the customer rep can't or won't tell you what your total monthly bill is going to be, including all taxes and fees, think long and hard before signing up.

Since the telecom market is so competitive right now, you have strong negotiating power.

Don't Confuse Introductory Rates with Real Rates

Those $100 a month rates certainly sound great, but when you read the fine print you generally find that they are good only for the first few months. So make sure you know how long that low introductory rate will last and how much it might rise once the initial period ends. A good way to ensure transparency before you actually make the switch, especially if you are discussing the plan over the phone with a customer service rep, is to ask for exactly what you talked about in an email or letter. This way you always have something to refer back to. Some companies like have been offering price guarantees to customers willing to sign long-term contracts (typically at least 24 months). But what if you move? Or need to drop one of the three services? Or your situation changes and you can't afford the monthly charge? Don't assume you have to sign a contract; you may have more wiggle room than you think. You just have to be open to asking questions and know which questions to ask.

Find Out About Service Limits

When telecom companies say they will provide users with unlimited service, they are generally talking about normal users. Customers who make an unusually large number of phone calls or who routinely download a lot of big files may suddenly find themselves saddled with restrictions on their unlimited telephone-calling privileges or Internet upload and download speeds. So if you make a lot of calls and you download a lot of movies, be sure to find out in advance the provider's policy regarding usage limits. Any restrictions should be noted prominently in your contract, but if you don't see them, don't assume you're in the clear—call customer service and ask.

Hang on to Your Old Phone Number

Most companies will let you keep your old telephone number when you switch to a new service—even if you're going from a traditional landline to VoIP (voice over Internet) service. (You have to stay within the same local exchange area, though.) Still, some charge a fee to transfer (or "port") a number. If your provider does, ask them to waive it. Chances are, they will.

Check Your Bill—and Be Prepared to Fight

Even though the companies are always talking up the convenience of getting just one bill for all your telecom needs, the fact is that one of the most common consumer complaints about bundling is that the bills are confusing, difficult to read, and sometimes just plain wrong—and that it can take weeks or months to get them straightened out. In part, this is because the various telecom companies all offer so many different plans that even they get confused about what they're doing. Some companies offer their customers as many as six different bundles, and some of them look almost identical. So go over your bill carefully, and be prepared for a lengthy battle if you find mistakes.

Don't assume you have to sign a contract.

What to Do if Things Go Wrong

If you have a problem with a bundled service provider, your first step should be to contact the company's customer service representative. If you can't resolve the problem with them, you should file a complaint with the Commissioner for Complaints for Telecommunications Services (CCTS). The CCTS was set up by the telecommunications industry to deal with complaints about telecommunications services. Most of the major providers in Canada are members, but you should check to make sure, at the Commissioner for Complaints for Telecommunications Services web site at **www.ccts-cprst.ca**.

You can use the online complaint form or write to the CCTS at:

P.O. Box 81088
Ottawa, Ontario
K1P 1B1
Toll-free: 1-888-221-1687
Toll-free TTY: 1-877-782-2384

Industry Canada's Consumer Connection web site at **www.ic.gc.ca** includes advice on complaining effectively and provides steps to follow to file a complaint as well as contacts for the organizations, or local, provincial, and federal offices that provide help to consumers.

Fight for Your Money Action Steps

- ☐ Always inquire about total charges, including taxes, surcharges, and extras like cable boxes and remote controls.
- ☐ Find out what the installation and activation fees are and work them into your comparison or ask that they be waived.
- ☐ Understand what your *real* rate will be after the introductory rate expires. Get it in writing.

TRAVEL

Air Travel

For most of the last decade, I have virtually lived on airplanes. I have the frequent-flier points, the Platinum Level memberships, and the scars to prove it. Now don't get me wrong—I have a lot of sympathy for the flight attendants, gate agents, baggage handlers, and everyone else who is employed by the airlines. They are, for the most part, overworked and underpaid. But there is no getting around the fact that I have come to hate the airlines. It's not just that travelling by air has become a brutal, miserable experience that gets worse with each passing day. It's that in addition to collecting hundreds—sometimes thousands—of dollars for a ticket, the airlines now charge you extra for just about everything except the wings and your seatbelt.

You want to make a reservation over the telephone? That can add $25 to the cost of your flight. Planning to check luggage? On most of the major carriers, checking one bag will cost you at least $15, maybe more. Checking a second piece could set you back as much as an additional $80. Sending your unaccompanied child to visit the grandparents? Prepare to fork over an extra $40. And unless you're flying first or business class, forget about free drinks and hot meals. Figure on at least $2 for a soft drink and $5 for a cold sandwich. Some airlines even charge extra for water!

The Airlines Are in a Terrible Squeeze—and They Want Us to Pay

It sometimes seems like the airlines are deliberately doing everything they can these days to make the skies as unfriendly as possible. Fares are higher than ever, planes are more crowded and uncomfortable, and schedules are less convenient. With more people flying to more places than ever before (nearly 33 million people travelled between cities in Canada in 2007), flights are more likely to be overbooked, departures are more likely to be delayed, connections are more likely to be missed, and luggage is more likely to go astray. The good news is that Canada seems to rank better than airports in the United States when it comes to delays. According to FlightStats.com, more than 90% of flights between Toronto and Montreal, the busiest route in the country, arrive and depart on time. The bad news is that many travellers from Canada go to the United States, where nearly 30% of domestic flights failed to arrive on time in 2008.

To be fair, the airlines have been caught in a terrible squeeze. Even before the run-up in oil prices sent the cost of jet fuel soaring (it nearly doubled between 2007 and 2008, although it plummeted downward again later in the year), the nation's major carriers had been losing money for a decade.

That's their problem, you say? You're right. But it becomes ours when they try to solve it on our backs. And that's what the airlines have been doing.

Airfares jumped by 20% in 2008 and are expected to climb another 40% by 2012. And as I just noted, most major carriers now make a practice of charging extra for services and amenities that they used to provide for free.

Some people accuse the airlines of nickel-and-diming passengers, but this sort of thing adds up to an awful lot of nickels and dimes. You don't even have to count the fare increases. The new baggage fees alone cost North American travellers close to a *billion dollars a year*.

How to Fight for Your Money

Go Online to Find Real Bargains

Air travel may no longer seem like a bargain, but there are bargains to be had if you shop around. Online travel sites like Expedia (**www.expedia.com**), Hotwire.com (**www.hotwire.com**), Kayak (**www.kayak.com**), Orbitz (**www.orbitz.com**), Priceline (**www.priceline.com**), SideStep (**www.sidestep.com**), and Travelocity (**www.travelocity.com**) can find you airfares for a fraction of the airlines' own published tariffs. But not all the best prices show up on the independent sites, so don't neglect the airlines' own sites. And comparison sites like Farecast (**www.farecast.com**) and FareCompare (**www.farecompare.com**) can offer solid advice not only on where to get the best deals, especially if you're travelling outside Canada, but also on whether prices for your particular destination are trending up or down, so you can figure out whether it's worth your while to book now or wait a while.

Some deals are truly amazing. For example, in a May 2008 special promotion, Spirit Airlines was selling tickets for a flight from Los Angeles to Fort Lauderdale for just $18.

Subscribe to the airline weekly newsletters and you could wind up being offered discounts of 25% or more.

You won't find these sorts of special deals in Canada because of different rules in this country. However, if you live near the U.S. border and don't mind travelling to the airport in the nearest U.S. city, you can take advantage of some good deals on U.S. airlines like Jet Blue and Spirit. Check the airline web sites and sign up for announcements and other information. There's generally no charge, and you could wind up being offered discounts of 25% or more.

Look for an Unexpected Carrier or Airport

Another way to cut the cost of air travel is to look for airlines you wouldn't expect to service the destination you're headed to. For example, on a trip from Toronto to London, you could save money by taking Air New Zealand, rather than the more obvious British Airways or Air Canada. Similarly, Qantas could get you from Montreal to Frankfurt for $400 less than Germany's flagship carrier, Lufthansa. Again, if you can get to a U.S. airport, you'll often find cheaper fares for overseas trips than you get in Canada, although you'll spend more time travelling.

FLY THE UN-OBVIOUS SKIES

New York to London Economy Fare	
On British Airways:	$942
On Air India:	$689
You save:	**$253**

(one-way fare; as of September 2008)

You can also save as much as one-third on airline fares by using unexpected airports—usually smaller, regional airports that serve the same market as a big international hub. If you're heading from Toronto for Montreal, try Toronto Island Airport instead of Pearson, or if your destination is Los Angeles, think of Burbank or Ontario rather than LAX.

Finding these unexpected carriers and airports is easier than you might think. There's a web site called FlightStats (**www.flightstats.com**) that can tell you every airline that flies to most Canadian destinations from any U.S. airport.

If You're Travelling in the United States, Don't Buy Tickets in Bunches—Buying One at a Time Can Be Cheaper

If you're travelling in the United States with your family, there often won't be enough cheap seats available to fill your whole order. But instead of selling you as many cheap seats as they have and then charging you more for the rest, U.S. airline reservation systems will often just kick your booking up to the next price level and charge you a higher fare for *all* your tickets. The way to beat this system is simple: shop for your tickets one at a time.

THE SINGLE ADVANTAGE

LA-to-NY Reservation for Four Seats:	$619 each
LA-to-NY Reservation for One Seat:	$344
You Save:	**$275 per ticket**

Avoid Being Bumped by Nailing Down Your Seat Assignment

There's probably only one thing worse than getting a bad seat on a plane (say, one that doesn't recline or is right next to the galley). That's not getting a seat at all, even though you have bought and paid for a ticket. Most airlines routinely overbook particular flights based on the statistical probability that a certain number of travellers will not show up to claim their reservations. Occasionally, these calculations turn out to be wrong and there aren't enough seats to go around. What happens next can be ugly. If no one volunteers to give up his or her seat, the carrier will start bumping passengers—that is, denying them a seat on the flight even though they have a confirmed reservation.

There are a number of criteria the airlines use to decide who gets bumped first, but generally the most vulnerable passengers are those who don't yet have their seat assignments. So one simple way to minimize the odds that you'll ever be bumped from an overbooked flight is to make sure you get a confirmed seat assignment at the time you make your reservation.

This is also the best way to make sure you won't get stuck in a terrible seat or, if you're travelling with relatives or friends, that you will all be able to sit together.

Most airline web sites provide seating charts that show you exactly which seats are available on any given flight and where exactly on the plane they are located. To ensure you make the right choice, check with SeatGuru (**www.seatguru.com**), which provides seat maps for 300 different aircraft on 45 different airlines, along with expert commentary on which seats are best and which you should definitely avoid. It's a great resource for any air traveller who needs extra legroom or has vowed never to get seated next to a restroom ever again.

What to Watch Out For

Nontransparent Pricing

Once upon a time, the price of an airplane ticket included all sorts of services and amenities. Not anymore.

Needless to say, most carriers don't provide comprehensive lists of the extra fees they plan to charge. Nor when they quote you a ticket price do they spell out how much is for the airfare and how much is for the various extra charges already built in.

So the smart air traveller needs to ask a lot of questions about baggage allowances, check-in services, cabin amenities, and the like. Specifically, make sure you know how many bags (if any) you are allowed to check for free, how many you can carry on, and at what weight and dimensions. To keep from getting dinged too badly, plan on bringing your own food, pack as light and tight as you can, and unless your trip involves some horrendously complicated connections, try to book it yourself online through the airline's own website or through one of the major booking sites like Travelocity, Expedia, or Orbitz.

One web site that does a good job of keeping up with the extra charges is SeatGuru. In addition to providing seat maps, it also compiles the latest data on baggage allowances and restrictions as well as many of the fees you might get charged.

Incomprehensible Fare Rules

The rules governing airline fares can make the *Income Tax Act* look simple. Some fares apply only if you make your reservation at least 21 days in advance; others require a Saturday night stopover. Some allow you to change your flight but not cancel it entirely; others permit cancellations but assess a penalty fee.

In addition to being complicated and often hard to understand, the rules also change constantly. So before you buy an airline ticket, make sure to ask the following questions:

- Is there a penalty if I need to change my flight time or date?
- What happens if I need to cancel the trip entirely?
- If the fare is nonrefundable, can I apply it to another trip at another time?
- If I decide not to use it, can I transfer my ticket to someone else?

As a rule, the cheaper the ticket, the more restricted it probably is—meaning that the less you pay, the more locked in to a specific flight you're likely to be. If your plans are not likely to change, that's fine. But if you need flexibility, be prepared to pay for it.

Paying by Cheque and Buying Too Far in Advance

If you pay for your ticket with cash or a cheque, you're out of luck in the event something goes wrong with your flight—like, say, the airline goes bankrupt and ceases operations. Buying your ticket with a credit card, on the other hand, may protect you, since credit card companies will not force you to pay for a service you did not receive.

There is one catch with this. Most credit card companies will cancel a disputed charge only if you file a complaint within 60 days of when it first appeared on your bill. What this means is that if you buy an airline ticket six months in advance and then the carrier goes out of business the day before you're scheduled to take off, you're out of luck. So don't buy airline tickets too far in advance. Reserve them, if you have to—but try to avoid paying for them until you reach the 60-day window. If you're concerned about locking in a low fare, check with a web site like Farecast or FareCompare to get an indication whether fares on the route you're travelling are likely to rise or fall in the near future.

> **If something goes wrong with your flight, buying your ticket with a credit card may protect you.**

What to Do if Things Go Wrong

In general, if you have any sort of problem with an airline, you should register your complaint as soon as possible—ideally, giving them the chance to resolve your issue on the spot. If you're in-flight and find a fly in your orange juice, don't wait until you get home to file a complaint; ring for the head flight attendant and simply ask for a new drink. If you're at the airport, you should ask for the airline's customer service representative or a manager with the authority to address your problem.

If you cannot resolve your problem on the spot, start taking notes. Write down all the pertinent information that will help you accurately describe what occurred—names of airline employees involved, time and date of the incident, flight number, airport, exactly what happened, and contact information for any witnesses. You'll also want to hang onto receipts for any extra expenses (such as hotel stays, car rental, or meals) that you incur as a result of the problem.

For the most part, it's best to file a complaint in the form of a letter or email to the carrier's customer relations manager. You can usually find the manager's name and address by going to the carrier's website and searching for "customer relations."

Although complaining by telephone may seem easier and more convenient, it's always better to put things in writing. That way there's never any question about who said what to whom and when. Your letter should be clear about who or what caused your problem and what you would regard as a reasonable resolution. Include photocopies of all relevant documents (boarding pass, baggage checks, etc.). And always keep a copy for your files.

If you keep the text professional and to the point, chances are, the airline will do its best to make you happy.

If you don't get any satisfaction from the airline, you should file a complaint with the Canadian Transportation Agency. You can file a complaint with the CTA online at **www.cta-otc.gc.ca** or you can contact them at:

Canadian Transportation Agency
Air Travel Complaints Program
Ottawa, Ontario
K1A 0N9
Toll-free: 1-888-222-2592
Toll-free (TTY): 1-800-669-5575
Fax: 819-953-5686

Complaints filed with the CTA should include a concise description of your problem, including your name, contact information, airline, flight date and number, origin and destination cities of your trip, and copies of any tickets.

Fight for Your Money Action Steps

- ☐ Shop around—and go online to find real bargains.
- ☐ Save additional money by using unexpected airports or carriers.
- ☐ Protect yourself against being bumped by nailing down your seat assignment early.
- ☐ Always pay for your ticket with a credit card—never by cash, cheque, or debit card.
- ☐ Make sure you know the rules regarding checked baggage and other no-longer-free services.

Hotels

Staying in a hotel these days can be a lot like travelling on an airline. The service is indifferent, the facilities aren't always ship-shape, and if you're not careful, they will ding you with all kinds of unexpected extra charges—some of which are nothing short of outrageous. One guy I know got charged $16 just for taking a bottle of water out of a hotel-room mini-bar and then putting it back. It turned out the hotel tracked mini-bar usage with electronic sensors, and when my friend moved the bottle, the fridge rang it up as a sale. And don't get me started on the Internet charges and the $200 telephone calls.

Unlike the airlines, the Canadian hotel industry is solidly profitable. It generates total revenues of more than $18 billion a year, which have increased by 5% a year since 2005. So there's really no excuse for its habit of ripping off travellers. And make no mistake about it—hotels try to get away with whatever they can. According to a study by Corporate Lodging Consultants, which negotiates hotel rates for hundreds of companies, between billing errors and hidden fees, hotels in North America routinely overcharge business travellers by as much as $500 million a year. Another study by American Express found that hotel reservation systems quoted the wrong rates more than half the time—and the mistakes were almost always in the hotels' favour.

As one travel consultant said not too long ago, "These mistakes don't occasionally happen—they regularly happen." Here's how to keep them from happening to you.

How to Fight for Your Money

Don't Be Afraid to Haggle

For all the travelling that Canadians do, more than one-third of all hotel rooms sit empty every night. As a result, most hotels will cut you a deal—if you ask for it. In a 2007 survey, *Consumer Reports* found that 70% of travellers who asked for a better deal succeeded in getting either a rate reduction or room upgrade. This was the case even at the most expensive hotels. So don't hesitate to speak up and inquire because it will likely be worth your while.

I live by this rule. The fact is, many hotels are like used-car lots. I recently stood at the front desk of a hotel in Las Vegas negotiating with the desk clerk, who kept running back and forth to his manager in the back room. Was it worth it? I ended up with a 2,500-square-foot penthouse suite for $500 a night. (The standard room they'd originally offered me was priced at $395.) So, yes, it was worth it!

I get an upgrade at almost every hotel I check into simply by negotiating at the front desk and asking for one. I've been doing this since I was 18 years old, when I stayed in a hotel with my parents and wound up with a better room then they got. Trust me—this works.

And whenever you call to make a hotel reservation, be sure to tell the clerk you'd like the lowest rate he or she can give you. A lot of hotels will offer their discounted corporate rate to anyone who asks—whether or not you're travelling on business or even work for a corporation.

Book Early—and Then Book Again at the Last Minute

Since many hotels offer discounted rates for advance bookings, it's generally a good idea make your reservation as early as you can. But hotels also sometimes drop their prices at the last minute in an effort to fill vacancies. So you should call again a day or two before your trip to see if you can get an even better rate. In most cases, you'll be able to cancel your original reservation and get yourself a new one at the lower rate without having to pay any kind of penalty.

Make Sure You Know What You've Booked

As with the airlines, you can get all kinds of great hotel deals by booking online through travel sites such as Expedia (**www.expedia.com**), Hotwire (**www.**

hotwire.com), Kayak (**www.kayak.com**), Orbitz (**www.orbitz.com**), Priceline (**www.priceline.com**), SideStep (**www.sidestep.com**), and Travelocity (**www.travelocity.com**). But particularly if you are using a less well-known site, you want to make sure that the room you booked actually exists.

The daughter of a friend of mine, a student named Ellen, learned this the hard way not too long ago. While spending a semester in Europe, she arranged to meet three friends in Dublin for a few days. The place where she wanted to stay was booked, so she surfed the Web for a while until she found a slick-looking travel site that claimed to specialize in hostels for students. Ellen used it to reserve a room with four beds for her and her friends in a hostel called The Shining, using her credit card to put down a 10% deposit. But when the young women arrived in Dublin, it turned out that The Shining had no reservation for them. Nor did it have any four-bed rooms—nor any record of Ellen's 10% deposit.

There's a simple way to guard against this sort of disaster—or even the less dire but still extremely annoying problem of showing up at a hotel and discovering it's not nearly as nice as it looked in the photos. Whenever you're planning to stay at hotel you've never been to before, go online to a traveller-based review site like **Boo.com**, **Gusto.com**, **IgoUgo.com**, or **TripAdvisor.com**, to see what real travellers who've been there have to say about the place. You can even ask questions on the message boards.

Regardless of where you're going and whether you've made your reservation through a third party or with the hotel directly, always phone the hotel to confirm your booking a few days before you start your trip. And double-check that the room rate you were quoted by the reservations clerk is the rate you're going to be charged.

If There's a Problem, Don't Leave the Front Desk Until It's Resolved

Even if you book through legitimate channels and have a confirmed reservation, it's not uncommon to arrive at a front desk and be told there's no room in the inn. Again, like the airlines, hotels sometimes deliberately overbook. Unfortunately, unlike airline passengers, hotel guests don't have a law that protects them in the event they are bumped.

Most lawyers agree that it's a breach of contract if you've guaranteed your reservation with a credit card and the desk clerk tells you that the hotel doesn't have a room for you. To make sure no one questions the validity of your claim, you should always travel with copies of whatever emails or letters you may have received from the hotel or travel agency confirming your reservation.

In such cases, the policy at most major hotels is to find you another room at a comparable place nearby—and if the room there is more expensive than the one you reserved, to reimburse you for the difference. Customarily, the hotel that's turned you away will also pay for your first night at the other place, provide transportation there, and give you free phone service so you can call your family and business associates to let them know about the change. If the hotel fails to offer you any of these amenities, don't be shy about asking for them.

> **Customarily, the hotel that's turned you away will pay for your first night at the other place.**

Above all, do not leave the front desk until your situation has been resolved to your satisfaction. The front desk staff will probably ask you to step aside so they can register another guest or answer someone else's question. Don't let them push you around. Until you're taken care of, you have to remain the squeaky wheel who needs to be dealt with now. If the clerks say there's nothing they can do, ask to speak with the general manager or the manager on duty so you're dealing with someone who has the authority to assist you. But keep in mind that raised voices and sharp words are not likely to get you anywhere. The clerks at the front desk most likely didn't cause your problem—but if you are polite, as well as persistent, they may be the ones to solve it.

Watch Out for Those Outrageous Charges

Most hotels these days charge you for virtually every amenity they offer. Some are obvious and easy to avoid, but increasingly they sneak up on you—and the tab can be considerable. In all, North American hotel surcharges picked nearly $1.8 billion out of travellers' pockets in 2008. The most outrageous rip-offs include:

MINIBARS. With their $8 cans of Coke and their $12 bags of mixed nuts, hotel minibars have been ripping off travellers ever since they first appeared in the early 1970s. These days they're worse than ever, thanks to modern electronics. As my friend with the $16 bottle of water discovered, many have been equipped with sensors. If you even *move* a soda can or candy bar, it signals the desk that you should be billed for it.

RESORT FEES. Many hotels charge "resort fees" of $15 to $25 a day for facilities such as gyms and tennis courts that you may never use. There's generally no way to avoid them, except to ask, when you make your reservation, whether the daily rate covers everything. Mandatory tipping may also be another "resort fee" that you are unaware of, so ask before you leave tips (otherwise you are double tipping).

ROOM SERVICE. When is a cheeseburger and fries worth $30 plus tip? When you have it delivered to your room by a room-service waiter in most big hotels. Let's face it—if you are a business traveller and get in late in the day, ordering room service is more than likely the only way you'll get something to eat. But watch out for the double- and triple-tip factor. Most room-service bills include both a delivery charge and gratuity—but when the bill is handed to you, there's a blank line labelled "Tip." If you write in a tip here—on top of the delivery fee and gratuity that have already been included—you may wind up paying as much in service fees as you paid for the food.

TELEPHONE CALLS. The rates hotels charge for using their phones are nothing short of amazing. What really boggles my mind is not that hotels routinely charge five times what the phone company does for calls—or that they even charge you for toll-free calls. No, what I still have trouble believing is that some hotels will charge you upward of $7 just for picking up the phone *whether or not you complete a call!* So unless it's an emergency, never use a hotel phone. Make all your calls on your cell or a public phone.

IT'S WORTH THE ELEVATOR RIDE

Two-minute local call from your room:	$3.90
Cost from a pay phone in the lobby:	$0.50
You save:	**$3.40**

INTERNET CONNECTIONS. Virtually every decent hotel makes a big deal of advertising the availability of broadband Internet connections. But most of them charge you through the nose for it—often as much as $14.95 a day. (You can avoid this charge by using a nearby wireless hotspot. There are a number of online directories—such as www.jiwire.com, www.wififreespot.com, and www.wi-fihotspotlist.com—that can point you to the nearest one.)

PARKING. Particularly in urban locations, hotel parking is another huge rip-off. The hotel garage may be convenient, but at anywhere from $20 to $50 a night, it's probably the most expensive parking spot in town. You're generally much better off looking for a municipal lot nearby.

Review Your Bill Carefully

With all these surcharges and special fees, it's not surprising that hotel bills are often riddled with errors. So when you check out, be sure to review your bill carefully. I never leave a hotel without getting a printout of the bill and going through it line by line.

First and foremost, I check to make sure the room price matches what I was told. (Trust me—it often doesn't.) Next, I check every single charge against my receipts to make sure the bills from the restaurants, room service, bar, pool—you name it—match what I signed for. Did I rent a movie? Why were there two charges for a movie when I know I watched only one?

I almost never leave a hotel without finding a mistake in their favour—and I always get it fixed—that is, credited back to me—before I check out. The moral here is simple. Check your bill, verify, and rectify! When you check out is the time to argue—politely—if you find a charge you don't recognize. The longer you wait to dispute a bill, the less likely you are to prevail—which is one reason that you might want to think twice about taking advantage of the express checkout option so many hotels now offer. Express checkout can be great when you're rushing to catch a plane, but when you do it, you might not see your hotel bill for several days or weeks. By then, it may be too late to sort out a dispute—if you even remember which charges are right and which aren't.

I almost never leave a hotel without finding a mistake on my bill—in their favour.

What to Do if Things Go Wrong

If you have a problem with your bill—or any other issue, for that matter—and the front desk clerk can't resolve it to your satisfaction, discuss it with the manager on duty. If this gets you nowhere, settle your bill with a credit card and then dispute the charge with the credit card company when your next statement arrives. (For details on how to do this, see the section CREDIT CARDS on page 81.)

In general, any problem you can't resolve with the hotel manager should be brought to the attention of the hotel's owner—which in most cases will be a national chain that has a customer relations department listed on its web site. Most chain are fairly protective of their brand reputation, so unless your complaint is totally unreasonable, they'll probably try to make it up to you—if only by giving you vouchers good toward the cost of a future stay at one of their properties. Whether or not you'll ever want to use the vouchers depends on how bad your experience with them was.

In the case of really bad treatment, you should also file a complaint with your local Better Business Bureau (**www.ccbbb.ca**) and your province's consumer affairs department.

Fight for Your Money Action Steps

- ☐ Negotiate for a better rate.
- ☐ Book online for great deals, but always confirm your reservation and rate directly with the hotel.
- ☐ If your hotel has overbooked or has lost your reservation, see what is offered as a resolution. And if nothing is offered—ask.
- ☐ Be aware that hotels add mandatory extra fees to the room rate for almost all amenities. Ask if you're not sure, in order to calculate the real cost of your stay.
- ☐ Check your bill line by line and resolve any errors before you check out.

Travel Packages

Travel scams probably occur more often in North America than they do elsewhere in the world because of the sheer size of the United States and Canada, because people like to get away from Canadian winters, and because people in North America simply like to take vacations in warm places.

That makes us all vulnerable to the phony tour operators and the crooked travel agents who offer packages that seem out of this world. Like anything else that seems too good to be true, these travel offers usually are too.

The RCMP warns on its website against travel scams. They talk about "dishonest travel agencies" that "lure a victim to a remote destination and charge extra fees for features and services that were supposed to be included in the initial travel package, making your dream holiday into a very stressful experience."

These scam artists operate on both sides of the Canada–U.S. border. In fact, back in 1999 in the United States, the Federal Trade Commission and 21 federal and state law enforcement authorities thought they might have gotten rid of these criminal operations once and for all. They sprung Operation Trip Trap, a crackdown on 25 crooked travel companies that were swindling consumers with phony or misleading vacation packages. The rip-offs were all classics. The scammers promised consumers luxury accommodations that turned out to be vermin-infested shacks. They told people they had won free trips and then hit them with all sorts of hidden fees. And they charged travellers for products and services they never received.

The sweep generated a lot of headlines. Several of the companies wound up refunding hundreds of thousands of dollars to the victims. A dozen or so scam artists were barred from continuing to work in the travel business. And business went on as usual, in Canada and the United States alike.

Don't Be Fooled

Check out **www.ripoffreport.com** to get an idea of the types of fraudulent travel packages being sold over the Internet and telephone.

In fact, a decade later all that's changed when it comes to travel scams is that instead of sending potential victims postcards, the scammers now send them emails.

So if you're planning a vacation, don't let down your guard. Travel scams are the fourth most common type of consumer fraud in Canada and the United States, according to the Canadian Institute of Travel Counsellors, totalling an estimated $12 billion annually.

How to Fight for Your Money

Increased enforcement by postal authorities may have made travel scammers wary of using the mail to solicit victims. But the Internet is not subject to government regulation and slick web sites and well-crafted emails offering too-good-to-be-true deals on trips and tours continue to snag unwary bargain hunters. Here's how to avoid being taken.

Be Careful About Prepaying

Scam artists are well aware that most major credit card companies give customers only 60 days to dispute a charge. As a result, once they've gotten you to pay for some dream vacation, they will take their time providing you with written confirmation of your reservation. When you finally do get it—invariably, after the 60-day dispute period has ended—you'll find a different price than the one you agreed to on the phone or online as well as a list of mandatory extra charges you were never warned about. And when you try to cancel, you'll be told it's too late—if anyone bothers to respond to your complaints at all.

So be wary of deals that require you to pay more than 60 days in advance. At most, don't put down more than a deposit. In particular, be skeptical of any tour operator who tells you that you have to buy your tickets now because the deal is good only today. And if you are persuaded to put down a deposit, insist on getting a confirmation number along with immediate written confirmation of the terms, including how far in advance you can cancel your reservations and still get a full refund. If it is not forthcoming, send a certified letter cancelling your trip and demanding a refund. And do this well before the 60-day deadline so you can dispute the charge if they refuse to return your money.

Never Pay by Cheque

A tour operator who insists on payment by cheque and refuses to accept credit cards or PayPal is a tour operator you should avoid. Once you write a cheque, your money is gone. And be aware that you do not get credit card purchase protection when you pay for something using those low-interest cash-advance cheques that come with your credit card statement.

Ask the hotel sales department if they know the tour operator and what kind of reputation it has.

Ask Questions if You Prepay

Make a point of finding out what happens to the money you prepay. Is it held in escrow somewhere? What's the name of the bank? Check if the travel agency is a member of the Canadian Association of Tour Operators, and make sure it displays the logo of the provincial licensing agency on its web site and on its front door. The provincial agency maintains standards and also operates a compensation fund for consumers in case the travel agent, cruise operator, or airline goes out of business.

Double-Check Your Reservations

To be certain that you're not being scammed, check directly with the airlines and hotels the tour operator claims he is booking for your trip. Is there a confirmed reservation in your name? If not, demand an explanation from the tour operator, and if it sounds fishy, cancel. Ask the hotel sales department if they know the tour operator and what kind of reputation it has. Make sure you receive copies of each vendor's cancellation and refund policies.

Beware of Phony Travel Agent ID Cards

One of the most devious travel scams involves what are known as card mills that sell phony travel agent ID cards. These supposedly entitle the holder to all the discounts, upgrades, and other perks airlines and hotels usually offer real travel agents, and they are not cheap. They usually sell for close to $500. In fact, they are worthless.

What most real travel agents have is an ID issued by the International Airlines Travel Agent Network (IATAN). The IATAN ID card is the only form of identification most airlines and other travel suppliers will accept for discounts or free tickets. Back in the 1990s, it was relatively easy to get one of these cards. But in recent years the industry has cracked down. As legendary travel guru Arthur Frommer has noted: "Much more than an ID card is now required to qualify people for travel discounts. And companies that take $400 or $500 from you for an ID, without offering real instruction or operating a chain of active retail agencies, are scam artists."

Be skeptical of anyone who offers to sell you a card that will allow you to "travel like a travel agent," when your only "client" is yourself.

The IATAN is part of the International Air Transport Association (IATA), based in Montreal. To get an IATAN ID card, you have to meet a series of stringent criteria, including working at least 20 hours a week selling travel and earning at least $5,000 a year in salary and commissions. So be skeptical of anyone who offers to sell you a card that will allow you to "travel like a travel agent," even if your only "client" is yourself. If you qualify for an IATAN card, the annual fee is only $30. If you don't qualify, it doesn't matter how much you pay—you can't get real travel agency credentials if you are not a real travel agent.

Don't Fall for Those "Free" Timeshare Trips

One of the most common travel package scams is the free vacation that is constantly being offered by timeshare promoters. At first glance, these deals usually seem great. To get what's described as a free trip to resort destinations like Orlando or Cancun, all you have to do is agree to sit through a 60- or 90-minute sales presentation for the timeshare resort they're pushing. The problem is that most of these deals don't include transportation, the accommodations they do provide can be dicey, and those 60-minute presentations often turn out to be all-day ordeals in which you're badgered by a team of high-pressure salespeople who won't take "No, thank you" for an answer. So while it's true that you are under no obligation to buy anything when you accept one of these offers, you still usually wind up paying a real price for that supposedly free trip.

Legitimate Travel Packages Do Exist

If you're looking for a vacation deal, I recommend doing some comparison searches on the major travel sites, like **www.expedia.com, www.Travelocity.com, www.orbitz.com, www.priceline.com, www.sidestep.com,** and **www.kayak.com**. Click on "Vacation Packages" to see what specials are being offered. For last-minute getaways, visit **www.lastminute.com**.

What to Do if Things Go Wrong

When fighting to get your money back, you first want to try to resolve the problem with the vendor, whether it's a hotel, an airline, or a car-rental company. Tell them exactly what happened, why you are dissatisfied, and what you want done to rectify the situation.

As you work your way through the complaint process, keep copies of all relevant receipts, emails, letters, and notes on phone conversations, along with a narrative of who said what to you and when. Send everyone copies of your confirmation information and travel documents, but never send the originals.

If this does not resolve the problem, you should dispute the charge through your credit card company. In addition, you should complain to the Better Business Bureau (**www.ccbbb.ca**). Within two days after you've filed a complaint with your local BBB chapter, the group will forward your dispute to the vendor, allowing him 14 days to respond.

You should also file a complaint with your provincial consumer affairs department as well as with any professional association your tour agency happens to belong to, such as the Travel Industry Council of Ontario (**www.tico.ca**) or the Association of Retail Travel Agents—Canada (**www.artacanada.ca**).

You can contact ARTA by phone at 416-962-0700 or by writing to:

ARTA
2 Carlton Street, Suite 1000
Toronto, Ontario
M5B 1J3

If you think you've been scammed by a fraudulent tour operator or travel agent, you should also contact RECOL, which stands for Reporting Economic Crime Online and is operated by a variety of law enforcement agencies, including the RCMP and provincial police forces, at **www.recol.ca**.

Fight for Your Money Action Steps

- ☐ Don't fall for vacation offers from telemarketers or spam email.
- ☐ If you are pressured to make a quick decision, just say no. It's most likely a scam.
- ☐ Get all terms and conditions in writing, including date restrictions and cancellation policies.
- ☐ Confirm bookings directly with hotels, airlines, and car-rental agencies.
- ☐ Use a credit card for payment, never cash or a cheque.

Conclusion

You have reached the end of this book, but your FIGHT FOR YOUR MONEY is just beginning.

You have now read more about smart spending then most people will read in a lifetime. As a result, you now possess the ability to take more control over your financial life than most people ever will have.

As I said in the Introduction, you deserve to be in control of your money and not be ripped off. But as we've seen, the battle to protect the money you have worked so hard to earn is a battle you have to fight every day. And this battle for your money is not going to end anytime soon. If anything, it is likely to get harder.

The good news is that you are now wiser financially—and wisdom makes you strong. You no longer have to be a victim, either of circumstances or of legal scams perpetrated by big business to separate you from your paycheque. You have become an insider who knows the tricks that companies play. You know how to read the paperwork before you sign anything, how to calculate the real cost of what you're being offered, and how to negotiate for a better deal.

Live for Your Life

As I put the final touches on this book in the fall of 2008, the world is going through some of the most difficult financial times since the Great Depression.

By the time you read this, that crisis may have been dealt with. But others will be unfolding. The fact is that financial crises are a part of life and a part of history. And how we deal with them is also predictable. A lot of us complain about how unfair it all is and blame the politicians (many of whom deserve to be blamed), while the news media pundits jump up and down, looking for heroes and goats as if they were covering a sporting event.

The most important thing I can say to you as your financial coach and advocate is this—at the end of the day, the only one who really controls your financial life is YOU. And when you control your money, you control your life. This is a truth you can feel in your heart. It is why it is so crucial that you make use of the knowledge and the tools this book provides.

You are the one person with the best chance of helping you and your family when it comes to your money. It is not about which political party is in Parliament or which leader says what to whom. It is not about new rules and regulations to protect us. It's ultimately about YOU and what YOU do to protect yourself.

The fact that big business has no compunctions about doing whatever it can to separate you from your money does not have to be your downfall. You are now too smart to let others exploit you. This book has covered your entire financial life from automobiles to taxes, and then some. There are certainly more topics to be covered—and there will certainly be more games played on us—but I am confident that if you use the information you have gotten from this book to FIGHT FOR YOUR MONEY, no one will be able to take advantage of you financially.

Remember this—no one can control our future if we don't let them.

I wrote this book to give you the insight and advantage that millions of people simply don't have when it comes to their money. Now please go use it and share it. I congratulate you on your desire to live and finish rich by fighting for your money.

If this book has touched you, inspired you, and gotten you to take action, please let us know. I truly love and live to hear from my readers. Every day, I wake up to your emails and letters. It is your successes and challenges that motivate me and my team to keep doing what we do every day. You inspire us by your success and you force us to work harder when we hear about your hardships. You can reach me at **success@finishrich.com**.

Until we meet again, enjoy your journey—and make it joyful.

Your friend,
David Bach

APPENDIX: FIGHT FOR YOUR MONEY TOOLKIT

Airline Complaint Letter

[insert date]

Customer Service
[insert airline name]
[insert address] [Note: The appropriate address can usually be found on the airline's web site. If not, call the airline to find out where customer-service complaints should be sent.]

Dear [insert contact name],

I'm writing to report an incident that occurred during [insert flight information and date]. I have always been a loyal patron of [insert airline name], but this recent incident, which involved [briefly state problem], has left me with no choice but to file a formal complaint and request that you [insert what you want—e.g., give me a 50% discount on my next flight] in compensation for the poor treatment to which I was subjected.

What happened was this. [Describe the incident as clearly and succinctly as possible. Do not whine or use abusive language. Rather, tell the story logically and methodically, with an eye to proving why you should be compensated.]

In view of what I happened, I think it is only fair that you [state, clearly and specifically, what kind of compensation you want].

Please contact me to confirm that my requests will be honoured. My daytime phone number is [insert number with area code] and my email address is [insert email address]. If I do not hear from you by [insert date], I will report this incident to the Canadian Transportation Agency, [my province's consumer affairs office], and the Better Business Bureau.

Sincerely,

[your name]
[your address]

Enclosures: [List what you are enclosing—e.g., your airline ticket—and provide copies of those supporting documents.]

Source: Executive Travel Magazine, 2008. www.executivetravelmagazine.com

General Complaint Letter for Defective Product or Inadequate Service

[insert date]

[insert name of contact person (if available)]
[insert title (if available)]
[insert company name]
Consumer Complaint Division (if you have no specific contact)
[insert address]

Dear [insert contact name],

On [insert date], I purchased [or had repaired] a [insert name of the product with the serial or model number or service performed]. I made this purchase at [insert location, date, and other important details of the transaction].

Unfortunately, your product [or service] has not performed well [or the service was inadequate]. Instead of [describe what should have happened], it [explain what did happen].

To resolve this issue, I would appreciate your [insert the specific action you want]. Enclosed are copies of my records [receipts, guarantees, warranties, cancelled cheques, contracts, model and serial numbers, and any other documents].

I look forward to your reply and a resolution to my problem no later than [insert time limit]. If I do not hear from you by then, I will seek assistance from a consumer-protection agency or the Better Business Bureau. Please contact me at the above address or by phone [insert home or office numbers with area codes].

Sincerely,

[insert your name]
[insert your address]

Enclosures: [List what you are enclosing and provide copies of those supporting documents.]

New Car "Lemon" Letter

[insert date]

[insert manufacturer's name]
[insert address]
BY CERTIFIED MAIL
RETURN RECEIPT REQUESTED

Dear [insert contact name if available],
I am writing to notify you of the problems I have had with my [insert Year, Make, Model and VIN# of car].

I purchased my car from [insert Name of Dealership] on [insert date of purchase.] Approximately [insert amount of time] after purchase, I began having trouble with [insert description of problem]. I took my car back to the dealer on [insert Dates of Repair Attempts] to have this problem corrected but to date, the dealer has been unable to do so. Thus far, my car has been out of service for a total of [insert number] days/a dealership has attempted to repair this problem [insert number] times. Attached are copies of the repair orders that document the dealership's attempts to repair my car.

This problem substantially impairs both the use and value of my car. Therefore, unless you are able to correct this problem within 30 days of your receipt of this letter, I request that you [repurchase or replace] my vehicle.

Please contact me at the address below or by telephone at [insert number with area code] to arrange a mutually convenient date and time for you to inspect my car and make the necessary repairs.

Sincerely,

[insert your name]
[insert your address]

Enclosures. [List what you are enclosing and provide copies of those supporting documents.]

Source: http://www.oag.state.md.us

Credit Card Charge in Error

[insert date]

[insert name of creditor]
Billing Inquiries
[insert address]

Dear [insert contact name if available]:

I am writing to dispute a billing error in the amount of [insert amount] on my account. The amount is inaccurate because [describe the problem]. I am requesting that the error be corrected, that any finance and other charges related to the disputed amount be credited as well, and that I receive an accurate statement.

Enclosed are copies of [use this sentence to describe any enclosed information, such as sales slips, payment records] supporting my position. Please investigate this matter and correct the billing error as soon as possible.

Please contact me at the address listed below within 30 days.

Sincerely,

[insert your name]
[insert your address]

Enclosures: [List what you are enclosing and provide copies of those supporting documents.]

Source: www.FTC.gov

Letter to Correct Credit Report Errors

[insert date]

[insert name of credit agency]
[insert address]
RE: Request to correct errors in credit report # [insert file number on your credit report].

Dear [insert name]:
In reviewing the credit report you sent me on [insert date], I have noticed the following errors:

1. [Describe the first error—e.g., "You list my date of birth as Jan. 1, 1900"]

This is incorrect. The correct information is: [be very specific here and accompany it with proof if you have it—e.g., "As the enclosed copy of my birth certificate shows, my date of birth is July 25, 1963."].

2. [Describe the second error—e.g., "You list me as having an active charge account with Sears."]

This is incorrect. The correct information is: [be very specific here and accompany it with proof if you have it—e.g., "I closed this account on March 15, 2001. Please note the enclosed copy of the letter I sent Sears instructing them to close the account."].

3. [Describe the third error—e.g., "You list me as having made two late payments on my Royal Bank home mortgage."]

This is incorrect. The correct information is: [be very specific here and accompany it with proof if you have it—e.g., "I have made all my mortgage payments on time. Please note the enclosed copy of my latest mortgage statement as well as a letter from Royal Bank confirming this fact."].

Please respond to my request within 30 days. My contact information is: [insert mailing address and phone number].

Sincerely yours,

[insert your name]

Disputing a Rebate Rejection

[insert date]

[insert company name]
ATTENTION: Rebate Processing Department
[insert address]
RE: Failure to Receive Rebate by Offer Date

Dear [insert name]:
I purchased a [insert product details], on [insert date] at [insert store name] in [insert city and province]. My decision to purchase this product was based upon your offer of a mail-in rebate of [insert dollar amount] ("offer"). My purchase of the product constituted my acceptance ("acceptance") of your offer, creating a binding and enforceable contract between us.

I have performed my obligations under the contract. I paid the full purchase price and then proceeded to fill in the rebate form provided by you. I included all information requested to process my rebate, but to date I have not received a cheque in the amount of [insert dollar amount].

I respectfully request you process payment and mail it to me at the address indicated within 30 days. I have re-attached all information originally sent for your convenience.

If I do not receive payment in full by [insert date 30 days from mailing], I will begin legal proceedings against you and will file complaint reports with the Competition Bureau, the consumer affairs office in [province], as well as selected consumer advocacy publications and local and provincial consumer affairs advocates.

I am sending copies of this letter to these agencies and organizations to encourage your compliance. I am also filing a report with ConsumerAffairs.com for inclusion on their web site.

Thank you for your prompt attention and resolution of this matter.

Sincerely,

[insert your name]

cc: Competition Bureau
Industry Canada
50 Victoria Street
Gatineau, Quebec K1A 0C9

Consumer Affairs Office
[Provincial address]

Source: www.consumeraffairs.com

SOURCES

INTRODUCTION

In a single week in November 2008, the TSX plunged more than 10% while at the same time real estate prices in many cities across Canada were down 20% or more from their peak in 2005 and 2006: www.globaltv.com.

Telemarketing scams alone cost us an estimated $1 million a year: www.cbc.ca.

BUYING A NEW CAR

Canadians buy roughly 1.7 million new cars, minivans, SUVs, and pickup trucks each year: www.statcan.gc.ca/pub/11-621-m/11-621-m2008069-eng.htm.

On average a car buyer can save 60% on the cost of an extended warranty if he or she buys it over the Internet from a third party rather than the dealer: www.usedcartips.org/warranty.html.

New cars take their biggest depreciation hit in the first year after they roll off the dealer's lot, typically losing 25% to 30% of their value: www.edmunds.com/advice/strategies/articles/77147/article.html.

There are about 3,000 car dealers in Canada: www.cada.ca.

The invoice price of a car is not the dealer's true cost, since it generally includes what's called a holdback—a fee (usually 2% to 4% of the MSRP) that most car manufacturers pay their dealers each time they sell a car: www.edmunds.com/advice/incentives/holdback/index.html.

2009 VW Jetta costs: MSRP figure based on Volkswagon.com web site in November 2008. Invoice and dealer's cost figures from www.carquotes.ca.

More than one-quarter of car-dealers' profits come from what they call F&I—finance and insurance: www.nada.org/NR/rdonlyres/03470866-3B06-49A7-8412-1749A3C11CE1/0/NADA_DATA_2007_FI_Service_Contracts.pdf.

The automakers spend literally billions of dollars each year on advertising: www.tnsglobal.com/news/news-B1FAE5AC1091484-FA02D8B7F4F7EDDAD.aspx; www.businesswire.com/portal/site/google/?ndmViewId=news_view&newsId=20080924005132&newsLang=en.

Though most new cars come with six-year/100,000 mile rust warranties, many dealers will try to sell you on an $800 rustproofing treatment that costs them all of $40: http://editorial.autos.msn.com/article.aspx?cp-documentid=476382.

Cost of dealer's "Fabric Protection Package": $300: www.edmunds.com/dealerships/Chevrolet/Ohio/SenecaCounty/OldFort.html.

More new-car buyers than ever before—more than one-third these days, compared to only one out of five in the late 1990s—get suckered into purchasing extended service agreements: http://blogs.consumerreports.org/cars/2008/03/ex-car-warranty.html and see and see Phil Edmonstons' Lemonaidcars.ca: www.lemonaidcars.com.

The price tag on these plans average around $1,000, while the total repair costs they actually wind up absorbing are typically just $250 or so: www.consumersunion.org/finance/extend-warr-pr.htm.

BUYING A USED CAR

The average gross margin on a used vehicle last year in Canada was $2,500 versus $1,800 for a new car: www.financialpost.com.

The fact is that most modern cars will easily give you 200,000 miles or more: www.msnbc.msn.com/id/12040753/.

Craigslist carries ads for upward of 3 million used cars each month. For its part, eBay welcomes 11 million visitors each month and sells upward of about $18 billion worth of cars and related products each year: www.edmunds.com/advice/selling/articles/74786/article.html.

Rental cars are among the best-maintained vehicles on the road today: www.edmunds.com/advice/buying/articles/46537/article.html; http://www.bankrate.com/brm/news/auto/20000126.asp.

Every year, more than 89,000 vehicles with tampered odometers reach the Canadian marketplace—at a cost to Canadians of more than $3.56 million: www.canadiandriver.com/articles/lh/odotamper.htm.

CAR LEASING

About 20% of the new cars on the road are leased (and more than 40% of some luxury models) rather than bought.

Car dealers average twice as much profit on a lease as they do on a conventional purchase: www.carinfo.com/autoleasing.html.

The amount of leasing being done by all new vehicle dealerships in Canada is now less than half of what it was only four months ago. As of Aug. 17, leases represented 19% of new-vehicle transactions at dealerships nationwide, down from 41.9% in April: http://autos.canada.com/news/story.html?id=3935a856-2946-48c3-8f42-41409449eb2b.

Since a Honda typically depreciates by 40% over three years, the car will be worth just $15,000 or so when your lease ends: www.usatoday.com/money/perfi/basics/2004-10-08-mym-autos_x.htm.

Basically, 58.5 cents for every business-related mile they drive: www.irs.gov/taxpros/article/0,,id=156624,00.html.

In the first year or two, leasing usually costs you less, but around the third year the balance begins to shift in favour of buying: www.consumerreports.org/cro/money/credit-loan/auto-lease-or-buy-4-08/overview/auto-lease-or-buy-ov.htm.

CAR RENTALS

All together, they take in more than $20 billion a year: www.carrentalexpress.com/theproof.htm; http://naucarrental.com/article.cfm/id/284920.

Roughly one-third of all car-rental customers sign up for it—paying as much as $40 a day for coverage most of them don't need: www.usatoday.com/money/perfi/insurance/2007-12-10-car-rental-insurance_N.htm.

At Hertz you'll pay $7 a day more to rent a Toyota Prius over a Ford Explorer. But you'll get more than double the gas mileage!: www.hertz.com in September 2008.

Cost of GPS per weekly rental: $59.75: www.hertz.com at JFK International Airport, NY, NY in September 2008.

CAR REPAIRS

Car repair shops consistently rank among the Better Business Bureau's Top 10 most complained about industries: http://us.bbb.org/WWWRoot/SitePage.aspx?site=113&id=ec2f39d2-b948-4f54-9959-01130dde2f61.

Fifty-one percent of repair shop customers are likely to pay for for unnecessary repairs: http://strategis.ic.gc.ca/app/oca/crd/document.do?id=1588&lang=eng.

BANK ACCOUNTS

Canadian banks employ more than 250,000 people and operate more than 8,000 branches. They generated more than $19 billion in net income in 2007 and manage more than $2.7 trillion in assets: www.fin.gc.ca/toce/2002/bank_e.html.

The Canadian Bankers Association has said that service fees account for about 5% cent of total bank revenues. For 2007, that would mean service fee income of about $3.7 billion: www.cbc.ca/news/interactives/who-bank-profits/.

Canada has one of the strongest banking systems in the world. In fact, the World Economic Forum rated Canada's banking system as the best in the world: http://en.wikipedia.org/wiki/Banking_in_Canada.

DEBIT CARDS

Since 2001, Canadians have conducted transactions using their debit cards—which draw on an existing source of funds such as a chequing account—more often than they've used cash: www.interac.ca/media/researchfacts.php.

About half of all Canadians say they use a debit card most of the time compared to one-quarter of all Canadians who use cash: www.usemybank.com/news070605.asp.

Debit cards are particularly popular among young people between the ages of 18 and 25 who use them instead of cash, even for small purchases. (Around 60% of debit card transactions involve less than $25.): "Debit-card Smarts," *Kiplinger's Personal Finance* magazine, August 2007.

CREDIT CARDS

There are almost 65 million credit cards in circulation in Canada, about two for every Canadian: www.cba.ca/en/viewDocument.asp?fl=6&sl=111&tl=&docid=246&pg=1.

Most Canadians—about 75% of them—pay off their credit card balance every month. But the remaining 25% carry an outstanding balance. That means they're paying interest on the outstanding amount, sometimes at a rate as high as 20% or more: www.cba.ca/en/viewDocument.asp?fl=6&sl=111&tl=&docid=246&pg=1.

CREDIT SCORES

As of 2008, the median FICO score in the United States was 723—meaning that half of all Americans scored higher than that and half scored lower: www.myfico.com.

If it turns out you're right, the credit agency must correct or delete the bad information within 30 days: www.equifax.com/answers/correct-credit-report-errors/en_cp.

PAYDAY LOANS

Payday loans are used most by people who can least afford them. A study by Statistics Canada shows that young families are three times more likely to have used payday loans than people over 35: www.statcan.gc.ca/bsolc/olc-cel/olc-cel?catno=75-001-X20071049617&lang=eng.

Typically, payday lenders charge around $12.50 for every $100 you borrow, including interest and fees. On a 17-day loan, this is the equivalent of an annual interest rate of 1,242%! : http://dsp-psd.pwgsc.gc.ca/Collection-R/LoPBdP/PRB-e/PRB0581-e.pdf.

IDENTITY THEFT

Identity theft ranks among the most prevalent of consumer complaints in Canada. The Better Business Bureau estimates that Canadians lose more than $2.3 billion a year to the crime: www.ps-sp.gc.ca/prg/le/bs/report-en.asp#a04.

The RCMP and provincial police agencies receive more than 7,800 calls a year about identity theft on their PhoneBusters anti-fraud hotline and say that number represents only 5% of all victims of identity theft. That means more than 150,000 people a year have their identities stolen every year in Canada: www.ps-sp.gc.ca/prg/le/bs/report-en.asp#a04.

Each year Javelin Strategy & Research publishes their Identity Fraud Survey Report—said to be the largest, most up-to-date study of ID fraud in the U.S.: www.idsafety.net/803.R_2008%20Identity%20Fraud%20Survey%20Report_Consumer%20Version.pdf.

A scam dubbed "vishing" is even less sophisticated and low tech yet has increased from 3% of identity theft in 2006 to 40% in 2007: www.idsafety.net/803.R_2008%20Identity%20Fraud%20Survey%20Report_Consumer%20Version.pdf.

The Washington Post *recently ran an article on mobile phones—specifically "smartphones" like the Palm Treo and BlackBerry—that was quite an eye-opener:* www.washingtonpost.com/wp-dyn/content/article/2006/10/20/AR2006102001647_pf.html.

DIVORCE

The average woman experiences a 45% decrease in her standard of living after going through a divorce: www.divorce360.com/articles/56/financial-tips-for-women.aspx.

The average man experiences a 15% improvement in his standard of living: http://101familymatters.com/7/rebuilding-your-finances-after-divorce/.

Over the long term, U.S. government data show that a divorce reduces the average man's ability to earn a living as much as 40% below his married counterparts: "Handbook of Divorce and Relationship Dissolution," By Mark A. Fine & John H. Harvey, Routledge (2005), p. 393.

Separation and divorce procedures: www.divorceincanada.ca/general.htm.

LIFE INSURANCE

With a total of $2.9 trillion of life insurance, Canadians tend to be better insured than Americans, although even that enormous sum works out to only $148,000 in coverage per insured individual: www.clhia.ca/prov/Facts2006_ON.pdf.

ESTATE PLANNING

If a person dies without a will (intestate), the estate will be distributed according to the law: www.gov.on.ca/ont/portal/!ut/p/.cmd/cs/.ce/7_0_A/.s/7_0_252/_s.7_0_A/7_0_252/_l/en?docid=004689.

Trusts can eliminate virtually all need to probate a will; however, there are costs associated with establishing and maintaining a trust: www.fpsccanada.org/fpsc/articles/estate_planning_avoid_taxes_and_probate_fees.

SAVING FOR UNIVERSITY

On average, Canadian families have saved more than $10,000 in an RESP for their child's education, with some families aiming to save the maximum $50,000. At the beginning of 2008, parents of university-bound kids had invested nearly $109 billion in them—and the numbers are expected to keep rising: http://resps.org/stats.htm.

Your children's education is a good investment. Studies have shown that the annual return on an investment in post-secondary education in Canada can amount to 10% or more: www.hrsdc.gc.ca/en/cs/sp/hrsd/prc/publications/research/2002-000150/SP-504-06-02E.pdf.

HEALTH INSURANCE

By 2021, Statistics Canada says seven million seniors in the country—19% of Canada's total population—will place increasing demands on our health care system: http://dsp-psd.pwgsc.gc.ca/Collection/H88-5-3-2005E.pdf.

Studies have shown that one-quarter of all Canadians who visit an emergency room wait for four hours or more compared to 12% in the United States. Half of us wait four weeks or more to see a specialist compared to 23% of Americans: http://en.wikipedia.org/wiki/Canadian_and_American_health_care_systems_compared.

HEALTH-CLUB MEMBERSHIPS

The health-club industry in Canada rakes in revenues of close to $2 billion a year: http://cms.ihrsa.org/index.cfm?fuseaction=Page.viewPage&pageId=19014&nodeID=15.

Roughly 5,000 health clubs in Canada today: http://cms.ihrsa.org/index.cfm?fuseaction=Page.viewPage&pageId=19014&nodeID=15.

BUYING A HOME

Housing sales in Canada, particularly in major markets like Toronto, fell by 14% in October from the previous month, the biggest decline since 1994: http://creastats.crea.ca/natl/.

The amount of money paid for these houses fell by more than 17%. The number of houses sold was lower than it had been since 2002: http://creastats.crea.ca/natl/.

There are roughly 97,000 real estate agents in Canada: www.crea.ca/public/crea/who_we_are.htm.

HOME MORTGAGES

Banks in Canada account for the majority of mortgages that people use to buy a home: www.cimbl.ca.

Property title scams: www.consumerscouncil.com/site/Consumers_Council_of_Canada_69/pdf/Title%20Insurance'05.pdf and www.firstcanadiantitle.com.

HOME BUILDING AND REMODELLING

According to the Better Business Bureau, home renovations consistently rank among the top 10 causes for consumer complaints in Canada. In Ontario alone, the Ministry of Small Business and Consumer Services receives more than 2,600 complaints a year against contractors: www.ccbbb.ca AND www.gov.on.ca/mgs/en/ConsProt/STEL02_045911.html.

About three out of four Canadian homeowners make renovations or repairs to their homes at a cost of more than $50 billion annually: www41.statcan.ca/2006/2162/ceb2162_001-eng.htm AND www.homebuildercanada.com/2005reno-market.htm.

One of the main protections homeowners have is that a subcontractor or supplier can't file a mechanic's lien unless he previously filed a notice of intent when he first started work: www.asktooltalk.com/articles/construction/contractor/lien.php; www.abanet.org/rppt/meetings_cle/2005/fall/PauPeterson.pdf.

RPPS AND RRSPS

As of 2008, some 6.3 million Canadian workers had invested in RRSPs over the previous year. But the $34.1 billion that they invested in their plans amounted to only 6% of the total amount that eligible Canadians could have invested: www.cbc.ca/consumer/story/2008/11/05/rrsp.html.

As of 2008, the CRA allowed you to put 18% of your earned income, up to a maximum of $20,000 a year, into an RRSP. In 2009, the maximum rises to $21,000, and it goes up to $22,000 in 2010: www.cra-arc.gc.ca.

As of the summer of 2008, there were 36 target date funds in Canada offered by BMO, Fidelity, Clarington, London Life, Scotia, RBC and a few other fund companies: www.fundlibrary.com/funds/listing.asp?filtertype=preset&filterid=2&id=XO&t=12&l=all&lc=100&ps=25&p=2&s=F.EnglishName50&sd =asc.

PENSION PLANS

About 38% of employees in Canada belong to an employer-sponsored registered pension plan (RPP). The vast majority–about 80% of them, almost 4.6 million workers–belong to what's called a defined-benefit plan: www.statcan.gc.ca/daily-quotidien/080704/dq080704a-eng.htm.

The Bank of Canada said that more than six in 10 Canadian chief financial officers had reported their DB plans face severe problems: www.bank-banque-canada.ca/en/res/dp/2007/dp07-3.pdf.

CANADA PENSION PLAN AND OLD AGE SECURITY

Some people, including several actuaries who work in the field of pension-plan design, suggest that people can live comfortably on their income from the Canada Pension Plan and Old Age Security when they retire: See articles by Malcolm Hamilton, Mercer Consulting (www.readersdigest.ca/debate.html?a=v&di=161).

Rules for CPP and OAS: www.gov.on.ca/ont/portal/!ut/p/.cmd/cs/.ce/7_0_A/.s/7_0_252/_s.7_0_A/7_0_252/_l/en?docid=004617.

ANNUITIES

Sales in Canada of individual annuities totalled $15.1 billion in 2007. Annuities are more popular in the United States, for various reasons, but Canadians are buying them in greater numbers, as well, primarily for their retirement income: http://casualtyactuaries.com/education/spring/2008/handouts/lebel.pdf.

Variable annuities, seg funds: http://network.nationalpost.com/np/blogs/wealthyboomer/archive/tags/Variable+Annuities/default.aspx AND www.insurance-journal.ca/archives/2007/ 0709110904.asp AND www.sunlife.ca/plan/v/index.jsp?vgnextoid=c7478db531f56110VgnVCM1000002dd2d09fRCRD&vgnextfmt=default&vgnLocale=en_CA.

Insurance companies do pay agents upfront commissions as high as 15% of the amount of every annuity they sell

ONLINE SHOPPING AND AUCTIONS

In 2007, Statistics Canada estimated more than 8.4 million Canadians bought $12.8 billion worth of goods over the Internet: www.upi.com/Business_News/2008/11/18/Canada_wants_taxes_from_online_sales/UPI-25111227031622/.

The Edmonton Police department says more than half the population of the country have lost money to online fraud in Canada. Phonebusters, Canada's online crime fighting agency, reported that Canadians lost $4.6 million to just one type of fraud in the month of January 2008 alone: www.419legal.org/blog/2008/04/23/internet-fraud-in-canada-reports-predict-an-ominous-rise-in-online-crimes-in-canada/.

In June 2008, a French court ordered eBay to pay a $63 million judgement for allowing counterfeit Louis Vuitton bags, Christian Dior clothing, and Guerlain, Kenzo, and Givenchy perfume to be sold on its site. Luxury brands like Hermès and Rolex won similar cases against eBay in previous years: "Court fines eBay over fake goods," BBC News, June 30, 2008, http://news.bbc.co.uk/2/hi/business/7481241.stm.

APPLIANCE PROTECTION PLANS/ EXTENDED WARRANTIES

Consumers Union notes that profit margins on some warranties can be as high as 50%: www.cbc.ca/consumer/story/2006/11/15/consumer-warranty.html.

Americans buy upwards of 100 million appliance protection plans and extended warranties each year, spending a total of more than $9 billion annually: Leslie Pepper, "Should You Buy An Extended Warranty?" *Parade,* February 10, 2008, www.parade.com/articles/editions/2008/edition_02-10-2008/Extended_Warranty.

A retailer typically keeps at least half—and often more—of the purchase price of every extended warranty he or she sells: "Why you don't need an extended warranty," *Consumer Reports,* November 2007, www.consumerreports.org/cro/money/news/november-2006/why-you-dont-need-an-extended-warranty-11-06/overview/extended-warranty-11-06.htm.

Experts estimate that for every 100 warranties sold on electronics and appliances, only 15 people ever file a claim: Leslie Pepper, "Should You Buy An Extended Warranty?" *Parade,* February 10, 2008, www.parade.com/articles/editions/2008/edition_02-10-2008/Extended_Warranty.

According to the Los Angeles Times, ***Amazon.com's extended warranty lists 35 cases in which protection doesn't apply, including "plasma TVs used in altitude levels above 6,000 feet above sea level":*** Michelle Quinn, "Extended warranty firm touts quick fix," *Los Angeles Times,* December 17, 2007, www.latimes.com/business/la-fi-warranties17dec17,1,7648303.story?coll=la-headlines-business.

In 2007, an Ohio-based company called Ultimate Warranty went bankrupt, leaving nearly 140,000 customers who had paid upward of $45 million for extended warranties holding contracts not worth the paper they were printed on: Alina Tugend, "For Extended Car Warranties, Resist the Showroom Pitch," *New York Times,* August 2, 2008, www.nytimes.com/2008/08/02/business/yourmoney/02shortcuts.html?pagewanted=print.

Apple offers first-rate tech support for its Macs, but it's free only for the first 90 days. After that, the company charges $49 for every phone call—unless you buy its three-year AppleCare warranty, in which case you can make as many tech-support calls as you want for no extra charge: Apple Inc., www.apple.com/support/programs/.

GIFT CARDS

Ontario's newly updated Consumer Protection Act ***states that gift cards cannot expire, cannot be sold with a transaction fee, and cannot penalize shoppers for not spending their credit immediately:*** www.cbc.ca/canada/toronto/story/2007/12/06/gift-cards.html.

Canadians spend about $6 billion a year on gift cards. But one in four cards is never used, according to the Consumers' Association of Canada—meaning that gift card issuers wound up pocketing about $450 million: www.cbc.ca/marketplace/we-bextras/triclosan/giftcard_stats.html?triclosan.

Starbucks gift cards are not good at many Starbucks outlets in airports, supermarkets, and bookstores: "Watch for these gotchas," *Consumer Reports,* December 2007, http://www.consumerreports.org/cro/money/shopping/shopping-tips/gift-card-pitfalls-12-07/watch-for-these-gotchas/gift-card-pitfalls-watch-for-these-gotchas.htm.

After six months, if you haven't used the card, what's called a dormancy fee kicks in.

When Sharper Image declared bankruptcy in 2008, it stopped accepting its gift cards—leaving consumers stuck with an estimated $40 million of suddenly worthless plastic: Marty Orgel, "Not worth the plastic they're printed on," *MarketWatch,* March 3, 2008, http://www.marketwatch.com/news/story/bankruptcies-often-leave-consumers-holding/story.aspx?guid=DCBBEB36-F293-4EDF-B2DC-F515E91A746.

Starbucks won't replace a lost or stolen card unless it's been registered: "Watch for these gotchas," *Consumer Reports,* December 2007, http://www.consumerreports.org/cro/money/shopping/shopping-tips/gift-card-pitfalls-12-07/watch-for-these-gotchas/gift-card-pitfalls-watch-for-these-gotchas.htm.

REBATE OFFERS

"The redemption rate on these, I've seen figures of two per cent mentioned. And the maximum figure I've seen is, 50 per cent. Of course it depends on how much the rebate is worth. If you give people $500 off on a product through a rebate, most likely more people will turn them in. But for the typical rebate sizes that you see, the range is like from, two per cent to about 50 per cent.": www.cbc.ca/consumers/market/files/money/rebates/marketing.html.

TAX PREPARATION

32% of taxpayers themselves say they probably skip exemptions and writeoffs that they could have taken because they just can't figure out how to do their tax returns properly: www.tax-news.com/archive/story/Study_Highlights_Huge_Cost_Of_Maintaining_Canadas_Tax_System_xxxx27126.html.

Preparing, filing, and submitting our tax returns plus maintaining a government bureaucracy to manage and regulate our tax system cost Canadians between C$19 billion and C$31 billion in 2005: www.tax-news.com/archive/story/Study_Highlights_Huge_Cost_Of_Maintaining_Canadas_Tax_System_xxxx27126.html.

Tax rebate regulation: www.canadabusiness.ca/servlet/ContentServer?pagename=CBSC_ON%2Fdisplay&lang=en&cid=1081944202559&c=Regs.

CHARITABLE GIVING

One in four Canadians donated an average of $250 to charity in 2006, a total of $8.5 billion: www.cbc.ca/news/interactives/map-cdncharity/.

CABLE AND SATELLITE TV

Some 1.5 million Canadian households still get their TV the old-fashioned way—with an over-the-air antenna. But they are a dying breed. Roughly 8 million of the nation's 12.5 million TV households are wired for cable, while around 3.5 million homes subscribe to one of the nation's two DTH (for direct to home) services, Bell TV and Star Choice.: www.crtc.gc.ca/ENG/publications/reports/radio/cmri.htm.

CELL PHONE PLANS

There are now 3.3 billion cell phones

There are more than 21 million wireless subscribers in Canada—roughly 65% of the population—yakking away on their cell phones an average of 15 minutes a day, and that's expected to increase to more than 75% of the population by 2010: www.crc.ca/en/html/crc/home/info_crc/pres_presentations/wwrf_2008 AND www.ic.gc.ca/epic/site/oca-bc.nsf/en/ca02267e.html.

RESIDENTIAL PHONE SERVICE

Only 3.1 million Canadians households used land-lines exclusively at the end of 2007, while more than 9 million had at least one cell phone: www.ic.gc.ca/epic/site/oca-bc.nsf/en/ca02267e.html.

Of the households with cell phones in Canada, only 6.4% of them used them exclusively in 2007. So there are still a lot of Canadians talking on the phone in the old-fashioned way: www.ic.gc.ca/epic/site/oca-bc.nsf/en/ca02267e.html.

With Skype, you can make unlimited calls to anywhere in the United States and Canada for just $2.95 a month. What's more, for $9.95 a month, you can make unlimited calls to 34 other countries, including most of Europe, Australia, New Zealand, Chile, China, Japan, and Korea.

BUNDLED SERVICE PLANS

According to IDC Canada, 62% of consumers prefer to subscribe to bundled communications services: www.marketnews.ca/news_detail.asp?nid=2789.

AIR TRAVEL

Nearly 33 million people traveled between cities in Canada in 2007: www.tc.gc.ca/pol/en/Report/anre2007/add/table-a18.htm.

Nearly 30% of domestic U.S. flights failed to arrive on time in 2008: "Nearly 1 in 3 domestic flights late in February," Associated Press, April 3, 2008, www.msnbc.msn.com/id/23938695/.

HOTELS

The Canadian hotel industry is solidly profitable. It generates total revenues of more than $18 billion a year, which have increased by 5% a year since 2005: www.pkfcanada.com/trends_research/publications/canadas_lodging_industry.htm.

TRAVEL PACKAGES

Travel scams are the fourth most common type of consumer fraud in Canada and the United States, according to the Canadian Institute of Travel Counsellors, totalling an estimated $12 billion annually: www.citc.ca/tico/en/travel-scams-e.asp.

ACKNOWLEDGEMENTS

First and foremost, I want to thank you, the reader of this book and my past books. When I first began writing back in 1997, I never imagined the journey it would take me on—helping to answer your questions and address your need for more financial education. I thank you from the bottom of my heart for your trust in me, for your letters and emails of encouragement and thanks—and for the gift of purpose you have all given me.

All of my books—and so far there have been 10 in the FinishRich series, with more than 7 million copies in print—have been projects of love. My mission has always been to promote financial literacy—and in many ways, this book is the pinnacle of a decade of work. There is no way I could have done this alone, and I am grateful for the hundreds of people who over the years have helped me do what we do.

FIGHT FOR YOUR MONEY involved the biggest team of dedicated individuals we have ever assembled to put the best of what we know into a book that can help you. As a result, there are many, many people to thank.

I want to begin by once again acknowledging my grandmother, Rose Bach. She inspired me to write the first book in the FinishRich series, *Smart Women Finish Rich,* and now a decade later, as I put the final touches on this book, I just want to say to my grandma again how much I miss you and love you and know you are watching and cheering me on from heaven. You were the true inspiration behind FIGHT FOR YOUR MONEY—having grown up in the Depression era, you were the one who taught me that "cash is king, savings are golden, and there is no such thing as a fixed price."

To Allan Mayer, after a decade of working together, this was truly our most challenging book to date. Thank you for your trust and insight and commitment to this project. You are a consummate professional, and I am honored to have worked with you for so many years. Ours has been a fabulous partnership, one I truly feel grateful for.

To Liz Dougherty, this is now the eighth book since 2002 we have worked on together. I simply cannot thank you enough for your commitment on this one. You not only kept it all together and on time—but most important, you also made this book the best it could be with your guidance and love. You are simply the best, and I thank the angels every day for bringing you into my life.

To the team of researchers we leaned on for insight and expertise, thank you! In particular, I'd like to single out Dan Carney (for all things automotive, including car buying, car selling, car leasing, car renting, and car repairs), Diana Dawson (air travel, health insurance, home-based businesses, hotels, hospital bills, and travel packages), Phuong Cat Le (bank accounts, credit cards, credit scores, debit cards, identity theft, online shopping, payday loans, and refund anticipation loans), Marilyn Lewis (home buying and selling, home building and remodeling, and home mortgages), Kara McGuire (charitable giving, college saving, divorce, gift cards, gym membership, life insurance, rebates, and tax-preparation services and software), and Helen Huntley (annuities, estate planning, and pension plans).

To my team at Doubleday Broadway Publishing Group—this book has had your excitement and attention since the first day we presented it. Thank you for always believing in me, my missions, and my dreams. I feel so lucky to have been with one publishing company my entire career—and I am so excited to cap off a decade of success with you by launching *Fight for Your Money.* To Kris Puopolo—your wonderful editing hands were all over this manuscript from the beginning to the end, and this book would not be what it is without your brilliant insight. David Drake, every day I wake up feeling lucky and blessed to have had you promoting my books and missions for a decade. You are simply as good as it gets—with your feedback, creative ideas, and passion, you make me better with every book. To Stephen Rubin and Michael Palgon, as always I thank you for your unwavering support and commitment. And to the entire Broadway Team—Catherine Pollock, Rebecca Holland, Stephanie Bowen, and Chris Fortunato—thank you so much for your hard work and dedication to this project. Thanks, too, to Jean Traina for the jacket design and Ralph Fowler for the interior design.

To my literary agents, Suzanne Gluck and Jay Mandel at the William Morris Agency, you have championed this project from the first day I envisioned it. Thank you for getting this book off the ground so successfully and for guiding its development.

To Stephen Breimer, my attorney and confidante, you are always there for me and I am always truly grateful. In many ways, you have been like a father to me throughout my writing career, and it has been a pleasure and a delight to work with you.

To Elisa Garafano, thank you for managing me on a daily basis in what has been a really exciting and busy year. I am truly grateful to you for always being so committed to me and all I do. Your insight on this book was invaluable, and your constant enthusiasm has kept me going on the tough days. Thank you!

To my son, Jack Bach, you light up my life and make every day special and meaningful. Telling you I love you doesn't do justice to how much I love you, but I want you to know that you are the most important thing that ever happened to me in my life and I simply love you more than the "the whole world." To Michelle, I will always love you and I'm beyond thankful for the son you brought into our life.

Finally, to my family: my mom Bobbi and my dad Marty—thank you both for your constant love and support. I wouldn't be here doing what I do without your love and encouragement. And to my sister Emily, I am so proud of you—thank you for everything you do as my little "sis."

—David Bach
New York, October 2008

INDEX

I

J

K

L

P

R

ABOUT THE AUTHOR

David Bach has helped millions of people around the world take action to live and finish rich. He is the author of eight consecutive international bestsellers, including two consecutive #1 *New York Times* bestsellers, *Start Late, Finish Rich* and *The Automatic Millionaire,* as well as the national and international bestsellers *Go Green, Live Rich, The Automatic Millionaire Homeowner, Smart Women Finish Rich, Smart Couples Finish Rich, The Finish Rich Workbook,* and *The Automatic Millionaire Workbook.* Bach carries the unique distinction of having had four of his books appear simultaneously on the *Wall Street Journal, BusinessWeek,* and *USA Today* bestseller lists. In addition, four of Bach's books were named to *USA Today*'s Best Sellers of the Year list for 2004. In all, his FinishRich Books have been published in more than 15 languages, with more than seven million copies in print *worldwide.*

Bach's breakout book *The Automatic Millionaire* was the #1 Business book of 2004, according to *BusinessWeek.* It spent fourteen weeks on the *New York Times* bestseller list and was simultaneously number one on the bestseller lists of the *New York Times, BusinessWeek, USA Today*, and *The Wall Street Journal.* With over a million copies in print, this simple but powerful book has been translated into 12 languages and has inspired thousands around the world to save money automatically.

Bach is regularly featured in the media. He has appeared six times on *The Oprah Winfrey Show* to share his strategies for living and finishing rich, along with numerous appearances on CNN's *Larry King Live,* ABC's *Live with Regis and Kelly*, *The View*, NBC's *Today* and *Weekend Today* shows, CBS's *Early Show*, Fox News, and CNBC. He has been profiled in many major publications, including *The New York Times, BusinessWeek, USA Today, People, Reader's Digest, Time, Financial Times, Washington Post, Wall Street Journal, Los Angeles Times, San Francisco Chronicle, Working Woman, Glamour*, and *Family Circle.* He is also a featured contributor and columnist with *Redbook* magazine.

David Bach is the creator of the FinishRich® Seminar series, which highlights his quick and easy-to-follow financial strategies. In just the last few years, more than half a million people have learned how to take financial action to live a life in line with their values by attending his Smart Women Finish Rich®, Smart Couples Finish Rich®, and Find The Money Seminars, which have been taught in more than 2,000 cities throughout North America by thousands of financial advisors.

A renowned motivational and financial speaker, Bach regularly presents seminars for and delivers keynote addresses to the world's leading financial service firms, Fortune 500 companies, universities, and national conferences. He is the founder and Chairman of FinishRich Media, a company dedicated to revolutionizing the way people learn about money. Prior to founding FinishRich Media, he was a senior vice president of Morgan Stanley and a partner of The Bach Group, which during his tenure (1993 to 2001) managed more than half a billion dollars for individual investors.

As part of his mission, David Bach is involved with many worthwhile causes, including serving on the board for Habitat for Humanity New York and co-founding Makers of Memories, a charity organization dedicated to helping women and children who are victims of domestic violence.

David Bach lives in New York. Please visit his web site at www.finishrich.com.

NEW!

Now Is the Time To FIGHT FOR YOUR MONEY AND FINISH RICH!

Start Today with a FREE...

FINISH**RICH**coaching

Consultation

Call now to schedule your FREE consultation and learn to fight for your money!

- Determine your debt-free date!
- Be prepared to handle any financial emergency!
- Know when you can retire comfortably!
- Learn how to reduce the amount you pay in taxes!
- Discover the best way to manage your income, assets and debts!

"I've designed this program to help you save a fortune...and Finish Rich!"

— #1 New York Times Bestseller David Bach

Dramatically change your financial future with 1-on-1 financial coaching. Call or visit us online and register for a **free 30 minute consultation.**

VISIT
www.finishrich.com/ffymcoaching

CALL
1-866-528-6312

"*Go Green, Live Rich* gives great tips, useful to everyone, about how to save money and the planet at once."
—ROBERT F. KENNEDY JR.

INSTANT BESTSELLER
NEW YORK TIMES
WALL STREET JOURNAL
USA TODAY

Let David Bach show you a whole new way to prosper—by Going Green.

50 Simple Ways to Save the Earth (and Get Rich Trying)
Go Green, Live Rich
AUTHOR OF 5 *New York Times* BESTSELLERS
DAVID BACH
with Hillary Rosner

Most people think that "going green" means sacrificing their bottom line for a healthier planet. But David Bach proves you can have it both ways—if you put the great ideas in his acclaimed book to work for you...

- **Bring your lunch to work. Save $2,250 a year and together we'll reduce our landfills by 1.8 million pounds of trash.**
- **Pay your bills online. You'll save $400 a year and together we'll spare 18.5 million trees.**
- **Turn your savings into millions by catching the "green wave" of investing.**

IN STORES NOW

The Bestselling Series by David Bach

with over **5 MILLION** books in print!

No matter where you start, David Bach can help you Finish Rich!

www.FinishRich.com

EXCLUSIVE BOOK SPECIAL

It's time to take the battle to the next level...

FIGHT FOR YOUR MONEY AND RETIRE A MILLIONAIRE

FIGHT FOR YOUR MONEY POWER PACK

A 13 step battle plan for living a debt-free lifestyle!

- How to get a quick start on the road to financial freedom!
- A proven roadmap to a lifetime of wealth and financial freedom!
- The ultimate weapon to radically improve your financial future!

GO TO

www.finishrich.com/ffymdownload

TO GET STARTED!